SOUL SALSA

Learning to Savor Every Season

By Elisa Juarez

SOUL SALSA
Learning to Savor Every Season
By Elisa Juarez

Cover Design: Destined Designs

Cover Image: Rebecacovers

Published by Collette Portis and Co. LLC, P.O. Box 674, Arlington, Texas 76004.

For general information on our other products and services, please contact us at (410) 914-7543, or fax (419) 821-8930.

Table of Contents

DEDICATION

This book is dedicated to my late mother, Janice Rand Tucker, who instilled in me a love of life, learning, and writing from an early age. She was an artist and a writer who loved gardening, cooking, and serving others. She had a deep and determined faith that carried her through a 40-year battle with scleroderma. She is my inspiration, my heroine, and my guardian angel.

ACKNOWLEDGMENTS

To my husband, Art, who has supported this dream and every one before it. Thank you for always believing in me and honoring the time and space required for me to accomplish this. You are my hero, my dream partner, and my rock.

To our daughters, Taylor and Lauren, who fill my soul with joy and love. You humble me and inspire me with your wisdom, creativity, and grace. Thank you for cheering me on and sharing your input and ideas.

To my father, Tom Tucker, whom I have always adored. He provided a foundation of love, joy, faith, and compassion for my life and work. As I walk with him along the path of Alzheimer's, I am amazed and inspired by his ageless spirit and relentless optimism.

FOREWORD

Elisa Juarez is the real deal.

We are both spiritually oriented; we are both social workers; we both like to write, and we both love to cook! So, it's only natural that I appreciated each and every one of these essays (and look forward to the recipes when the book is in print!) But it is more than just those commonalities that make this a book I would highly recommend. Elisa is the real deal because her honesty, vulnerability, and transparency shine through every page.

Mental, emotional, and spiritual health is the ability to feel what you feel and know what you know. Elisa takes a third step – to write it down.

This book can be used as a daily devotional, a book to tuck in your suitcase when you have a plane ride ahead, or a book by your bedside to calm you down when anxiety strikes. Much more than that, however, I hope Elisa's honesty will encourage you to bring forth yours. You are who you are. If I had a wish for the book, it would be to add a couple of blank pages after each essay so readers could jot down their own experience of the essay they just read.

Often another writer's words clarify the fuzzy feelings roaming around in a person's body and soul and motivate further reflection or writing.

That happened for me in her essay "Season of Lights," in which she wrote about Jesus saying, "I am the Way, the Truth, and the Light." She pointed out that the first part of that statement is, "I am," which is the name of God. If I had followed up with my own essay, I would have written about my belief that the One God was here long, long before the law or Jesus, telling us through Abraham that God would bless *all* people. Followers of Jesus were commonly called "People of the Way." Jesus' "way" was to accept and bless *everyone*, just as Abraham said. It breaks my heart — as it does Elisa's — to see how many people take that verse to mean that nobody but Christians can be loved by God. I could sure write 500 words about that!

I'm sure many readers will resonate with "String of Pearls" where Elisa writes about a hard day. By the end of that day, she writes about the cleansing value of tears. You might follow that one up with a little essay of your own about a bad day in your life and what it was like to just be at one with it.

We each live our very own story every day. In this book, our stories can intersect with Elisa's because hers is straight from the heart.

Janice Harris Lord,
MSSW, LCSW/ACSW, LPC\Christian, clinical social worker, author, and pretty good cook

PREFACE

The writing for this book has taken place over several years, but primarily the past four. My essays express the reflections, insights, questions, and longings of my soul as I continue to discover, create, and celebrate an authentic life. Writing has kept me connected to my soul and stretched me on many levels. It has helped me to navigate this adventure through many ups and downs without losing my compass or my compassion. In fact, living from a deeper awareness has increased my capacity, my faith, and my passion.

This book is being completed and released in the middle of 2020, a year that has brought us a global pandemic, an economic recession, and a powerful movement for racial justice and equality. People have had to adapt to new ways of working, learning, and communicating while also examining their long-held beliefs, attitudes, and perceptions. We have seen a diverse populace come together in response to these challenges, demonstrating the power of compassion, collaboration, and courage. At the same time, the carcasses of prejudice, hatred, avarice and fear have been rattling loudly, threatening the opportunity to heal and recreate our country.

These immense challenges have resulted in a sense of fatigue and a hunger for hope and renewal. Our souls are weary and longing to find meaning, purpose, and expression in the midst of it all. This book recognizes our collective hunger for these elements and provides spoonfuls of "salsa" to awaken, enliven, and empower us at that level of our being. At a time when the outside world is filled with confusion and crisis, and we don't know what to believe or who to trust, it is essential for us to connect to our inner wisdom. We have an inner compass and source of strength that will support us through this difficult season.

My hope and vision for our world as we pass through this upheaval is that we come to a greater awareness of our shared humanity and create new pathways that will take us to higher ground. This is a time of breakthroughs and new discoveries, healing and transformation. It is a passage through darkness and light, fear and courage, grieving and rejoicing. As with every season of life, I remind myself that *this, too, shall pass,* and I choose to believe that life can be *better* than before if we *learn* from this and *love* our way through it.

> "Never lose hope, my dear heart; miracles dwell in the invisible." — Rumi

May this book meet you wherever you are with the nourishment you need and the *spice of life* that your soul is seeking. May it inspire and empower you through every season with reminders of your innate wisdom and wholeness.

— Elisa J. Juarez

INTRODUCTION

For as long as I can remember I have loved to write. When I was in grade school, I wrote poems and stories. I started writing in a five-year diary given to me in second grade by my mother, also a writer. She planted the seed early!

The other seed she planted was an interest in nutrition and healthy eating. She used to grind her own flour for fresh-baked bread, get milk from a local dairy farm, and make nasty tasting concoctions in the blender every morning which she called "Pick Up Drinks." We had a small vegetable garden and three plum trees in the backyard. I grew up eating fresh, "real" food and learning about the health benefits. As a teenager, I started doing my own research on nutrition and fitness. I ran, swam, and cycled all through high school and college.

I considered a college major that combined psychology and physiology but ended up going for straight psychology. My fascination with people and human behavior has always pulled me in that direction, and after college I worked for three years, then went back to school to get my master's degree in social work.

My husband Art and I met in the restaurant business, and we dreamed of owning our own restaurant. We both have an entrepreneurial spirit and a willingness to live on the edge and outside the box to pursue our dreams. After working as a counselor for about three years, I gave birth to our first child, Taylor, and left my job to stay home with her. Three and a half years later we had another daughter, Lauren, and I was looking for ways to work from home. I tried a variety of things and stayed busy with volunteer work in our church, schools, and community. All the while I continued to write, and the hunger for a writing career grew stronger.

Fast-forward to the girls' teen years, and Art and I decided it was time to pursue our restaurant dream. Knowing what a huge commitment of time, energy, and money it required, we had put it on the back burner for many years. We spent two years preparing for it through market research, brainstorming, and planning. We found two investors and two cooks, and opened a fast-casual Mexican restaurant called Cumino's. The food was fresh, authentic, and delicious, and we soon had a loyal following of regular customers. Unfortunately, we were underprepared for the challenge and experienced problems with finances, the location, and some of the people involved. We ended up having to close it much too soon, and it was heartbreaking.

I continued to make salsa and share it with friends, and I got many requests for it. When I decided it was time to launch my blog, Taylor helped me put it all together and come up with a name. My idea was to create a website that combined my three passions: food, nutrition/wellness, and writing. We decided the name should include the word "salsa" ... and *Spoonful of Salsa* was born. It has been one of the most fun, creative, and interesting projects of my life and continues to "feed" me and my passions. It also provided the foundation for this book, a collection of essays and recipes to nourish your mind, body, and soul through every season.

When we have health and vitality, we can do more, give more, and live well. Salsa adds spice, flavor, and zest to our food and to our lives.

Not only do our bodies crave flavor; our minds and souls do, too. When we find that which uplifts, energizes, and inspires us, we have found the "salsa" of our lives. That nourishment and encouragement add "spice" which is reflected in our lives as vitality, energy, and wholeness. We have each been designed to seek and fulfill our passion and our purpose, to live fully and freely.

> "When we align our thoughts, emotions, and actions with the highest part of ourselves, we are filled with enthusiasm, with purpose and meaning. When the personality comes to fully serve the energy of its soul, that is authentic empowerment."
> — Gary Zukav, *Seat of the Soul*

Author Sarah Ban Breathnach (*Simple Abundance*) refers to the authentic self as "the soul made visible." It is the real and eternal part of us which is both unique and universal. As we are each a unique expression of Divine Love which is universal, we are all part of the same Whole. We come "alive" when we discover our passion and our purpose and allow the creative energy of the Universe to live and move through us.

> "When you become authentic, you become greater than you ever thought you could be, and this greatness allows you to heal yourself, your family, and your world."
> — Sarah Ban Breathnach, *Simple Abundance.*

The characteristics and qualities of the soul include authenticity, love, joy, wonder, compassion, wisdom, and generosity. All of these arise from our source, Divine Love. This is the truth of who we are; it is our essence. There are many things in this life which nourish, renew, and enliven our souls. These include passion, purpose, service, relationships, silence, nature, creativity, and play. Through these elements and activities, the soul (or authentic self) discovers, develops, expands, and fulfills itself.

> *"Love is something alive, living, personal, and true, the*
> *creating and nourishing power within life. It is patient, free*
> *to all, and it is medicine and food."*
> — Anne Lamott, *Almost Everything.*

Love is the connecting cord between our divinity and our humanity. As we discover it within ourselves and our relationships, it starts showing up in unexpected times and places. We realize that it is always here as a pulse that gives energy to all that we do. The world would have us believe that we are separate from Love, from God and good, and from each other. Belief in this lie is the source of all fear and suffering. We need regular reminders, encouragement, and soul food to stay grounded in the awareness of Love.

These essays provide *spoonfuls of salsa* to sustain your soul and to help you savor every season. It is in sharing our lives, our love, and our stories that we deepen our connection to each other and to our authentic selves. My desire and intention is to inspire, encourage, and empower you to create a truly authentic, rich, and joyful life.

— Elisa J. Juarez

Note: This book is organized according to the calendar year, but start in whatever season you find yourself, physically or spiritually. Let it be a tool, a guide, and a companion for every season.

For Everything There is a Season

"For everything there is a season, and a time for every
matter under Heaven:
a time to be born, and a time to die;
a time to plant, and a time to pluck up what has been
planted;
a time to kill, and a time to heal;
a time to break down, and a time to build up;
a time to weep, and a time to laugh;
a time to mourn, and a time to dance;
a time to cast away stones, and a time to gather stones
together;
a time to embrace, and a time to refrain from embracing;
a time to seek, and a time to lose;
a time to keep, and a time to cast away;
a time to rend, and a time to sew;
a time to keep silence, and a time to speak."
— Ecclesiastes 3:1-7

CHAPTER ONE: WINTER I

Winter I

> "Learning the soulcraft of seasonal healing can bring new depth to our journey toward Wholeness. In the natural world, winter is the season of rest, restoration, and reflection."
> — Sarah Ban Breathnach, *Simple Abundance*

All life begins in darkness, silence and mystery. Winter is the season of darkness, dormancy, stillness, and inner growth. We experience darkness and doubt before a breakthrough in awareness and understanding, before a growth spurt, before new life is expressed through us.

It is in the middle of this season that we cross over into a new year with bells and sparklers and champagne toasts. It comes at a time when we need a lift, a glimmer of light, a boost of confidence and hope. January offers us a fresh canvas on which to create our lives. It beckons us inward to the sanctuary of creativity where we find our souls awaiting expression. February delivers the celebration of love, reminding us of that which we *are* and inviting us to share it.

Winter draws us to the hearth of our being for warmth, wisdom, and wonder. It bids us to be patient and savor the time of inner growth. Embrace this season and its gifts of guidance and grace. This is a time for our roots grow deeper, resulting in greater strength and stature in the months ahead. Trust yourself and the Love that created you. As with every season, this, too, shall pass. Know that *wonders are unfolding* in you, through you, and for you.

New Year's Day

*"You can have anything you want if you want it
desperately enough. You must want it with an exuberance
that erupts through the skin and joins the energy that
created the world."* — Sheila Graham

As a new year begins, there is a part of me that is reluctant to let the holidays go and put away the Christmas tree and décor. At the same time, I feel ready for a fresh start with new ideas, possibilities, and opportunities! Instead of making resolutions, I choose to imagine the life I want to create and experience, then set my intentions accordingly.

What do you really want this year? Have you taken the time to ask yourself and really listen? What is your dream for this year? What inspires you? What can you do today to move in that direction?

*"If one advances confidently in the direction of his dreams
and endeavors to live the life which he has imagined, he
will meet with a success unexpected in common hours."*
— Henry David Thoreau

Advance confidently. One step at a time. Love will show you the way, for Love created you and knows your destiny.

We're all aware of how fast the time goes, from week to week, month to month, and year to year. We know how precious and unpredictable each day is as we move forward into an unknown future. As you glance back across the past year you see evidence of this. The one thing of which we can be certain is change. There are those things we cannot control and those that we can. Our job is to take ownership of our lives in a conscious and creative way, choosing how we respond to what life gives us. As we answer the above question about what we really want, let's get honest about what we are doing (or not doing) to create and attract our heart's desires.

Set aside some time this week to take an inventory of each area of your life: physical, mental, emotional, financial, and spiritual. What is working in each area, and what is not? Where can you improve or increase your health and well-being? What do you need to release and move beyond? Set your intentions in each area and decide on a specific action you can take in each one. Imagine yourself healthy, happy, and successful. It all starts with a *decision*, and sometimes a change of *direction*. Keep your thoughts held high and you will rise to the occasion each day, overcoming your inner and outer obstacles and creating the life you desire!

January Joy

"The first month of the year, A perfect time to start all over again, changing energies and deserting old moods, New beginnings, new attitudes." – Charmaine J Forde

What is it about January that is so special to me? We cross a threshold into a new year after spending a few weeks celebrating the holidays with family and friends, suspending our regular routines and living in the rich present. We step into January with a mixture of fatigue and anticipation, somewhat reluctant to resume our work routines, yet ready for a new beginning and another chance to realize our dreams.

When we were raising our girls, January was typically a calmer month in terms of extracurricular activities. The new semester ramped up gradually, making it a golden opportunity for renewal and reflection. That feeling continues now that the girls are grown; the afterglow of the holidays warms my soul and illumines my path into the new year. I focus on gratitude, goals, and a vision for the future. The cold weather inspires me to cook, especially soups and stews, and get back on track with healthy eating. It also inspires me to curl up with a warm blanket, a good book, and my journal.

This month I also celebrate my birthday and reflect on all the goodness and simple abundance in my life. As my awareness of the presence of God increases and deepens, I find that every year is better than the last. The sacred is found in the ordinary and life continues to unfold with mystery and beauty. This awareness brings gratitude which draws even more goodness into my life. I continue to be amazed at the work of Divine Love, order, and grace. They are within and around us, always guiding us to the highest good. The more I surrender to this reality, the greater my experience of life!

As I seek to serve, grow, and fulfill my purpose in this life, I am called to discover, develop, and use my gifts. I am challenged to focus and balance my time and energy between outer work and inner work. When I am rested and healthy with a full tank, I can give and serve fully and freely. I am learning to design my life in a way that creates and attracts beauty, love, and fullness of joy. Now that I am an empty-nester, I have the gift of more time and energy to pursue my passions and contribute something of value and significance to the world outside this home. Every season brings new and different opportunities, lessons, and challenges which stretch us and open us to a greater experience of life and love.

Embrace the joys of January and new beginnings in this season of renewal and reflection!

Masterpiece

"There is a vitality, a life force, an energy, a quickening that is translated through you into action, and because there is only one of you in all time, this expression is unique." — Martha Graham

January brings each of us a blank canvas, beckoning for a masterpiece! Consider the empty space and the materials you have to create something new this year. Although we can do this any time, January is a perfect opportunity as a new year sprawls out before us. We each have our own dreams, desires, gifts, tools, and experiences with which to create. If you've never considered yourself an artist, now is the time.

We have been created by Love, for Love, and infused with creative energy. All that we learn and experience goes into our toolbox to be used to create a masterpiece of our lives. Take a look at where you've been, what you've endured, how you've lived, and who you are becoming. Pain creates intense color and texture in our lives, so embrace the gifts it brings and the beauty that comes from it. Pain cuts through the outer layers of our being and reveals a deeper reality, awakening us to previously undiscovered strength and grace. It is through pain, struggle, loss, and brokenness that we find what is real and lasting within us. Hope and healing transform our lives and shine on those around us.

Whatever season you find yourself in, you have the opportunity to redesign yourself and your life in alignment with your passions. The new year holds abundant possibilities for your life! If you are in a time of grief, allow your tears to water the seeds of new life within you. We may or may not feel ready for a new season. It doesn't matter. We are here, and life is unfolding before us, offering a blank canvas for us to paint with all the love, joy, pain, humility, strength, compassion, and beauty we have within us.

The world needs us and what we have to give more than ever. Our experiences have shaped us, strengthened us, empowered us, and humbled us. We have beauty and wisdom to express from our authentic selves. So, take this blank canvas and celebrate the new year with every cell of your being!

Realize that you were created for a time such as this, and you are called to create something of beauty and value for yourself and the world around you. Your Creator is your source of inspiration, wisdom, and grace. Pull out all your tools and materials and roll up your sleeves! This is your year, your life, your time, your season!

Vision, Part 1: Imagination & Intention

As a new year begins in the middle of winter, we are nudged by Mother Nature and our divine nature to turn within ourselves for inspiration and reflection. Allow the season of dormancy to draw your attention inward for renewal and rebirth. What is your vision for the coming year? How is your authentic self growing and evolving? Instead of setting resolutions, create a vision for your life. When we have a vision, we use our imagination and intention to create something we desire. This serves as a roadmap, giving us direction toward a destination. It also inspires us with a sense of purpose which can pull us forward into a greater experience of life.

If you have not yet taken the time to create a vision for your life, this is the perfect time to do so — regardless of how far along the path you may be. None of us knows how much time we have here, but we each have an opportunity and a responsibility to make the most of what we have been given.

The thoughts, ideas, beliefs, and images that we hold in our minds have the power to create, attract, and manifest. *If we only realized the power we have, then we would pay more attention to how we use it — or fail to use it!* Writing in a journal and articulating our vision on paper will raise our awareness and give us clarity.

Just as important as our vision of *where* we're going and *what* we want to create is another type of vision: *how* we look at the world around us. In our daily lives, what we see reflects our beliefs, expectations, judgments, and self-talk. I've heard it said that we generally see what we expect to see. *That deserves pause.* There are many obstacles to clear vision, such as fear, anger, resentment, ignorance, arrogance, pride, and greed. The factors that support our vision include focus, clarity, openness, awareness, attention, understanding, and faith. This quote from the Talmud says it well: "We don't see things as they are; we see things as *we* are."

What if you went out into the world expecting to find what you're seeking? Maybe it's a solution, a helper, a new sweater, or a great sale. What if you carried this thought with you: "Help is everywhere!" Or, "Love is everywhere!" I challenge you to try it as an experiment. Do you see what you expect to see?

Yesterday I was out for a walk, and as I crossed the parking lot, a man in a truck smiled and waved as he waited for me to cross. Kindness is everywhere. Can you see it? Can you *be* it? Sharpen your vision and keep your eyes open to the countless wonders and gifts of grace that surround you each day!

Vision, Part 2: Preparation

As I continue to contemplate vision this month, more ideas and examples keep popping up in my life like hot kernels in a corn popper! My pastor dished up a spoonful of wisdom on Sunday that gave me more thoughts to ponder. He talked about how we *get ready* to live a life of purpose. Let's apply this notion of *preparation* to the vision we are creating and living in, the intentions we are setting, and the steps we are taking.

Once we have created a vision for our lives and written it down, what's next? Cross our fingers and hope for the best? Our thoughts, words, and feelings have power; they are the raw materials of our experience. To these we add the right tools, resources, and actions which will prepare us for what's ahead, no matter what hills and valleys we travel along the way. Although each path is unique, there are universal elements which determine our direction and our destination. I've put these into 4 categories that can provide a framework for our preparation and fulfillment: Learning, Loving, Living, and Letting go.

1. **LEARNING** is essential to discover and fulfill your purpose and vision. Adopt the mindset of a lifelong learner by staying curious and open-minded, asking questions, and seeking understanding. This can be accomplished by reading, listening to others, and experiencing new things. Look for books, articles, online courses, and other materials that will support your vision and personal growth. Listen to others' stories to increase your understanding and awareness. Be willing to try new things, meet new people, and consider new ideas.

2. **LOVING** yourself and your life *right where you are, as you are,* gives energy to your vision and your passion. This is easier said than done, but you have within you all the love you need. Begin by accepting this love, even when you don't feel it. Meditation and other spiritual practices will expand your

awareness and your capacity for love, which is the lifeblood of all that we dream and desire. Spend some time each day sitting in silence, imagining yourself filled with light and love. This will connect you to the source of power, creativity, and wholeness, which is the best preparation for your day and your vision.

3. **LIVING** what you are learning and living the *love* that you *are* will open the way for your vision to become reality. Living fully involves taking action, taking risks, giving back, and paying it forward. Passion and purpose are energizing and empowering! They will guide you into a greater expression of your authentic self and your best life.

4. **LETTING GO** is the final step in the fulfillment of any dream or vision. Once you have prepared yourself to experience and express your vision, it's time to let go of the outcome and the timetable. This requires patience and faith. When we have a vision, a desire, a dream, it is hard to wait for its fulfillment, especially in this fast-paced, instant results world. Can you trust and affirm that divine order is bringing all the elements of your vision together in the best possible way? Can you muster up a sense of glad anticipation as you wait, watch, and wonder? I use affirmations daily to remind myself of how truly *amazing* this life is and to attract the highest and best. I also give thanks in advance for the good that is unfolding in my life.

One of my favorite devotionals, *God Calling*, says this repeatedly: "Claim big things, really big things, now. Have a big Faith, and expect big things, and you will get big things."

How big is your vision? As we commit to learning, loving, living and letting go, we find the things that matter, the "really big things," like peace of mind, joy, relationships, energy, well-being, and wholeness. They are woven into our purpose and our passion. When we hold a vision for our lives that includes these, we will experience freedom and fulfillment.

Casting a Wider Vision

As we sharpen our vision by using the powers of intention and imagination to shape our experience, we become agents of change in our own lives and in the world around us. Our vision is created and sharpened from within and provides a roadmap for our lives.

Today we're going to cast a wider net by taking *vision* to a higher level. The power within us is designed for more than just our own lives; we are part of a larger whole. Who we are, how we live, and the vision we hold for the world can make a *significant* impact on a wide scale.

This week we honor Martin Luther King, Jr., who demonstrated the power of a vision, a dream, a higher level of thinking and being. His dream was backed by courage, hope, faith, and action. He paid for it with his life and left a legacy for all of us. He held a bold vision of equality for our country. We, too, are called to cast a vision that goes beyond ourselves, to hold the highest and best thoughts of and for humanity, and to let our intentions guide and empower our lives.

Can you imagine a world in which people trust, respect, and encourage each other? Can you imagine people around the globe working together creatively and courageously to heal our planet, our countries, and our communities? Can you imagine a world in which all people have access to clean food and water, education, meaningful work, a comfortable home, and affordable healthcare? Does it seem impossible? Everything starts with an idea, a bold vision, and faith. What if we began to imagine and focus on these ideas? What would they inspire us to do?

When we are bombarded daily by news, words and images that are upsetting, violent, hateful, divisive, and fearful, it can be very difficult to hold a higher vision of beauty, love, peace, healing, and unity. We may begin to wonder if there is really any "good" news out there, any cause for hope. I recently discovered a source of good news that I now follow on Facebook and email, and I am happy to share it with you. I have realized that the more we expose ourselves to stories and images of nature, healing, courage, kindness, and faith, the greater will be our hope, happiness, and overall well-being. We need to build our belief in the divinity within humanity and nature like building muscles to be healthy and strong. The Good News Network, www.goodnewsnetwork.org, has positive, uplifting stories and articles that will renew your faith in humanity. Check out their website and follow them on Facebook! I also nurture my soul and calm my mind by watching the nature programs on BBC America and Netflix e.g., *Planet Earth, Blue Planet, Nature's Great Events,* and *Seven Worlds, One Planet.*

Consider that you are on a heroic mission simply because you came to the planet at this time in history. You are here for a purpose, a unique and amazing assignment. Your life matters, and your vision is critical. Don't underestimate your purpose or your power! Take some time each day to connect to your divine center and ask for wisdom and guidance. We all need to do this to create a momentum of healing energy on the planet.

The Jigsaw Puzzle

One of our holiday traditions is to make a 1,000 piece jigsaw puzzle while the girls are home. It is a relaxing, fun, and even therapeutic activity. I think it uses a different part of the brain than other tasks, so it gives my thinking mind a rest as I focus on matching shapes, colors, and patterns into a larger whole. When we dump out all the pieces, we know that they fit together to create the big picture; it just takes time, patience, and focused attention. The process itself is both fun and frustrating, and we have to regularly step back and look at the big picture to see what goes where. As the picture comes together, the momentum increases until we finally complete it and feel the joy of accomplishment!

This week we had a real life puzzle to put together. As we looked at all the pieces, we knew there was a solution, a way for each part to fit together, but we couldn't quite see how. It was a puzzle that affected and involved the whole family, so we all gave input. There were different sections of the puzzle that needed to connect, so we had to step back and visualize the full picture to navigate the process. There were moments of frustration when it looked like some of the pieces were not going to fit, but then we found new pieces that connected the sections of the puzzle and created a beautiful picture! For me, this was another example of how trust, patience, faith, and vision can work together to bring order, beauty, and abundance into our lives.

We are all working on some kind of puzzle in our lives. Maybe we are dealing with relationship challenges, health issues, or situations at work or home that need our focused attention. We must start by setting our intention to find solutions and by working on ourselves to bring more order, harmony, and abundance into our lives. We need to step back from time to time and look at the bigger picture of what we want to create. There are always pieces that are not visible to us until we start working on the puzzle with patience and persistence.

When frustration sets in, it helps to take a break and let go for a while. When we return to it, we will have a fresh perspective, renewed energy, and clarity. This requires trust and faith that there *is* a beautiful picture unfolding, one that we only have to discover. Divine order is always at work, but we need to claim it and trust in it first.

Puzzles take time, so relax and rejoice in the process. Things *will* come together for you as long as you ask, believe, and open yourself to receive. Don't give up on yourself or your dreams. Trust that the bigger picture is even more beautiful than you imagined! You are part of a larger whole, and the Universe is supporting you!

I Think I Can, I Think... I Can!

Creating space, order, and simplicity in our homes is a physical and mental necessity if we are to experience more life and energy. It is so easy to get distracted and drained when we have multiple projects, demands, and responsibilities, and we may tell ourselves that we don't have time to clear the clutter, to organize the closet, to sort through and eliminate *stuff!* Having been through a move from a house with three bedrooms and an office into a two-bedroom apartment, *let me tell you how liberating it is! You can do it!* Just use the mantra, "*I think I can, I think I can, I think I can... I know I can!*" Where there is a will, there is a way. You will make time for something when your reason is strong enough. I'm not saying you should move! We had multiple reasons to sell our house at that time and to simplify our lives, and we could see and feel the end result: more time, more energy, and more money! We stayed focused on the goal and pushed through all the work that was required. It was exhausting, but *so* worth it!

What I have realized is that clearing the mental and physical clutter created space for something new, and for that which I had been imagining and desiring for a long time. I had to be willing to let go of the old for the new to show up and take shape. When we work for something and use the power of imagination and faith, we can overcome all kinds of obstacles and challenges and create something amazing. At the same time, we need to take a look at our lives to see what can be released so that we are ready to receive that which we desire. It takes energy to hold onto things, mentally, emotionally and physically. I used the following affirmation for months before the move: "I release anything that no longer serves my highest and best good." I found myself releasing thoughts, feelings, ideas, and material things that no longer had a place in me or my life. What came in their place: new energy, ideas, joy, and freedom. Everything seemed to fall into place in my life and so much *good* starting showing up.

It's January. Take inventory of your thoughts, habits, and relationships and *decide* what stays and what goes this year. What is your heart's desire? What is keeping you from experiencing it? Look for ways to create space, order, and simplicity in your home and in your life. Let go of anything that is taking energy away from you or distracting you. When you are living fully and freely, you will make an impact on the planet. Set your intention in this first month of the new year and use the gifts of imagination and faith to chart your course. When your *why* is strong enough, the *how* will become easier. You've got this. Just claim it, own it, and *go for it!*

Passion

"When you are inspired by some great purpose, all your thoughts break their bonds. Your mind transcends limitations, your consciousness expands in every direction and you find yourself in a new, great, and wonderful world. Dormant forces, faculties, and talents become alive, and

*you discover yourself to be a greater person by far than you
ever dreamed yourself to be." — Patanjali*

There comes a time in one's life when one's passion can no longer be contained or adjusted to fit one's environment, and the resounding "*yes*" becomes louder and stronger. It builds and gathers energy and moves one at the deepest level of being, and with it the desire for one's gifts to be shared in a way that impacts others' lives, making waves across the world. There comes a time when one's voice must be heard, the song of one's heart must be sung, and the purpose of one's life must be fulfilled.

When this happens to us, we are faced with releasing the habit of making sure everyone else is okay first, without guilt. We can come into our own fully, freely, and joyfully, without any fear of lack or failure. In so doing, we answer the call of the Universe to become that which was placed within us before we were born. It is time to move beyond the barriers we have created and break through to a higher level, thereby uplifting and empowering others along the way.

*"If you... follow your bliss, you put yourself on a kind of
track that has been there all the while, waiting for you, and
the life that you ought to be living is the one you are
living." — Joseph Campbell*

Step forward into your destiny and see yourself empowered, enlightened, and magnetic to abundance in every form. This is your life.

Discovering Our Gifts

"The world needs your gift as much as you need to bestow it." — Sarah Ban Breathnach

From an early age, my parents instilled in me an appreciation for and awareness of my personal gifts, helping me to embrace them. It was hard for me to keep from comparing myself to others — especially my older sister, the embodiment of perfection! I didn't want to *be* her, but I perceived her gifts as being better than mine, and I rarely saw her make a mistake. Thankfully, my mother made it very clear to me that we each had valuable gifts and that it was my responsibility to be *myself* fully and freely.

So, what does it mean to embrace our gifts and be true to ourselves? What are our gifts, really? Talents, skills, blessings, dreams? No matter how we think about them, we can agree that a gift is something *given* to us, not earned or acquired through work. Our personal gifts are planted in us before birth, and then we have the opportunity to recognize them, develop them, and share them with others. Why is it important to honor our personal gifts? According to author Sarah Ban Breathnach, *"discerning our personal gifts is essential if we are to experience harmony in our lives (Simple Abundance).*

What if our dreams and desires are also planted within us and bound to our gifts for the purpose of fulfilling our destiny here on Earth? What if each of us was sent here on a mission, and to complete it, we have to find and use our gifts, like super powers?

31

ELISA JUAREZ

> *"...Our gifts carry us out into the world and make us*
> *participants in life..."* so *"uncovering them is one of the*
> *most important tasks confronting any one of us. When we*
> *talk about being true to ourselves – being the persons we*
> *are intended to be - we are talking about gifts. We cannot*
> *be ourselves unless we are true to our gifts."*
> — Elizabeth O'Connor, *Eighth Day of Creation*

I believe that finding and using our gifts *is* the key to empowerment! When we are being and doing what we were created to be and do, we are energized, we are in harmony with life and love, and we are unstoppable!

> *"Whatever you can do or dream you can, begin it; boldness*
> *has genius, power and magic in it."*
> — Johann Wolfgang von Goethe

We have a responsibility to find and share our gifts; they are an expression of who we are, a part of our unique design and purpose. When we connect to our gifts, our authenticity, we are filled with energy, enthusiasm, and passion! We begin to live life more fully and freely, to give and serve more generously, and to experience joy, peace, and power! Life becomes more vibrant, exciting, interesting, and rich! This is how we were each designed to live. This is the key to abundance and fulfillment.

How do we recognize, discover, and connect to our gifts? It happens when we turn within and recognize the presence of the Spirit, our Creator, our God. We are never separate from the Love that created us; it continues to guide, inspire, and empower us every day. We just need to ask for guidance from within and learn to identify what brings us joy, peace, and energy.

"All we need to know is that the Spirit knows what we don't. If we get out of the way, we'll be shown the next step, including how not to sell ourselves short as we gracefully grow into our gifts."
— Sarah Ban Breathnach, *Simple Abundance.*

When we are aligned with the Spirit and intentional about connecting to our gifts, we can trust and follow our intuition. Look for clues every day through your feelings and self-awareness. And remember this:

"Love wants, wishes, and wills nothing less than your unconditional happiness, harmony, Wholeness. Commit to discovering, acknowledging, appreciating, owning, and honoring your personal gifts."
— Sarah Ban Breathnach, *Simple Abundance*

Begin with an open and grateful heart and a willingness to serve. Whenever we extend ourselves for others, we step out of our own limits and allow the Spirit within to work through us. The experience of giving and serving enlivens us, uplifts others, and increases our capacity and compassion. Service is one of the best ways to discover and share our gifts because it shifts our attention from ourselves and our circumstances onto others. When we realize that we can make a difference in the life of another, our sense of purpose and responsibility is strengthened.

In addition to service, we can tap into our gifts through creative collaboration with others. As we work together, we can learn how to develop our gifts and use them productively. We get feedback by engaging with others and discovering our skills and talents. Opportunities arise for us to continue our growth and development and strengthen our gifts through education and experience. When we commit to personal development, we seek and find the people and resources that will help us, support us, and lead us in the direction of our dreams and desires.

Discovering and developing our gifts, therefore, begins within and extends into our living. It requires a commitment to self-awareness, lifelong learning, openness, and service. We need to connect to the Giver to best use and express the gift. The more we commit to the inner and outer work for which we were created, the more our life will be filled with opportunities, healthy relationships, positive experiences, creativity, and abundance.

Soul Stirrings

It's a cold, gray, January day and the trees are barren. There is virtually no color outside, no warmth; nature is dormant. Stillness and starkness prevail. Yet it is this time of year that I cherish most for what it offers my soul. Life stirs within me; warmth rises from my heart and soul. The presence of Spirit wraps around me like a blanket and sends ripples of joy throughout my entire being. In response to the gifts of Spirit, I create a place of comfort and joy for others — especially my family. The physical nourishment that we enjoy in winter is symbolic of the greater comfort that comes from spiritual soul food. The outside world offers no fulfillment, so it must come from within.

As the season of winter is passing, so is our life on this earth. So how do we connect with the reality that is eternal and remember who we are? This life is an opportunity to learn and grow spiritually, and we can only do this when we consciously connect with the Divine Love that dwells within and around us. We cannot do it on our own, or by following earth's wisest. Our truth comes from the source of life, and we are here to find it and follow it back home.

It's so easy to forget. We forget who we are and where we came from. We forget what's real and settle for temporary illusions. We search for meaning and fulfillment outside ourselves, and it is nowhere to be found.

It's like being in a dream and thinking it's real. I can think of many times when I have had a dream in which I realized it was a dream, and then felt free and unconcerned about what might happen. I could sometimes wake myself. I especially remember when I was a child, having repeated dreams of being chased by a witch in a castle in which hallways wrapped around the interior on several levels. Then I would remember that I could wake myself up by sitting with my knees pulled up and my head down, and my arms wrapped around my knees. The witch would be fast approaching, and I would do this and wake up *just in time*. *Saved!* Saved by what? By remembering. By remembering that it was a dream, and I had the power to wake myself up. She couldn't touch me in reality; who I was in the dream was an illusion, not the real me who was asleep in my bed, safe and sound.

Such is this life. What an analogy. It takes a stretch to really get that, to let that realization transform your life, but it will. We may not be able to *leave* this earth as easily as I was able to leave the dream, but we can *wake up* in the sense that we begin to live in the awareness of who we really are, unmoved by the trials of this earth life, unafraid of what might happen here. We are here to deepen and expand our awareness of God, and to learn to forgive. I can, in fact, live my motto: "Live fully, love freely, laugh often." Live in the fullness and freedom of joy and love. I am still trying to grasp a lot of things, but this much I know: *Love and laugh. Relax and rejoice. Give thanks. There is One Spirit in which we live and move and have our being.* We shall know the truth, and the truth shall set us free. Free to live and love and laugh and be. Free to let go of any and all attachments to this earth. Free to forgive and be forgiven.

As I look out at the bleak appearance of winter, the light shines in my home. The eternal light of God shines in and through me, and all is well. All is gift. This season shall pass, and new life shall burst forth with joy and song... and "I shall dwell in the house of the Lord forever."

Wellness Wisdom

Today we are heading home from San Antonio where my mother-in-law was admitted to the hospital last Thursday with pneumonia and flu-B. We spent two and a half days in the hospital with her, following all the precautions to stay well during this "flu pandemic." We were clearly significant support for her, and now she is back home, continuing her recovery, as my sister-in-law comes to care for her this week.

I think we can all agree that our health is something we take for granted until we get sick. I was raised by a mother whose chronic illness drove her to study nutrition and seek out alternative medicine. She took responsibility for her health (and ours), teaching us what she was learning and trying out new things on us. We didn't always enjoy it (especially eating liver or gulping down a tablespoon of cod liver oil mixed with orange juice!) but I know that it made a difference in my overall health and well-being. She inspired me to continue learning about nutrition and wellness and living a healthy lifestyle.

In the month of January, most people I know are trying to get well or *stay* well! We often get depleted during the holiday season and enter the new year with a compromised immune system. It's a good time for some tips and reminders to boost your overall health! We all tend to neglect ourselves in one way or another without realizing it, so give yourself some TLC with these ingredients of a healthy, balanced life:

1. **MINDSET**: This is the place to start. What are you thinking and telling yourself about your health? The body follows instructions and suggestions from the mind, so keep your thoughts and beliefs in check! Tell yourself daily (multiple times), "I am healthy and strong!" and "Every day, in every way, I am getting better and better!" Positive thoughts and affirmations give the body signals that assist in healing and staying well!

2. **REST**: Sleep is one of the most important factors in keeping our immune systems strong and counteracting illness. Do everything you can (naturally) to get a good 7 to 8 hours of sleep each night. I use essential oils in a diffuser and on my body every night and try to turn off TV and electronic devices at least 30 minutes before bed. There are many things we can do to improve our quality and quantity of sleep at night; I recommend doing some research on your own if you need some help here!

3. **NUTRITION**: Boost your immune system with plenty of fruits and vegetables *and* quality, whole food supplements! Drink plenty of purified water with lemon! Plan your meals and take the time to sit down and enjoy them! It's so easy to grab something on the go and miss out on the full benefit of a meal. Don't cheat yourself here; if you have a short time in which to eat, then choose a healthy, high protein option, packed with as many nutrients as possible. Good nutrition is also essential for our mental health, cognitive function, and emotional well-being! There is plenty of information available about health and nutrition, so be open and willing to learn and try new things. An investment in yourself will pay dividends for years to come. *You are worth it!*

4. **SPIRIT**: Carve out time each day to feed and nurture your spirit, especially at the beginning and end of the day. Sit in silence, read, meditate, write in a journal and list the things for which you are grateful each day. This practice will reduce stress, increase awareness, and calm the mind and body in a way that has a direct positive effect on your physical health.

5. **EXERCISE**: Find ways to get moving each day. Stretching, walking, climbing stairs, doing yoga, cycling, dancing... or whatever you enjoy most and can fit into the day that will get your heart pumping and your energy flowing! Exercise is a great stress buster and strength builder. You will find that you feel more balanced, confident, and happy as a result!

6. **EMOTIONS**: Keep your emotions in check and don't let negative feelings stay for more than a few minutes. Notice them but move through them without giving them any power

over you. Repeating negative thoughts, feelings, and experiences will magnify them and create toxins in the body. What we think about will expand, and hurt feelings, resentments, anxiety, and other negative emotions will wreak havoc on our health if we dwell on them.

Pay attention to your choices, your feelings, your relationships, your finances, and your mindset. Attitude is everything, so don't underestimate the power of a positive mental attitude! All of these aspects of ourselves and our lives are connected and can be developed with intention and action, so be grateful, be happy, and be well!

Passages

It's a cold, rainy day as I sit in my warm kitchen looking out at the stark silhouettes of trees. The world is painted in various shades of brown and gray. It misses the bright red cardinals and their song. Even the squirrels are huddled in their cubbies today, feasting on the morsels they have gathered over the past several months. The earth is still and cold, accepting this necessary passage through the dark and dreary when all signs of life are hidden. Nature knows and trusts the seasons through which it must pass; the seasons that symbolize a greater reality which encompasses us all. It is a manifestation of our inner journey, our spiritual unfolding through the seasons of life.

We all experience darkness and doubt before a breakthrough in awareness and understanding, before a growth spurt, before new life is expressed through us. We must turn within, shifting our focus to that inner sanctuary where we find the source of Life and Love, and

ELISA JUAREZ

our true identity. Here we know the truth that sets us free from the lies and limitations that face us on the outside. Here we are eternally kept, held, protected, guided, loved. Secure at last. Nothing to fear. Each season is a passage, and an opportunity to find something new within and around us. The cardinal will soon return with its bold color and song. Keep your eyes and ears open, always.

Giving Birth

It was a Sunday afternoon in the middle of the NFL playoffs when the contractions started. As instructed by my doctor, I grabbed a notepad and started timing them. Art noticed that I was making a notation about every five minutes. He asked, "What are you doing?"

I said, "Timing my contractions."

He was startled. "What? They're that close together?!"

"Yep," I said, sprawled out on the futon in our little townhome living room. We had put the overnight bag in the trunk of the car earlier that day, just in case. It was still a few days before my due date, and the doctor had told me a week ago that the baby would be late. I would have none of it. We went walking at the mall the night before, and I mean *intentional* walking! "Bring on the baby" walking! Well, it seems to have worked. I went into labor the very next day. Later that afternoon my water broke suddenly, and I flew off that futon and into the bathroom. That was the beginning.

We checked into the hospital at 10:00PM, and our first child, Taylor Brooke, was born at 3:30AM. My parents were on their way, driving from Indiana, but that night it was just Art and me and an amazing nurse.

It was a rough delivery for Taylor, as she had the umbilical cord wrapped around her, and it took considerable time and effort to bring her out. She was not breathing when she arrived, but they didn't tell me since they didn't want me to *freak out!* They just called NICU nurses to the room to scoop her up and take her. I begged to hold her for a minute first, having waited for nine months for this moment. They nervously passed her to me, and I could feel the sense of urgency in the room. After they left I slept for a few hours before they let me see her. There she was, hooked up to a ventilator and monitor, asleep. I held her little hand and talked to her. She was okay; they just needed to clear her lungs and help her breathe until she could breathe easily on her own.

Today she is a healthy, strong, happy, and thriving young woman, living her best life. For me this is always a special day, as it marks the beginning of the most sacred and challenging journey of my life. As much as I tried to prepare for it, I never could have imagined the depth of love this experience would carve into my heart and soul. I didn't realize how much she would teach me and shape me as a parent. What I have learned along the way is that giving birth to a child, or a dream, or our authentic selves, takes courage, humility, surrender, and faith. There is always more to it than we can imagine, and it will increase our understanding and our capacity when we are open to the lessons and the blessings it brings.

Every journey is designed to take us places within ourselves that we have yet to discover. This is the *real* adventure in life, and it is full of mystery and wonder. It may be painful and difficult at times, but this is the path to wholeness. When you find your authentic self, hold it and love it fiercely. Trust it and allow it to show you the way to joy and healing.

Celebrate Your Life!

"Age has given me what I was looking for my entire life - it has given me me. It has provided time and experience and failures and triumphs and time-tested friends, who have helped me step into the shape that was waiting for me. I fit into me now. I have an organic life finally. ... not necessarily the one people imagined for me or tried to get me to have. I have the life I longed for. I have become the woman I hardly dared imagine I would be."
— Anne Lamott

This is the week of my birthday, and I believe in celebrating every day in some simple way. As a lover of life, I experience birthdays as an opportunity to honor and give thanks for the life I have been given. I also like to set new intentions for the year ahead and refresh my dreams! I think it is easier for us to celebrate others than ourselves, so I have a few ideas for you that you can use throughout the year, not just on your birthday! These are things I have learned over time as I continue to discover how to love and accept myself more fully. The more we love ourselves, the more we can love others.

One of the best guides for discovering and embracing your authentic self is *Simple Abundance* by Sarah Ban Breathnach, and I refer to it often. Knowing what we love is the key to bringing more happiness and enjoyment into our lives. Sarah provides all kinds of ideas for how to do that!

I have always known what I liked, but Art, on the other hand, had parents who *told* him what to like, what *not* to like, what to do, and what *not* to do. When he expressed an interest in something, they would often say, "You don't want to do that." This included both school and career interests. When I met him, he was still trying to figure out what he really wanted to do and become. No surprise! Perhaps you, too, were influenced by your parents or other adults who had definite ideas of how you should be, what you should like, and who you should become, and as a result, you're not in tune with or confident in your own instincts.

For today, start with what you *know* brings you happiness and enjoyment and make a list. Mine includes starting my day with coffee and journal writing; doing crosswords and jigsaw puzzles, taking a walk, doing yoga, meeting a friend for coffee or wine, cooking, watching HGTV, browsing at World Market and farmers' markets, and exploring new places. Your list is something to continue to add to and choose from as you plan your days each week. Be sure that you are including at least one thing from your list every day! This is one way to love and honor your authentic self. Take time, make time, to do what you love. Every day.

The next tool comes from Julia Cameron's book, *The Right to Write*. This is a big one which will take more than one sitting to complete. Find a quiet time and space, a good pen, and a notepad or your journal. Number a page from 1 to 100. Go back through your life and list a full 100 things you are proud of.

> *"These do not need to be what you should be proud of or what other people may tell you [that] you should be proud of. Some of what you're proud of may even be antisocial or even illegal. It's your list. Let yourself be particular and personal."* — Julia Cameron, *The Right to Write*

Don't let the number 100 overwhelm you. Just get started.

Remember that *this is your life!* It is your gift, your creation, and your responsibility. It is yours to enjoy, discover, and celebrate. Stay curious, grateful, and open, and the Universe will continually surprise and bless you.

January Closure, Inventory, & Imagination

January is winding down and it's time to take a quick inventory of where we are with our intentions for the new year! Time slips through our fingers so fast; before we know it, spring has sprung and summer is around the corner! So, take a few minutes today or this week and review your goals, dreams, ideas, and intentions. We all need to do this weekly and monthly anyway! Before January is gone, take the time to do at least one thing on your list. Whenever we clear space in our lives and our homes, we invite something new! That is what I did a little over a year ago, and I am enjoying the time and creative energy that was freed up when I made space for it!

As a part of this creative process, begin to find and cut out pictures of things and places you want to attract into your life. Include physical, mental, and spiritual conditions which create quality of life and love. You might cut out or write words that represent these aspects of your life. Perhaps you have heard of or created a vision board at some time in your life. You can do this on a poster board or in a blank 8" x 12" sketch book. The idea is to choose and focus on the images that you wish to manifest in your life, because whatever we think and imagine *repeatedly*, we attract and increase in our lives! Have fun with this and realize that to attract something *new* you need to release that which no longer serves you, and especially anything that is keeping you from experiencing your best life!

The Starting Gate

It seems like I've only blinked twice since we rang in the new year, and the first month is already over! Now that we are out of the starting gate, it's time to look at where we are and whether we are on the right footing. How is your vision shaping up? Have you taken some steps toward it? The path you've chosen does not require huge leaps, just daily steps. The best way I've found to stay on track is to start each day with a morning routine that supports my total well-being and focuses my attention on my vision.

My vision includes every part of me – physical, mental, spiritual, and emotional. It starts with self acceptance, where I am, as I am, which is a daily practice. I think as we get older we get better at it, but it's still a challenge at times. From a place of self acceptance and love, I see *all of me* as healthy and whole, filled with energy, vitality, and joy. Holding this vision of myself increases the likelihood that I will make choices that support it. My morning routine touches all four corners of my being, giving me a solid start to the day. You may already have a morning routine that works for you, but here are 7 things I do every day to give myself the best start possible. Perhaps you can incorporate a few of them.

1. Drink a glass of room temperature water with a tablespoon of organic apple cider vinegar, half a fresh squeezed lemon, and a generous drizzle of raw, local honey. This is an excellent morning tonic to detox and refresh your system! When I don't have lemons, I just mix the apple cider vinegar and honey. Drink this first, before eating or drinking anything else.

2. Make your bed! This is a great way to bring order and beauty into your day from the start, and it only takes a few minutes.

3. Stretch! Since I do yoga, I choose some of those stretches to start my day and get my blood flowing.

4. Brew your favorite morning drink. For me it's coffee. The sound and aroma of the brewing gives me a good feeling, not to mention the satisfaction of drinking it. A cup of tea or a smoothie are other good choices!

5. Sit down with a daily devotional or anything inspirational, and a journal. *This is your mental and spiritual breakfast!* Sit in silence with your books, your drink, and a fleece blanket if it's cold. Be still and breathe. Relax. Meditate. Write. Author Julia Cameron recommends a daily ritual called "the Morning Pages" to clear our heads of the clutter that consumes our attention and energy. Whatever is in your head or your heart, just write it. Let it go; make room for creativity and productivity instead.

6. Make a list for the day as a guideline to help you focus and get things done. Set your priorities.

7. Give thanks. Ask for guidance, protection, and grace. Claim divine order. Give thanks again.

I recommend doing these 7 things *first*, before turning on the television and getting onto the computer or any electronic device. This can be hard. But you know as well as I do that once you engage with any of your devices your attention gets pulled in multiple directions. You lose focus and time gets away from you. When you open the door to the outside world, it quickly invades your inside world and disturbs your peace of mind. *It can wait!*

There is a saying: "How we spend our days is, in fact, how we spend our lives." How we *start* our days can also determine the course of our days, and therefore our lives. Life is unpredictable, and the starting gate is a sacred space in which to prepare ourselves for whatever the day brings. We need to fill our tanks first by giving love and attention to all four corners of our being. Learn to savor the morning and don't rush it. Get in alignment with the highest and best, establish your footing, and step into your vision!

Home

It is a gray, cold morning in Texas and the sky looks like winter. I snuggled a bit longer than usual on the couch this morning with my coffee and blanket. The present moment was so rich and full as I listened to the clock ticking, watched the fish dart around the aquarium, and felt the softness and warmth of the blanket around me. I didn't want to move. In the stillness, I began to consider the sacred space in which I live, the comfort it brings me, the beauty that surrounds me, and the simple abundance of home.

Our homes are a reflection of who we are and what we love. What does your home look like? How have you created a home within your house or apartment? If you have children at home you've created a space that is safe, comfortable, happy, and fun. If your children are grown and gone, how has your space changed? It feels different now. Is it more your own? Does it feel full or empty? Does anyone live with you? Tap your writing and creativity well with a reflection on your home. Choose one or two things you especially love about it and write. Write in your journal or a notebook, whatever is most comfortable. There is tremendous potential for inspiration and creativity within our homes because they hold not only our bodies but our souls, our love, our dreams, our energy. Cherish that sacred space in which you live and allow it to inspire you to write!

Perhaps you can begin to see your home with fresh eyes and discover the sacred in the ordinary. Take a closer look at your space today and give thanks for it. Realize you can recreate it at any time. Find simple ways to refresh your home and bring more beauty, order, and harmony into your life! In the process, you will discover the luminous threads of your inner world woven together with your surroundings in a rich tapestry of contentment and wholeness.

Spoonful of Love: Savor the Juice!

Art and I both enjoy cooking, and sometimes on the weekends will prepare a meal together. This works for the most part, but we have different ideas about cooking that don't always "blend" well. For example, I love using fresh herbs and he doesn't. He likes to cook almost everything with tomato sauce. And when we cook ground beef, I drain the fat and he likes to keep it! He'll say, "Look at all that *love*!" One time he caught me draining the fat and he said, "What are you doing!? You're pouring off all the *love*! That's what makes it so good!" He argues that the fat from grass fed beef must be good for us since the beef is! I don't know about that, but I have learned to relax a little when it comes to saving the "juice." My mother used to drain it and pat it so much that it was dry. That's where I learned it.

The theme for February is *love*. I don't know anyone who doesn't long for more love in some area of their lives. The truth is, Love is what we are made of; it is our source and our essence, so we are never truly without it! Our thoughts, ideas, and beliefs can get in the way of experiencing more love.

For fun, let's use the fat analogy. I had a belief that the fat was "bad" or that I shouldn't eat it, so I made sure to drain and remove as much as possible while cooking the meat. Now I am not here to argue whether or not to do that, but to use it as a metaphor for how we live our lives. What are your beliefs around love? I bet you have some definite ideas about what it "should" look like in your life.

49

Perhaps the biggest obstacles to experiencing love are our beliefs about ourselves. Yep, that's the clincher. How do you see yourself? How do you *love* yourself? Do you believe you are worthy of love? *What are you telling yourself?*

If you believe that you came from Love, exist in Love, and therefore are forever worthy of Love, then you will embrace your true self more fully, and your true self is Love. This is the starting point to increase the love in your life. It *all* starts within. That's where Love resides and abides, always. Let's imagine love is like fat, the juice that gives the meat its flavor, moisture, and goodness. It is part of the meat until we remove it, right? So, what happens if you stop removing it? Soak it up and savor it. Realize it doesn't come from outside yourself, or from anyone or anything, but from you, through you, and for you. Mmm, good!

Once you learn to accept, embrace, and live the love that you *are*, you will naturally attract more love into your life, because love is energy, and like attracts like. Take a look at the areas of your life that may need more love: health, relationships, work, finances, etc.

I found a powerful affirmation that I have placed on my bathroom mirror and memorized. It is my gift to you today: I know Love as absolute freedom in every area of my life. I release any sense of struggle, lack, or wrongdoing. I live in an abundant universe, where there is more than enough for all. I experience freedom in every moment by always having more than enough money, vibrant health, and loving relationships. I am rich; I am blessed; I am free. And so, it is.

Let Love fill you and your life until it is overflowing. Ask, believe, receive. It is yours, and it is *you*.

Presence of Love

February is full of symbols and reminders of love with the observance of Valentine's Day right in the middle of the month. It is an opportunity to celebrate the presence of *love* in our lives, in all its different shapes and expressions. When we truly learn to embrace and celebrate life, we will find countless opportunities to do so. Whatever we think about and focus on *expands* in our lives, and who wouldn't welcome an abundance of *love*?

Think of love as energy. It is creative energy, a life force, magnetic and powerful. Think of increasing *that* in your life. What would that look like? How would it impact your work, your relationships, your health, and your everyday life? Take a few minutes to really think about this idea and imagine it! Then realize this energy is always available to you; you just need to connect with it. Plug into it. Allow it to flow through you, letting go of any thoughts, feelings, attitudes, or beliefs that might block it. Anytime you feel a lack of love and energy, it is time to identify those blocks and release them. It can take time, awareness, and discipline, but it's not hard. It's worth it.

Enjoy any and all symbols and gestures of love, beauty, and affection that you give and receive this month. At the same time, realize the energy of love within and behind these symbols is the real gift, the one that lasts, and the one that is present in the *present*. The now. *Be* present and attentive with yourself and your loved ones, and you will experience the presence of Love. That awareness will be followed by gratitude and joy.

The Kitchen Sink

*"My whole life, in one sense, has been an experiment in
how to be a portable sanctuary—learning to practice the
presence of God in the midst of stresses and strains for
contemporary life."* — Richard Foster

I have had this little paperback entitled *The Practice of the Presence
of God* for many years. First published in 1958, it is a collection of
letters and conversations with and by Brother Lawrence. It contains
simple yet profound insights for all of us — regardless of our religious
background.

The one illustration that I have carried with me through the years
is about working in the monastery kitchen. It was there that Brother
Lawrence experienced the presence and peace of God just as much as
anywhere else. He prayed, *"Lord of all pots and pans and things... make
me a saint by getting meals and washing up the plates!"* As one who has
spent a considerable portion of my life in the kitchen, I find this
example relevant and enlightening. The kitchen is, for me, somewhat
of a sanctuary.

Brother Lawrence, on the other hand, had "a great aversion" to
working in the kitchen, but he used the time to practice the presence
of God, doing his work prayerfully with humility, grace, and
excellence. As a result, he found everything easy during the 15 years
he was employed there. He discovered that his times of "business"
were not different from his times of prayer, and that, by doing his

work mindfully with love and devotion to God, he experienced deep tranquility and joy.

> *"All things are possible to him who believes, they are less difficult to him who hopes, they are easier to him who loves, and still more easy to him who practices and perseveres in these three virtues."*
> — Brother Lawrence, *The Practice of the Presence of God*

When I stand at the sink after supper, washing dishes and wiping counters, I feel a sense of serenity and gratitude. I have just enjoyed a meal and conversation with my husband in our simple but lovely surroundings; my heart and belly are full. Time spent in the kitchen and around the table is rich with life's goodness as we share food, stories, laughter, ideas, and love. When we learn to pay attention, to *notice* and *savor* the simple pleasures, the aromas, textures, and flavors of our food, our homes, and our lives, we will discover the *sacred* in all of it. We will experience the presence of God.

Knowing how swift and uncertain life is, we long for a sense of peace and security. We may feel more *absence* than *presence*, or a hunger for something real and lasting. Brother Lawrence found that *something* in his daily life by turning "the most commonplace and menial task into a living hymn to the glory of God." That example has helped me to find the sacred in the ordinary, even at the kitchen sink! As I bring more love and attention to my daily routine, I catch the sweet music and rhythm of Spirit. I get a taste of the divine.

ELISA JUAREZ

> "The presence of God is thus the life and nourishment of
> the soul."
> — Brother Lawrence, *The Practice of the Presence of God*

It is that which alone can satisfy our hunger, and yet we forget that we are in the midst of it every day. It takes practice to bring love into everything we do until it becomes a natural expression of who we are. Start by bringing your full attention to your surroundings and the task at hand. Smile and say *thank you* under your breath. Gratitude is the gateway to greater awareness of all good, and the kitchen is one of the best places to practice it.

Writing Life

> "Writing is a rare treasure - for if it is done right, it can
> empty you and fill you up at the same time."
> – Taylor Juarez

Ever since I was in grade school, I have loved to write. I enjoyed writing fictional stories and poetry, and started keeping a diary in second grade. My mother gave me a five-year diary at that time to get me started. As a seven year old, my handwriting was rather large and the lines in that diary were very narrow. Most days I could only write one or two sentences. Here is one I remember well from that year: *"Today at recess we played Boys Chase the Girls. Mike Evers caught me and kissed me on the back of my hat."* I guess I remember that entry because of the feeling attached to it. I had a crush on that blond haired boy and never forgot that day!

The cool thing about a five-year diary is that for each date, you can see the previous years on that same page and see what you were doing, what was going on in your life. As I got older, I learned to write smaller and fit more in! I think I was in junior high when I started writing in a journal. These were blank books in which I could write as much or as little as I wanted, whenever I had the urge to write. On those pages I would pour out my heart or simply write the highlights of the day. During high school and college my writing became a valuable dialogue with myself and my spirit. It helped me work through the myriad of feelings, experiences, relationships, and complex issues of growing up. It helped me see things clearer at times, listen to my inner wisdom, and develop a language for my thoughts and feelings. It was just for me, so there was no judgment, critique, or pressure. This is what makes journal writing so therapeutic and necessary in finding our authentic voice.

We each have a unique and yet universal story to share. The first step is to just write it down for our own understanding and reflection. Julia Cameron says that writing is how she metabolizes her experiences.

> "Just as walking aerobicizes the physical body, producing a flow of endorphins and good feelings, writing seems to alter the chemical balance of the soul itself, restoring balance and equilibrium when we are out of sorts, bringing clarity, a sense of right action, a feeling of purpose to a rudderless day." — Julia Cameron, *The Right to Write*

We all tend to process things in our heads, and sometimes verbally with others. Our feelings, ideas, experiences, annoyances, relationships, challenges, disappointments, all get processed somehow in our minds. Without a healthy outlet for all this activity we can easily become overwhelmed, confused, discouraged, depressed, anxious, and exhausted. Writing gives us an easy and natural outlet for all the noise in our heads and feelings in our hearts. It is something we do alone. When we sit down to write we connect with our inner selves.

> *"What writing brings to a life is clarity and tenderness.*
> *Writing, we witness ourselves."*
> — Julia Cameron, *The Right to Write*

There is something about putting pen to paper that activates the creative process in each of us. Don't be intimidated by it; just start writing whatever is on your mind. Don't judge it. Consider it an exercise in clearing your head and let it come out. This is the first step. Julia Cameron recommends writing three pages every morning as soon as you get up. She calls these the "Morning Pages," saying they might also be called the "Mentoring Pages" because they help you access a warmer and wiser part of yourself. It is like crossing a threshold into your inner world with open eyes and ears, connecting to the Wisdom and Love that created you. It is there within you, ready to speak to you and through you. Once you begin this daily practice, it will become easier and ever more valuable to you. You will learn to let the writing flow through you.

I have this experience often; it feels like it is coming from a larger presence that is both within me and beyond me. The more I engage in this daily writing, the easier it flows. My awareness expands and the connection grows stronger. Writing is a touchstone for me. It brings me back to myself and my inner wisdom and helps me to focus on the present moment as I put pen to paper. It is a comfort and an anchor for me. At 56 years young I am still growing into my authentic self and learning to love her fully. Writing helps me in this process, like an old friend who is sharing the journey. It is always there for me, no matter how I am feeling or what is going on in my life. I can pick up my journal at any time and just write a few sentences or a few pages. It grounds me while opening me up to insight and inspiration, wisdom and healing.

Writing the Morning Pages clears the clutter from our minds so that we can see, think, and act more clearly. It also creates space for listening, imagining, and allowing the creative process to become active within and through us.

> *"Writing gives us a place to say what we need to say, but also to hear what we need to hear."*
> — Julia Cameron, *The Right to Write*

It brings our attention to the present moment, to what is happening in our heads, in our environment, and in our lives. It helps us to see it and to cherish it.

> *"Writing is the act of opening the eye to the absolute beauty of ordinary things."*
> — Julia Cameron, *The Right to Write*

From the practice of Morning Pages may come a newfound comfort and joy that leads you into new avenues for writing. You will discover and develop your voice and the power to use it in new ways. You may be inspired to expand and share your writing and connect with other writers. The most important journey is the one that leads you to your authentic self, and writing will carve out the path and lead you gently. Just let go and trust the process. There is mystery and magic in it.

Reading can inspire our writing by giving us ideas for how to tell our stories and articulate our thoughts and experiences. I have found that reading is essential for me as a writer, as it expands my vocabulary, understanding, and perspective. It also generates new writing ideas and inspires me to become a better writer. So, each day I read a little and write a little. I *listen, learn,* and *live.* These three actions inform and shape my writing. They provide content, character, and substance. It is not mine to measure my worth or my impact. It is mine to give voice and expression to that which is within me (*listen*), that which I am learning (*learn*), and that which I am experiencing (*live*). All three are woven together to create a rich tapestry that reflects both a unique and universal experience.

Each of us has been designed to participate in the creative process and share this with the world in our own unique way. Writing can open you to the discovery of your purpose, your voice, and the Wisdom and Love that abide within you. In this way it becomes an avenue for healing, creativity, clarity, and empowerment. It can help you sort through the messiness of life, the chatter of the world, the confusion of competing and critical voices in your head, and the barrage of information you receive every day. The world is too much with us, and we need to retreat, release, and reflect. We need to write. When we write through it all, we find our way. We find our voice. We remember that we are okay, we are loved, and we have something to give to the world.

"If you do stick with writing, you will get better and better, and you can start to learn the important lessons: who you

really are, and how all of us can live in the face of death,
and how important it is to pay much better attention to
life, moment by moment, which is why we are here."
— Anne Lamott, *Almost Everything*

Perhaps writing is somewhat new to you. Perhaps the voice in your head says you're not a writer, you're not good at it, or you can't do it. *Disregard.* Your authentic self is waiting for your attention and trust. *Just start.*

> *"Each time you experience the new, you become receptive to*
> *inspiration. Each time you try something different, you let*
> *the Universe know you are listening. Trust your instincts.*
> *Believe your yearnings are blessings. Respect your creative*
> *urges..."* – Sarah Ban Breathnach, *Simple Abundance*

Dragon Slayer

My day starts in the quiet, in solitude, with books, pen, and paper. Here I find rest and comfort for my body and soul. Here I connect to my inner wisdom and the abiding presence of Divine Love and Light. Here I practice stillness, listening, and focused attention. Here I am empowered. It is vital to my existence and my work.

From here I go forth to write, create, connect, serve, and inspire. On the battlefield of the soul I fight off self doubt, self criticism, disappointments, discouragement, failure, weakness, and weariness. I have to slay these dragons at the start of the day so they are out of my way. I have work to do.

I am bigger than these little demons, dragons, and distractions. I can rise above them, but I need to face them and slay them or they will sneak up on me throughout the day, hanging in the shadows, whispering in my ear, pulling me down, interfering with my goals and my creativity.

> "Our dragons are our fears: our day stalkers, our night
> sweats. Fear of the unknown. Fear of failing. Fear of
> starting something new and not finishing. Again. Or the
> real fear, the one that sends shivers up our spines: the fear
> of succeeding, of becoming our Authentic Selves and facing
> the changes that will inevitably bring."
> – Sarah Ban Breathnach, Simple Abundance

I use my words and my attention to master this challenge, saying No to that which robs me of energy and power and Yes to that which energizes and empowers me. It is focus, faith, and action in alignment with my purpose and passion that allow me to slay the dragons and awaken the goddess within me.

> "Women have always known how to deal with dragons
> hiding under beds or lurking in closets. We turn on the
> lights and reassure worried souls with love. We need to slay
> the dragons in our minds the same way."
> – Sarah Ban Breathnach, Simple Abundance

Draw your sword from within your sacred soul where true power and courage reside. It is there for you always. As we draw our power and wisdom from within, we become transformers of our lives. We remember who we are.

*"How could we be capable of forgetting the old myths that
stand at the threshold of all mankind, myths of dragons
transforming themselves at the last moment into princesses?
Perhaps all dragons in our lives are really princesses just
waiting to see us just once being beautiful and courageous."*
— Rainer Maria Rilke

Awakening to Beauty

"Beauty arises in the stillness of your presence."
— Eckhart Tolle

It's a beautiful February morning with sunshine illuminating the
Spanish tile rooftops. As I look out and take in the beauty of the here
and now, I also imagine waking up to a panoramic Hill Country view
every morning. I realize that to attract my dreams and desires, I must
first see the beauty and wonder of my present circumstances by
accepting and giving thanks for them. I have joy and peace and
abundance right here, right now. From this awareness I am receptive
to increase. It is from a consciousness of abundance and gratitude that
we attract, become, and experience *more*. "More" is always within us,
as is the *capacity* for more. As we stretch, grow, and give, we increase
our capacity. We were designed for this.

Take a few minutes each day to pause, look, and listen. Find at
least one thing for which to give thanks. Start where you are and open
your mind to new ways of seeing the world and experiencing life. Look
for beauty and you will find it. Begin to notice more by becoming

aware of what's around you. For example, sometimes I am struck by the way the sunlight streams in across the room, the shadows it casts, and the soft glow it creates. In these moments I stop and really look at it. I absorb the beauty of it and the light reaches into me. Practice this pause and gratitude in your daily round and you will soon discover the sacred in the ordinary. You will have touched the "more" that is already present in your surroundings and your inner self. As your awareness expands, so will your experience of life. As within, so without. More life, love, beauty, wisdom, creativity, and energy are awaiting our discovery in every moment.

Taste & See

Love yourself first, and everything else falls into line. You really have to love yourself to get anything done in this world." — Lucille Ball

This week I came across a quote by Eleanor Roosevelt: *"Friendship with oneself is all important, because without it one cannot be friends with anyone else in the world."* In this month of valentines, sweethearts, and all things *love*, let's say it this way: *Loving oneself is all important, because unless we love ourselves, we cannot truly love anyone else in the world.* We are so programmed to look for love and happiness outside ourselves, we feel disappointed and inadequate when someone or something falls short or doesn't show up for us. We may believe another person will make us complete. I am here to remind you that the Love that created you makes you complete. It breathes through you, flows through your veins, and abides with you always. It is the stuff of which you're made, the essence of who you are, and the highest and best love you can imagine. *Taste and see that this Love is good, and it is Life, and it is enough.* You are enough. Period.

But it's Valentine's Day, and you have wishes and expectations! Okay, of course! What you really want is love, beauty, appreciation, and chocolate. Maybe a bottle of wine. This is no problem, because once you've discovered and embraced the Love that is *in you*, you will be empowered! You will be connected to the source, and you can enjoy that wine and chocolate, with or without someone else giving it to you! In fact, if *you* give it to someone who may be feeling alone, then a greater gift will be yours. *Taste and see*; try it out! Express the love that you *are* by giving more to others. Let this Valentine's Day be an opportunity to make someone else's day.

If you are feeling a lack of love, take some time to sit in stillness and focus on your breathing and your heartbeat. Relax. *Hold your sweet heart tenderly and say, "I love you."* Ask that your eyes, heart, and life be opened to a greater experience of love. Ask how and where you can give more love. Say aloud, "I am love," and "I am open and willing to give and receive more love."

As we learn to truly love ourselves, we will attract, experience, and enjoy more *love!* You probably already know this, but do you *really* know it? I have come to know this a little more every year. It is such a central theme to everything else in life that I come back to it again and again. No matter how old you are, I'm guessing you are still working on accepting and loving yourself. I know I am!

"Start to treat yourself more generously. Begin with $5.
Buy one beautiful flower for your desk, enjoy a French

ELISA JUAREZ

*pastry with your morning coffee, stop at a fancy salon and
get yourself some almond-scented shampoo. Just do
something out of the ordinary that you normally wouldn't
do that will lift your spirits."*
— Sarah Ban Breathnach, *Simple Abundance*

I have embraced this approach to life, and now it comes easily.
I've noticed that when I am feeling good and treating myself well,
more energy, joy, and love flow through me to others. Some of the
ways I care for myself are by starting each day with quiet reflection,
writing, and coffee; getting a one-hour massage twice a month,
keeping my favorite foods and wine in the pantry, exercising almost
every day, and doing a crossword puzzle in the evening. I have learned
to listen to my inner wisdom, trust my intuition, accept me where I
am, and laugh at myself.

In this time of turmoil, division, and anxiety, it is ever more
important that we commit to and connect with the Love that we are.
The world needs it desperately, and we can increase our awareness
and capacity a little each day. Nurture the friendship with yourself
with kind and loving thoughts, words, and actions. Let Love comfort,
heal, and strengthen you. Let it swell within you and spill over into
every area of your life. Taste and see and savor it. It's better than
chocolate!

What's New?

"What's new?" Have you heard that phrase lately? Do people still use it as much as they used to? I know I hear, "What's up?" often, but that's different. Today let's consider the common question, "What's new?" and ask *ourselves*.

Winter is winding down in much of the U.S., and we are all anticipating the arrival of spring. Spring is all about new life, renewal, freshness, and change. It's the perfect time to take a look at ourselves and our lives and find or create something new! How can we keep it fresh and fun?

It's interesting and sometimes amazing how life can bring us a new idea or perspective through a person, book, program, or experience that opens our eyes and our minds in a new way. Sometimes these encounters and experiences inspire us in such a way that we decide to change our direction or make a lifestyle change. Have you ever had an experience that altered the course of your life? Maybe it was someone you met, a class or program you took, or a service project in which you participated. I believe these are intended to awaken us to a part of ourselves that may have been asleep or unfulfilled. It is important for each of us to be alert and receptive, to pay attention to the clues the Universe is providing to us. Every day brings with it something fresh and new and an opportunity to awaken to the ever-unfolding design within us. I have found that each day is also a chance to move through our fear and self-doubt and release anything that may be holding us back. We have to do this to make room for the new.

Today and this week, look for a new idea or experience that can give you a different perspective on yourself and your life. I just finished a book by Dr. Christiane Northrup, *Making Life Easy*, that gave me a fresh perspective on this stage of my life. It was liberating! Reading, listening to audiobooks, meeting new people, and trying new things are all great ways to open and expand our minds. Try at least one this week and notice what you learn from it. Write it down. Now when someone asks you, "What's new?" you will have something to share. Make it a fun and interesting week by renewing yourself and your mind each and every day!

On Love and Marriage: 50 Things I Learned from My Parents

I wrote this for my parents in 2009 as a gift for their 50th wedding anniversary. They had a beautiful marriage based on a strong faith. I share it here with the intention of adding some value to your relationships, whether or not you are married. It is important to note that there was never any abuse or infidelity in my parents' marriage. These lessons are what I learned growing up, not a universal prescription for marriage. However, I think you will find most of these to be universal principles.

1. Love is a gift.
2. Love creates, supports, and sustains life.

3. The best relationship is based on genuine respect and affection.

4. Marriage calls for unconditional love and acceptance.

5. When you open your heart, you experience both joy and pain.

6. Life is meant to be shared.

7. Love is a decision you make each day, and a commitment you renew continually.

8. Anger can be expressed without hurting the other person or yourself.

9. Forgiveness is absolutely necessary for a marriage to last.

10. Sharing your thoughts and feelings is an integral part of marriage.

11. Listening is more helpful than talking.

12. Marriage is about partnership, friendship, and trust.

13. A healthy marriage requires effort, patience, and faith.

14. Prayer is a powerful way to connect to God and each other.

15. Sharing dreams and a vision for the future creates a sense of purpose and hope.

16. It's more important to be loving than to be right.

17. Each day is a chance to begin again, to renew your love.

18. A happy home is a safe haven from the world.

19. Family is a treasure beyond measure!

20. If you want to get the best out of someone, look for the best in them.

21. It's best to ignore little irritations.

22. Happiness and joy come from within, not from the other person.

23. A healthy relationship is the result of a series of choices, day after day, year after year.

24. Your partner and your children will become that which you see and affirm in them.

25. When you recognize the Spirit of God in someone, their light will shine like the sun.

26. You build strong relationships by building people up, not tearing them down.

27. Marriage is to be enjoyed, cherished, and nurtured.

28. A marriage will grow deeper and stronger when each partner is committed to their own spiritual growth.

29. Love is about bringing out the highest and best in each other.

30. Marriage is like a garden that needs tending. Weeds need to be pulled regularly; seeds planted and watered, and space allowed for the seeds to grow.

31. Marriage is a sacred union that needs to be guarded.

32. Marriage is an investment that rewards the partners and their children.

33. A husband and wife need to have fun together, to laugh, play, and relax together.

34. Balance is the key to health and happiness: time with your partner, time with friends and family, and time alone. A person needs all of these to be fulfilled and balanced.

35. When your partner is having a bad day, don't take it personally.

36. When your partner is having a bad day, give him/her space. Be patient; it will pass.

37. Marriage requires creativity and resourcefulness!

38. It's best to discuss and resolve conflicts in private, not in front of children or others.

39. Keep negative comments and opinions to yourself.

40. Be intentional about the marriage and family you wish to create.

41. At the end of the day, let it go. Let go of everything but the joy, the love, and the lessons.

42. Work together, play together, and pray together.

43. Give your best to your partner and the relationship. You will reap an abundant harvest.

44. In relationship things take time. Love is cultivated. Trust that the Spirit is at work.

45. Be a student of life, always open to learning and growing.

46. Wisdom comes from being open to the Spirit within, and open to a full experience of life.

47. Be practical and purposeful in all that you do, but also flexible.

48. Keep a sense of humor, no matter what life brings!

49. Hold your partner loosely; they do not belong to you.

50. A happy marriage is the best gift you can give to your children, and a lasting legacy.

On Love & Marriage

"Let there be spaces in your togetherness and let the winds
of the heavens dance between you. Love one another but
make not a bond of love: Let it rather be a moving sea
between the shores of your souls. Fill each other's cup but
drink not from one cup. Give one another of your bread but
eat not from the same loaf. Sing and dance together and be
joyous, but let each one of you be alone, Even as the strings
of a lute are alone though they quiver with the same music.
Give your hearts, but not into each other's keeping. For
only the hand of Life can contain your hearts. And stand
together, yet not too near together: For the pillars of the
temple stand apart, And the oak tree and the cypress grow
not in each other's shadow."
— Kahlil Gibran, *The Prophet*

Winter / Finale: Perspective

As winter winds down and early signs of spring arrive to give us a prelude to what's ahead, pause and reflect on what you have already learned and accomplished so far this year. Make a few notes in your journal or planner. Give yourself credit! It's so easy to overlook our little accomplishments, steps taken toward our goals, and challenges endured and overcome. We need to stop regularly and make note of these wins, however small (or large!) they may be. It's also too easy to let time slip away without taking any action toward our goals, so be honest with yourself right now and see where you have yet to take action.

Now look forward. I don't know about you, but my calendar is filling up! This is the time each year that I begin to get busier as more and more activities, commitments, and events consume my time and attention. I try to keep spaces in my calendar every week so I don't overdo it, since I have a long history of overcommitting and just trying to do too much. Be honest with yourself here, as well. What is coming up for you? Where are you headed? And how do you plan to get to it and through it? You see, getting there (to it) is one thing, but we also need to be intentional about how we get there (through it).

We each choose our direction, our destination, and how we navigate the journey. When we do it mindfully, we are more receptive to gifts and guidance along the way. Although looking back and looking forward are useful and valuable, we ultimately want to stay grounded in the present. The here and now is all we have and all we need. Bring from the past what you have learned and gained; it will give you perspective. Look forward with glad anticipation and vision; it will fill your soul with energy and purpose. Then sharpen your focus on the rich and vibrant present. Celebrate it, savor it, and give it your all!

WINTER I RECIPES

Tortilla Soup

By Elisa Juarez

- 1 lb. ground turkey or cooked, shredded chicken
- 1 medium onion, chopped
- 1 clove garlic, minced
- 1 cup salsa or Rotel (diced tomatoes and green chiles)
- ½ cup finely crushed tortilla chips
- 2 cans chicken broth
- 2 cans water
- 2 cups frozen corn
- 1 large can black beans
- ½ cup uncooked rice
- ½ teaspoon ground cumin
- ½ cup chopped cilantro

INSTRUCTIONS

1. Sauté ground turkey or chicken with onions and garlic in a large pot.
2. Add all other ingredients, stir, and simmer for 15-20 minutes.
3. Top with tortilla strips, fresh cilantro, and sliced avocado (if available).

Favorite Gingerbread

This was one of my childhood favorites and is truly a comfort food for me!

- ½ cup soft shortening
- 2 tablespoons sugar
- 1 egg
- 1 cup dark molasses
- 1 cup boiling water
- 2 ¼ cups sifted flour
- 1 teaspoon soda
- ½ teaspoon salt
- 1 teaspoon ginger
- 1 teaspoon cinnamon

INSTRUCTIONS

1. Mix shortening, sugar, and egg thoroughly.
2. Blend in molasses and boiling water.
3. Sift together flour, soda, salt, ginger, and cinnamon, and stir in.
4. Pour into well greased and floured 9" square pan.
5. Bake at 325 degrees F., 45-50 minutes.
6. Cut into 3" squares in pan. Serve piping hot with sweetened whipped cream, applesauce, chocolate sauce, or vanilla ice cream.

Favorite Pancakes

This is the recipe my mother used as I was growing up. It is an adaptation of a recipe from her trusted and well-worn *Betty Crocker Cookbook*. It became our family favorite when I had children.

- 1 egg, beaten well
- 1¼ cups buttermilk, sour milk, or almond milk
- 2 tablespoons soft shortening
- 1¼ cups sifted whole grain flour
- 1 teaspoon sugar
- 1 teaspoon baking powder
- ½ teaspoon soda
- ½ teaspoon salt

INSTRUCTIONS:

1. Heat griddle slowly while mixing batter.
2. Beat all ingredients with rotary beater (or whisk) until smooth.
3. Pour batter onto hot griddle and cook until edges bubble on first side, then turn over and cook for about a minute until golden brown.

BLUEBERRY PANCAKES:

Follow directions above, except add ½ cup drained fresh or frozen berries to batter, folding in carefully at the last.

Full of Life Minestrone Soup

By Elisa Juarez

This recipe can easily be made meatless and still be very hearty. Just use vegetable broth in place of beef broth and leave out the meat.

- 1 lb. ground turkey, beef, or fresh chicken sausage (anything you like)
- ½ onion, chopped
- 2 stalks celery with leaves, chopped
- 1 clove garlic, minced
- 2 carrots, peeled and chopped
- 1 cup fresh (or frozen Italian) green beans, cut
- Fresh spinach or chard, chopped
- 1 small can tomato sauce
- 2-3 tablespoons tomato paste
- 4 cups (32 oz) beef stock
- 1 zucchini, sliced in half moons or chopped
- 1 can red kidney beans or cannellini beans
- Fresh herbs, if available (otherwise dried): basil, Italian parsley, oregano
- Multicolor shell pasta (2 cups cooked)

INSTRUCTIONS:

- Brown meat in stock pot.
- Add onion, celery, and garlic. Sauté together for approximately 10 minutes.
- Add potatoes, carrots, green beans, tomato sauce, tomato paste, and beef stock.
- Cook on medium heat for about 10 minutes.
- Add greens and zucchini.
- Add herbs and seasonings according to your taste.
- Reduce heat to low.
- When vegetables are soft, add kidney/cannellini beans and cooked pasta.
- Add water if necessary so it is soupy.
- Let simmer for 10-15 minutes before serving.
- Serve with fresh grated Parmesan or Parmigiano Reggiano cheese and crusty bread.

Italian Meat Sauce

From my Italian friend, Susie, who taught me how to make this. The cloves give this sauce a wonderful flavor! However, you may want to remove them before serving if you can find them!

- 1 – 1½ lbs. ground beef
- ½ medium onion
- 2 stalks celery
- 2 carrots
- 2 cloves garlic
- 2 tablespoons olive oil
- 3 - 4 cans (28 oz each) whole tomatoes
- 3 tablespoons tomato paste
- 3-4 whole cloves
- Fresh parsley, chopped (a few sprigs)
- Salt and pepper

INSTRUCTIONS:

1. Brown ground beef in large pot.
2. Finely chop onion, celery, carrots, and garlic and add to meat.
3. Add olive oil to pot. Stir and sauté together.
4. Drain canned tomatoes and save juice. Chop in blender. Add tomatoes and juice to pot, then tomato paste and cloves.
5. Let simmer for a few hours. then add parsley, salt and pepper.
6. Skim fat off top during cooking.

Moist & Marvelous Chocolate Cake

Adapted from a recipe by Nestle, "Moist and Tender Chocolate Cake"

- 2 cups unbleached flour
- 2/3 cup dark chocolate baking cocoa
- 1 teaspoon baking powder
- 1 teaspoon baking soda
- ½ teaspoon salt
- 1 cup water
- 1¾ cups granulated sugar
- ¾ cup (1½ sticks) unsalted butter, softened
- 2 teaspoon vanilla extract
- 2 eggs
- Cream Cheese Icing (recipe below)

CREAM CHEESE ICING:

- 2 cups confectioner's sugar, sifted
- 1 stick unsalted butter, melted
- 1 - 8 oz package cream cheese, softened
- 2 teaspoons vanilla

INSTRUCTIONS:

1. **COMBINE** flour, cocoa, baking powder, baking soda and salt in medium bowl.
2. **BEAT** sugar, butter, and vanilla in a large mixer bowl until creamy. Add eggs one at a time, beating well after each

addition. Alternately beat flour mixture and water into sugar mixture until well blended. Pour into well greased Bundt pan or 9" x 13" pan.

3. **BAKE** in preheated 350 degree oven for 25-35 minutes or until a wooden toothpick inserted in center comes out clean.

4. **COOL** in pan for 15 minutes. Invert Bundt cake onto plate to cool completely. If using a 9" x 13" pan, leave in pan or turn upside down onto board.

5. **FROST** with cream cheese icing.

Makes 10-12 servings.

Oatmeal Banana Muffins

This is a family favorite that I found and started making when my girls were young. These muffins are moist, nutritious, and delicious!

- ½ cup butter, softened (or coconut oil)
- 2 eggs
- 1 cup bananas, mashed
- ½ cup raw, unfiltered honey
- ¼ cup plain yogurt
- 1 teaspoon baking soda
- 1½ cups whole wheat or oat flour, or any combination of whole grain and regular unbleached flour)
- ½ teaspoon salt
- 1 cup rolled oats

INSTRUCTIONS:

1. Preheat oven to 375 degrees
2. Grease 12-18 muffin tins.
3. Combine butter, eggs, bananas and honey in a mixing bowl.
4. Mix yogurt and baking soda together and add to butter mixture. Cream well.
5. Sift together flour and salt. Add to creamed mixture, mixing until just blended.
6. Stir in oatmeal.
7. Fill muffin tins 2/3 full of batter.
8. Bake 18-20 minutes. Remove from pans and cool.

Super Bowl Shrimp Slaw

By Art and Elisa Juarez

- 4 cups chopped green cabbage
- 2 green onions, sliced thin
- 1½ stalks celery, diced
- 1-2 tablespoons cilantro, chopped
- 1 small banana pepper (pickled), finely chopped
- ½ red or orange bell pepper, chopped

DRESSING:

- ½ - ¾ cup Hellman's mayonnaise
- 2 tablespoons apple cider vinegar
- 1 teaspoon dill relish
- 1 - 2 teaspoons sugar
- sea salt
- fresh ground black pepper

INSTRUCTIONS:

1. Mix together and stir in dressing.
2. Stir in 15-20 cocktail shrimp with tail removed, sliced in half.

ELISA JUAREZ

Torta de Canela (Cinnamon Cake)

I got this recipe from my sister, Catherine, who got it from her husband's Peruvian aunt. My family loves it! It is so simple to make and can be made relatively healthy. It's not too sweet but chock full of cinnamon, and we enjoy eating it at any time, including breakfast! It's especially good warm.

- 2 cups flour (I like to use whole grain flour or a combination of whole grain and unbleached flour)
- 1 stick, plus 1 tablespoon butter
- 1 cup sugar (not too full)
- ¾ - 1 cup milk
- 2 eggs
- 3 heaping teaspoons cinnamon
- 3 teaspoons baking powder

GLAZE:

- 6 tablespoons butter, melted
- 1 cup confectioner's sugar, sifted
- 1 teaspoon vanilla
- 1 - 2 tablespoons milk, as needed, until smooth

INSTRUCTIONS:

1. In a mixing bowl, combine butter and sugar; beat very well, until creamy.
2. Add eggs one at a time, beating between each.
3. Sift together flour, baking powder and cinnamon. Add to creamed mixture alternately with milk. Beat well.
4. Pour mixture into greased and floured cake pan (rectangular or Bundt)
5. Bake at 350 degrees about 30 minutes.
6. Cake is done when toothpick inserted in center comes out clean.
7. Top with glaze.

ELISA JUAREZ

CHAPTER TWO: SPRING

Spring

"The beautiful spring came, and when nature resumes her
loveliness, the human soul is apt to revive also."
— Harriet Ann Jacobs

Spring's return is inevitable and insistent, arising from cold, barren earth with a steady pulse of the life force. Gentle yet persistent, she gradually transforms the landscape and fills the air with sweet aromas and wisps of warmth. Something within us stirs as well, in response to this awakening and renewal of life. Our own spirits drop the extra blanket of winter that has kept us safe and warm. There is a lightness of being, a spring in our step, and a sense of anticipation and gladness. We see in the natural world a reflection of our souls, an awakening beauty and strength that lay dormant for weeks or months. The time of inward focus and growth begins to produce buds and blossoms in our lives, opening to the light which increases by the day. The spring storms bring forth resilience, courage, and grace. Behold, all things are made new and wholeness is restored.

"And Spring arose on the garden fair,
Like the Spirit of Love felt everywhere;
And each flower and herb on Earth's dark breast
rose from the dreams of its wintry rest."
— Percy Bysshe Shelley, *"The Sensitive Plant"*

Themes for this season include renewal, resilience, planting, growth, home, connection, and wholeness.

The Dance

It's a chilly, rainy day here as March moves in, gently nudging winter aside. The transition is like a dance between two seasons, with spring gradually leading winter to the edge of the dance floor. I love this dance, the music, the movement, and the rhythm of nature as one season graciously enters and escorts the outgoing season off the stage. The dance is often tumultuous, passionate, and riveting. I witness this with wonder every time as nature reveals her strength, beauty, and persistence.

On my walks this past week I have caught the sweet aroma of spring blossoms and noticed that several trees are already budding. Many of them, however, are still stark and bare, with no evidence of new growth on their branches. Grass is greening in some areas but remains brown in others. Isn't this how our lives look at times? The more awake and aware we become, the more we notice the subtle changes within and around us.

The fragrance of spring greeted me before I saw the blossoms. There are days when I can sense or smell the approaching good before I see any evidence, and I am filled with *glad anticipation*. When we learn to trust life, practice gratitude, and choose joy, a sweet fragrance fills our world. It is a sign of renewal, hope, and healing. The time of darkness and dormancy is subsiding as the life force ushers in abundant growth.

Transitions are filled with uncertainty and sway as the dance between what was and what is coming keeps us on our toes. Just when

I think spring has finally arrived, here comes a blast of winter. When I release my resistance to what is happening and let go of expectations, I am free to join in the dance. I become attuned to the music and rhythm of life. I am lighter on my feet and less likely to stumble. Every season has its own energy and mystery, drawing us in to receive its gifts. We are more receptive when we are flexible, humble, and patient. These lessons can be hard to learn and may even take a lifetime. *I've been working on patience my whole life.* The seasons of nature offer us much wisdom and healing as we learn to breathe deeply, listen intently, look closely, and dance lightly.

Curiosity & Imagination

This past week I finished reading *The Right to Write* by Julia Cameron, which will continue to be a guide, workbook, and inspiration for me, and I started *Fearless Writing* by William Kenower. These books remind me that writing is an extension of being human. It is a pathway to deeper understanding of ourselves and our lives. In *Fearless Writing*, Kenower says that the only way to write is to consult our own curiosity and imagination. That is a great place to start, whether you write regularly or not.

If you consider yourself a lifelong learner, as I do, then you will continue to use your curiosity to ask questions, seek answers, observe people and situations, and become a better listener. Ask yourself what interests you most. If you choose not to write, then at least be willing to pay more attention to that which interests you. Become an observer with an eye for detail and an ear for the whisper of your authentic self.

Perhaps one day you'll decide to just jot down something you noticed, felt, experienced, and thought about a piece of your life. If you can be more curious about the magic and mystery of writing, then maybe you'll be willing to sit down to a blank page with pen in hand without even knowing what you want to write. You can start with a question to yourself, and just see what happens. Why not?

When you pick up the pen, let go of any and all judgment about your writing. If and when you decide that you want to share something you've written, then you'll need to give up caring what anybody else thinks. I know that's hard. But the more you write, the more confidence you will gain and the easier it will become. My guess is that if you do *not* write, you may be telling yourself that you can't, or it's too hard, or you don't like it. Well, here's the thing, those messages are deceptive and they're blocking you. Ask yourself where they came from and how they are (or *aren't*) serving you. Be curious. Write about it. Have some fun.

> *"We have to cultivate the habits of curiosity and paying attention, which are essential to living rich lives and writing."* — Anne Lamott, *Almost Everything*

Every year when spring arrives, I experience the awe and wonder of creation as new life appears after months of dormancy. This season always inspires me to do something new and different. I feel a sense of renewal, creativity, and hope. Let's use our curiosity and imagination to discover something new, within ourselves and the awakening world. Each day gives us another opportunity to learn, listen, love, and live well.

The Choice

I've been thinking a lot lately about how we can bring more light and love into this crazy world. It's easy to get discouraged by all the negativity that comes across the airwaves and the internet, and into our own thoughts! We are influenced by many voices, circumstances, and relationships in our world, and it can be a challenge to discern what to tune in to and what to tune out. How can we respond consciously while staying true to ourselves and our values?

I remember when Taylor was in junior high and some of her "friends" were saying and doing hurtful things to her. It was hard to see her wrestling with that pain and anger. After giving her some time, I told her that she had a decision to make: She needed to decide who she wanted to be in response to this. She could only control herself and her choices. Her power was in taking responsibility for herself, not taking revenge against them.

I clearly remember that moment, realizing that, as her mother, I needed to give her the tools to deal with hurt, anger, betrayal, and pain more than I needed to give her sympathy. The darts and stings of adversity are part of life, and it is our job as parents to equip our children, to encourage and empower them to stand up for themselves and work through their challenges.

The other element of that situation was the emphasis on *being* rather than *doing*. Choosing who we are going to *be* in response to someone or something is more important than choosing what we are going to *do*. Our doing will come out of our being, but the first questions we need to ask ourselves are who we are and how we can be the best version of ourselves.

When you are in an argument, ask yourself this: "Is it more important to be *loving* or to be *right?*" That's a great example of this principle. It takes discipline and maturity to live this way, to think before we react, and to choose and create consciously.

I'll end with a funny story from when Taylor was only 3 years old. She was a very intense and energetic child who pushed all the boundaries. One day when her daddy came home from work, she was bouncing around, maybe on our bed; I don't recall exactly, but he said, "Taylor, you're making me mad!" She said, "No, Daddy, I don't make you mad. You make yourself mad!" (I had told her something like that, probably when she was mad at me!) I had to restrain myself from laughing out loud because he did *not* find it funny!

It goes back to taking responsibility for our behavior, our feelings, and our lives. We all need to be reminded at times, as our society teaches us to blame others for nearly everything. We cannot control others, only ourselves. We create our world through our thoughts, beliefs, feelings, and actions. We create ourselves this way as well. How can we be agents of light, love, joy, and healing? That is a question for us to ask ourselves each day.

> *"You must be the change you want to see in the world."*
> — Mahatma Gandhi

As a wise teacher of mine once said, "Live the question."

ELISA JUAREZ

Welcome, Morning

Darkness still lingering in anticipation of awakening light,

Clocks ticking steadily, faithfully,

Coffee waiting to be brewed.

Stillness envelops me with the same softness and comfort as this
fleece blanket.

Rest for body and soul,

Renewal for mind and spirit.

Listen within, breathe deeply,

Give thanks.

Morning awakens with fullness and emptiness,

Full of possibility and empty space in which to create.

Morning gently beckons me into her warm embrace,

Opening my awareness to her beauty and grace.

Welcome, Morning.

I treasure your gifts.

Growth, Grief, & Grace

*"Only knowledge gained through experience, the fruit of
living and suffering, fills the heart with the wisdom of love,
instead of crushing it with the disappointment of boredom
and final oblivion. It is not the results of our own
speculation, but the golden harvest of what we have lived
through and suffered through that has power to enrich the
heart and nourish the spirit."*
— Karl Rahner, *Encounters with Silence*

As a new season begins to awaken with warming temperatures and
early signs of spring, I think of the many parallels of changing seasons
in my life and relationships. For me, observing and understanding the
seasons in nature has deepened my acceptance of the seasons in my
life. Nature speaks to me continually, showing me her wisdom and
beauty, her resilience and fortitude, her simplicity and grace. I have
received her bounty as an increase in my own awareness,
understanding, and gratitude.

Over the past several years, I have experienced a considerable
change in seasons as my parents moved from East Texas into a
retirement community here, and then my mother passed away two
years later. The following year, Lauren graduated from high school
and Taylor graduated from college. As they launched into their new
lives away from home, I became the caregiver to my dad who has
Alzheimer's dementia. This season has been one of significant growth,

grief, and grace in every aspect of my life and all my family relationships.

Growth came from my new role as a caregiver for my parents as they struggled with significant health issues and disabilities. I embraced this sacred responsibility one day at a time, doing what needed to be done, responding with love, patience, and compassion. I was still working full-time, but eventually had to go part-time to give my parents the attention and assistance they needed. I was also stretched and challenged by my job and a new business that I decided to pursue on the side. There were countless demands on my mind, body, and spirit, but I just pushed ahead each day, praying for strength, wisdom, and guidance. I had to get out of my comfort zone regularly. In fact, my comfort zone became a thing of the past. Still, as I look back, I see myself filled with energy and joy. It was a conscious choice and a gift of grace.

> *"Grief can be the garden of compassion. If you keep your heart open through everything, your pain can become your greatest ally in your life's search for love and wisdom."*
> — Jalal Ud-Din Rumi

Grief was my quiet companion for several years as I watched my mother decline, struggle, and suffer day after day. I felt like I was watching her die. My grief was compounded by the realization that I was also losing my father, the man whom I had admired my whole life. Seeing the stress and strain of their combined disabilities was exhausting. Mom needed so much, and Dad was not capable of grasping that reality or helping her. She was heartbroken by the loss of her companion who could no longer carry on a meaningful conversation or support her in the ways that she needed.

When she passed away, I stepped into the role of Dad's advocate and caregiver, tending to his mental and emotional needs and ensuring that he could maintain the highest possible quality of life without having to move to another facility. The time and energy I've spent with Dad these past few years has helped him maintain some stability and security amid increasing confusion. He is in many ways like a child now, depending on me and others to stay on track and hold onto reality. As his world becomes more and more uncertain and fragmented, he grasps to hold onto his memory, his family, and his sense of identity.

My grief was exacerbated by the changing relationships with my siblings who live many miles away. As I navigated that first year after our mother's death, I had to make decisions and choices that were often difficult, and which they didn't always understand or accept. I was in a tough financial situation after quitting my job to care for my parents, and ended up having to borrow money from my dad. Although I had Power of Attorney and consulted both the estate lawyer and the financial advisor regarding my decisions, my siblings felt angry and betrayed. The situation damaged my relationship with both of them, and it took a long time to heal. The more I was questioned and challenged, the more I began to question and doubt myself at every turn. I ended up exhausted and crushed mentally, emotionally, and spiritually. I gave my power to my siblings, and this added a third layer of grief, I lost a part of myself.

Grace has held me, guided and strengthened me throughout the storms of the past several years. Grace lifted me out of the pit and set my feet upon a rock. Grace gave me a husband who is fiercely supportive of me, who believes in me more than anyone on the planet, and who loves me unconditionally and wholeheartedly. His support of me is all encompassing and unwavering. It is emotional, mental, physical, and spiritual. He is my rock on this earth, my comfort, my companion, my forever love. God loves me through him, that I know. He sees in me a strength and beauty I do not see in myself. He acknowledges it and calls it forth. That is a gift of grace.

As we grow through the different seasons in our lives, we experience grief and grace. We must let go of the old and embrace the new. It is inevitable that our family relationships will change, and we will have an opportunity to stretch and grow as we accept and honor these changes. We are called to become more in our relationships with others. As our parents age, they will need us more than we need them. We are called to respond with love and attention, as they did for us when we were growing up. They still have so much to teach us, and we have the chance to give back.

As our children grow into young adults, we have the opportunity to see and experience the fruits of our labor, a return on our investment, by allowing them to develop their gifts and pursue their dreams. There is an element of grief that accompanies this transition, as well; we must let them go out into the world and make decisions and choices without us. At times we may not agree with or accept those decisions, but they are not ours to make. It is a season of intense growth for them, and we can continue to encourage them, believe in them, and honor the divinity within them. We can recognize and call forth their beauty and strength. That is a gift of grace.

Change is the one thing we can count on in this life, and it can be difficult, exciting, painful, and liberating. When we learn to accept and embrace change with courage and optimism, we will experience growth and grace.

Signs & Rituals

One of my favorite seasons is opening up before us, and that is literally what happens in March. Nature begins to awaken and open up her treasures after a season of dormancy. I think we are all ready for more light, warmth, and color in our world. Winter has its own special treasures and celebrations, but now we look ahead to everything spring!

This week I took the flannel sheets off the bed and bought a floral sprig/bouquet for the front door. Lauren will be flying home from Indiana this weekend for Spring Break! The flowers on my patio are blooming again, and a dove came and perched on the railing the other day. These are signs of spring that renew my spirit! Rituals of spring include planting, cleaning, redecorating and refreshing the house, and packing up the winter clothes. Rituals carry us into each new season and remind us how time rolls along from one season to the next in our lives. They can give us a sense of stability and security in the midst of all the changes and uncertainties in our world.

What are your spring rituals? How about meals and treats that you like to make? What about Easter and Passover? These are sacred holidays surrounded by tradition and family. If you still have children at home, or grandchildren, perhaps you dye Easter eggs or make Easter baskets. I have many memories of those days when our girls were young, as well as memories of my own childhood. Rituals can connect us to our past, giving meaning to our lives and enriching our relationships with family and friends. As our children grow up and leave the nest, we learn to adjust our expectations and embrace a new season in those relationships. They will carry on some of those traditions while creating some of their own, and it's all okay. Seasons change, and we experience renewal and release.

As you see the signs of spring all around, take some time to look within for signs of renewal. Consider what needs to be released or put away for something fresh and new to come forth in your life. Old habits, beliefs, and attachments can block our good and hold us down when we were made to rise and shine! Do some inner spring cleaning this month. Sweep out the corners where dust and dirt can accumulate. Let your inner beauty and strength come forth by removing self-doubt, worry, anxiety, and negativity. This is your season!

The Gift of Rest & Renewal

I'll never forget the summer afternoons of my childhood when my mother would call my siblings and me in from playing outside with the neighbors to take a half hour nap. Our friends didn't have to go in for a nap, why did we? It was kind of embarrassing since we weren't toddlers anymore, we were in grade school. We didn't have to sleep, we just had to go to our own rooms for half an hour and do something quiet. It was "rest time," for my mom as well. She told us when we got older that she did that so that we would learn to value quiet time alone.

When I got married and started a family, I carried this forward. It wasn't easy to get my spirited daughter to settle down for an afternoon nap — even when she was a baby! However, I needed it more than ever as a mom, and I was a firm believer in the importance of quiet time for both of us.

Our second child, Lauren, was wired differently, and often initiated her own naps. I'll never forget the day she and Taylor were playing next door and she came trotting down the sidewalk, up the driveway, through the front door, and straight into her room where she lay down on her toddler bed and went to sleep. She was two years old. What a contrast! Her body told her it needed to rest, and she listened!

My regular practice is quiet time alone in the early morning before anyone else is up. I read, meditate, and write in my journal. I started doing this in my mid-twenties and haven't stopped. It provides physical, mental, and spiritual renewal and overall well-being. The benefits of regular meditation are now widely recognized as individuals and organizations seek to reduce stress and improve health, wellness, and productivity. I have even heard that 10 minutes of meditation has the same benefits as an hour of sleep!

Rest and renewal are essential to our health and well-being, and yet we live in a society that never sleeps. We have 24/7 news coverage, fast food, retail shopping, and internet surfing. As a result, we have information overload, work overload, stimulation overload, and stress! Even when we do lie down to sleep, it is hard to turn off our brains. It is directly impacting the health of our children as well as *us*, as we take continual shortcuts to keep up the pace. We cut short our meals, our rest time, our play time, our exercise; and in the end we cut short our lives!

A visit to Europe and other parts of the world reveals a different way of life, a slower pace, and a healthier population. There are times in the middle of the day when businesses close for two hours for lunch and rest! People take more time to eat, and they eat fresh, whole foods. People do more walking and cycling and drive smaller cars. They live more simply and life is good. They seem to understand something that we don't here in the U.S. Therefore, it is not a universal human condition to live like whirling dervishes! We can choose a different path than the one our society prescribes for happiness and success which often leads to pharmaceutical prescriptions, addiction, and *unhappiness!*

How we choose to live and work is really up to each of us. I have had several different work situations throughout my adult life and have learned the cost and benefit of each one. Many women feel that they do not have a choice, or that their choices are limited. We all have financial responsibilities that we need to fulfill, and we negotiate those with our career choices and family responsibilities. I believe that no one need be unhappy in their work. We can choose to make the best of where we are and what we are doing, or we can change it. We *do* have the power to create our experience from the inside out. We can't change others, but we can be a positive influence that changes the environment in which we live and work, and we can always change ourselves through intentional personal growth.

This brings us back to rest and renewal. We were designed for health and happiness. We were designed for work, play, and rest. To restore balance and wellness in our lives, we need to first become aware of the choices we make every day. We cannot separate our body, mind, and spirit; they are all interconnected. We have within us both power and peace. We have wisdom and intelligence. We have unlimited, 24/7 access to our Creator and our creativity. When we stop, rest, and listen, we will receive wisdom, renewal, and peace. It is simple and fundamental to our well-being. As my favorite devotional advises me repeatedly, "Relax, rejoice, and be thankful all the time." Life is overflowing with beauty, joy, and creativity. When we take the time to look, listen, learn, and be fully present, we will experience it all.

Dove Love

Something interesting and heartwarming happened this week. I heard the cooing of doves for the first time in months. Two doves showed up on my balcony, chatting and cooing as they hopped around and investigated my planter, filled with raggedy pansies. There are some early signs of spring popping up in Texas, and the doves are among them.

Last spring, we were privileged to provide a nesting spot for these doves as they took turns sitting on their eggs for several weeks. Since doves pair for life and are likely to return to a familiar nesting site, I have reason to believe these two doves are the same ones we hosted last year. It was amazing to witness the whole process right outside our living room window. The eggs hatched in early June, and once those baby birds grew in size, strength, and restlessness, they were gone. The mama dove returned the next day and then disappeared... until now.

ELISA JUAREZ

In nature we can see the divine order of things, and when we pause to notice and reflect on it, we are struck with awe and wonder. Art and I love watching the *Planet Earth* series for this reason. It is a reassuring reminder that there is something greater than us, present and active within all life. When much of the world around us seems to be going crazy and life gets overwhelming, nature provides a healing balm for our ills and anxiety. Doves in particular are a symbol of peace, and they certainly bring that awareness to me as they nest on my balcony.

Here are some of my observations from watching them last spring:

1. The doves work together to build the nest, bringing twigs, grasses, etc., for days and creating a bed.

2. The mama dove can sit still for hours on end. I mean *hours*. Now I wasn't watching constantly, but I can safely say that she rarely moved at all. Her partner brought her food, and at times took her place so she could get some exercise! Thank goodness she got a break once in a while because she showed incredible patience!

3. Once the mama dove laid those eggs, she did not move, and I could slip out there very gently and sit in the chair without startling her. I talked softly to her, and after a time, she let me take a few pictures. I always moved very slowly and quietly. However, once the babies were born, she was extremely protective, keeping them covered every time I stepped outside. A few times I noticed she left them alone to get food, and I carefully took a few photos.

Watching those doves, and other animals with their young, assures me that within the parenting instinct that nests, broods, protects, nurtures, feeds, and leads, is the presence of Divine Love. I mean, that is what love looks like, right? It is our instinct, our essence, and evidence of the divine within all life. It is present in the smallest of creatures and the grandest. It is present in the environment that surrounds all of us, the awesome creation that was designed to support and sustain life. All of it is truly beautiful and amazing, and it is wise for us to take the time to notice, absorb, and appreciate it.

The doves have come earlier than last year. It is a joy to see them, to hear their chattering and cooing, and to consider the sacred task they are about to undertake. It takes preparation, partnership, and patience. I think about the dreams I am carrying and brooding over, eagerly and patiently doing the daily work that will help them develop, break through their shell, grow in strength and stature, and then take flight. Dreams take time, patience, and a lot of love. They take energy, intention, persistence, and faith. They require the work of our minds, hearts, and hands. We must protect them from our own and others' doubt and discouragement, and the harsh environment of the world which can destroy hope and optimism. Like a mother bird, we must brood over our dreams with the determination and commitment required to bring them to fruition.

In the days and weeks ahead, as I watch the doves tend to their nest, I will again be filled with wonder, gratitude, and joy. I will remember that the same Divine Love that watches over the doves is watching over me. I will find renewed strength, patience, and peace as I give expression to my authentic self. I will take some time to be still, listen, and observe.

Beauty arises within me and around me. The wings of my soul flutter and lift me up, reminding me of the fullness and freedom that are mine when I surrender to Love. Life gives us many opportunities to remember this and break through the shells that hold us back. Divine Love, like dove love, creates a space for us to come into the fullness and freedom of who we are. Our dreams were planted in our souls with wings designed for fulfillment and flight. Trust in the Wisdom and Love that created you, the divine life that pulsates through all creation and connects us. Then you will recognize it in the rising sun, the budding trees, and the singing birds. Life is good.

The Power of Connection

Today started early as Art and I got up at 5:00 AM and drove to the airport in the dark. He had an 8:00 AM flight to Cleveland. My head felt tired and achy, so when I got home I made coffee and sat on the couch with a fleece blanket around me. I just wanted to go back to sleep, as I hadn't slept well through the night. I gave myself about 30 minutes before forcing myself to get going to the Alzheimer's symposium I had been looking forward to attending. It started at 8:30, and traffic across town at that hour was heavy and slow. But when you are as hungry to learn as I am, you do what it takes, and I am so glad I did. It was an amazing day.

Each session I attended was very valuable and informative; I took lots of notes and photos of the slides. I was happy to see that this time they had two sessions about the connection between lifestyle and Alzheimer's, including nutrition and exercise, backed by science and impacting the future direction of research and treatment. Finally, a shift from a pharmaceutical focus to a holistic lifestyle focus! The research and implications give hope and encouragement. It was empowering for all of us to learn how we can change the trajectory of our own lives as well as the Alzheimer's epidemic.

At lunchtime we each received a box lunch in the convention hall which was set up with round tables. I felt a bit like a student in the cafeteria, looking for whom I might sit with since I didn't know anybody. I said a quick prayer for guidance under my breath and saw a woman sitting alone, so I chose that table.

I said, "Hello," and immediately another woman sat down. They were each looking at their phones, but I asked, "So, are you family caregivers or professionals?"

They each said, "Family," and began to share that their husbands had early onset Alzheimer's.

Whoa. Both of them.

It was like I opened the door to their lives, and their stories started pouring out. I was amazed. I asked questions, I listened, and I shared a little about my dad. One woman's husband was diagnosed at age 48, and the doctors believed it resulted from environmental toxins, since he had worked in two different manufacturing plants where he was exposed to fine particles of heavy metals. On top of that, he worked the night shift at one job and never could adjust to sleeping during the day, so he also had sleep deprivation. He is now 55 and unable to feed or take care of himself, so his beautiful wife cares for him at home, along with her mother who lives with them. Double duty.

The other woman was only 44 years old. Her husband, age 51, was diagnosed a little over a year ago. His diagnosis came on suddenly after years of other health problems for which he took multiple medications. He can still care for himself physically, but cannot be left alone while she works at her full-time engineering job, so she had to put him in memory care.

I couldn't help but think of all the dreams that died for those couples when they received that diagnosis. They had a future that must have looked much brighter than the one they have now. Their lives will never be the same as their husbands continue to decline, and are no longer able to share the conversations, activities, and dreams they once had. These brave women are losing their life partner to a debilitating disease that could last for years. One of them has already lived with it for seven years; the other is just starting on this road. My heart breaks for them. I had to fight back tears as we sat together in the next session listening to Martin Schreiber, caregiver and author of *My Two Elaines*, talk about his journey with his wife who was diagnosed at age 65. I was and am deeply moved by the stories I heard, and the awareness, yet again, of how uncertain and fragile life can be. It is hard enough seeing my dad decline at age 87 and realizing that he could live for several more years. I still have my life with Art which is illumined by shared dreams and mutual support. That and my faith are what give me strength and joy.

Everyone has a story, and we all have something to learn from each other, which is why I am compelled to write. Julia Cameron says writing is how she metabolizes her life. I feel the same. It allows me to take an experience and process it, reflect on it, and find the gem within it. By writing, I can take that gem, hold it, look at it, polish it, and share its beauty with others.

Life offers countless opportunities to listen, learn, observe, and discover. When we connect with people consciously, with presence, genuine interest, and compassion, we realize our oneness and the universal experience we all share. We receive an unexpected gift that may inspire us to respond with creativity through art, music, or writing. The process of creating in response to our experience connects us to our Creator and the energy in all creation. We discover beauty, wisdom, and joy.

Welcome Spring!

Happy first day of spring! Are you doing something to celebrate? I hope it is beginning to look and feel like spring where you are. I notice a different smell and feel in the air as the trees begin to bloom and the birds return. Mornings are still pleasantly cool and afternoons are comfortably warm. This is a *golden* time in Texas, before the sweltering heat returns for what seems like an eternity. Once summer arrives there is little change in the weather; it's just *hot*, morning, noon, and night. So I *love* springtime!

Planting herbs and flowers is one of my favorite ways to welcome the spring. I was able to keep my rosemary, thyme, and mint alive through the winter by bringing the planters inside, and now I am ready to add a few new herbs. I've decided on lemon verbena since it is so good for making tea! I think I'll plant lavender this year as it is a blooming herb, bringing color as well as fragrance. Herbs are treasured for their wealth and variety of aromas, flavors, and health benefits. Another wonderful thing about herbs is how easy they are to grow, regardless of your space and climate. I live in a third floor apartment with a small balcony facing south, so I have a container garden. In the winter I bring the herbs inside and continue to enjoy them. Consider trying something new this spring; after all, that's what this season is all about! It is time for planting, dreaming, and savoring in every area of our lives. Take the space you have and be creative with it. Bring a new idea, color, and flavor into your world. Refresh your home and your outdoor space! Your spirit will perk up and take notice, welcoming the oxygen of new life with gratitude and hope.

My mother used to say that the mind is like a garden; whatever we plant in it is what will grow there. She taught us to be selective, intentional, and aware of how and what we feed our minds. When we realize that we are the gardeners of our own lives, it can be exciting and fun to create a beautiful garden! We do tend to reap what we sow, and what we *think* about we *bring* about! So plant your seeds wisely, giving them the light and water they need to grow and blossom. Take delight in the whole process, giving thanks each day, and you will reap a bountiful harvest.

Spring Blooms

In honor and memory of my wonderful mother on this, her earth birthday, March 22nd. She was a true gardener in every sense of the word, planting flowers religiously and meticulously every spring, and planting seeds of love, faith, and gratitude every day of her life. She passed away in November 2015.

Spring was a long awaited and glorious season in South Dakota where I grew up. Winters were long and harsh, lasting about as long as summer in Texas with equal intensity. It could take weeks for the snow to melt as the temperatures gradually rose. I can remember how good it felt when the temps got up into the 60's with ample sunshine! Sweet aromas filled the air as trees began budding and blossoming. One of the first signs of spring was the return of the robin, "Robin Redbreast" as we called her. She was the first bird of springtime, bringing her song and the promise of a new season.

My mother was an avid gardener, planting iris bulbs that pushed their green stems through the earth and spread their delicate purple and white petals like open arms. They were the first flowers, followed by tulips and lily of the valley. I don't remember when the daisies bloomed, but they were one of mom's favorite flowers. We had a perimeter garden that wrapped around our house, along with a narrow cement walkway. I'll never forget the intoxicating fragrance of the lily of the valley! They were probably my favorite flowers, each stem adorned with a row of tiny, bell shaped, white blossoms. I used to pick several and place them in a small glass vase, bringing their beauty and aroma into the house for pure enjoyment.

Mom planted morning glories along the back screened porch and attached white string from garden posts to the edge of the roof. As the flowers grew, they would climb the strings, creating a beautiful, royal blue canopy across the screened windows. The blooms opened every morning and closed every evening, demonstrating the inherent wisdom and rhythm of creation.

On the west side of the house by the kitchen door she planted hyacinths. These small bushes boasted extravagant blooms that would often lean over the garden. They were a sharp contrast to the delicate lilies on the opposite side of the house and bountiful in a larger way. They had the benefit of the large elm tree that sheltered them from the afternoon sun. Next to them we grew mint, which we picked for iced tea and garnishes. In addition to these and many other flowers, we had three plum trees in our backyard. Since they were relatively small trees they were great for climbing! Although they only produced fruit every seven years, they donned a cloak of lacy white blossoms every spring, attracting birds and squirrels to their branches.

Our sense memories are stored in our cells as well as our brains. I imagine myself walking around the outside of my childhood home, taking in the sights, smells, and sounds, feeling the warm spring air after a long, cold winter. It feels like a lifetime ago, and yet it is a part of who I am. I am thankful for the many seeds my mother planted, in our garden and in our hearts and minds. Today is her birthday, right after the arrival of spring. I carry her spirit in mine, still living in the warmth and security of her love. Springtime brings cherished memories of her and the beauty she created within and around our home. *Welcome spring and Robin Redbreast and fragrant flowers and sunshine!* This is abundant life.

Simplicity & Abundance

"I have just three things to teach: simplicity, patience, compassion. These three are your greatest treasures."
— Lao Tzu

When Lauren was in her freshman year of college, we made the decision to sell the house we had lived in for 13 years and move into an apartment. There were multiple factors behind this decision, and Art and I agreed it was a wise and necessary move. As I remember the considerable stress and strain that led up to that move, and the immense effort it took to accomplish it, I am both amazed and relieved. During our 13 years there we watched the little oak tree we planted grow from about six feet tall to above the roofline. We went through seasons of growth and abundance, and seasons of drought. We birthed a dream and watched it die. We became caregivers for my parents, moving them from their home in Tyler, Texas, to a retirement community nearby. We put one daughter through college. We put our 13 year old German Shepherd down. We watched my mother die after a valiant 40-year battle with scleroderma.

There was a sea of change through those years – beginnings and endings, laughter and tears, struggle and determination, celebrations and joys, pain and loss. It truly was a full and abundant life, though difficult and painful at times. We shared stories, hopes, and dreams around the kitchen table almost every night.

But in the last few years, the weight of care became too heavy — physically, financially, and emotionally. We realized we had to make a change that would relieve our stress and strain. The real estate market was hot. We could sell the house. Brilliant!

The decision was made and shared with our daughters, and the work began: cleaning, clearing, sorting, tossing, packing, storing, multiple trips to Goodwill, furniture posted on Facebook and sold quickly, mostly to friends. Every day we focused on this huge project. We looked at apartments and found one that we loved, which was still being finished. We began to visualize a new, simplified life without stress or strain. The whole idea excited and inspired us: a new beginning, a new lifestyle, a lighter load. Freedom. This became the new face of abundance for us.

We sorted through years of accumulated papers, books, games, crafts, movies, projects, and possessions, choosing what we wanted to save and passing on the rest. The process was mentally and physically exhausting, but on the other end of it was simplicity, freedom, relief, and abundance. It changed our outlook, our perspective, and our definition of "the good life."

Today I read, "simplicity and abundance are soul mates." Yes! In simplicity we have found an abundant life with more time, energy, and money to enjoy it. We downsized to half the size of our house, putting our "extra" belongings in storage for now. We dream of living in the Texas Hill Country and building a house on an acreage. We have tasted the sweetness of simple abundance and discovered the priceless commodity of peace of mind.

Our society teaches us through words, images, advertising, and other media that bigger is better, more is mighty, and wealth is power. It is easy to get caught up in comparing ourselves and our lives to others and letting external measures define us and determine our value. This game creates stress, anxiety, discouragement, and jealousy. It is unproductive and irrelevant. Only when we go against the grain, choosing simplicity, harmony, peace of mind, and gratitude, do we experience true abundance. Only when we focus on the beauty and bounty all around us and choose to live by our own lights to be true to ourselves and our passions are we free and fully alive! Brilliant!

Simplicity and abundance go hand in hand. Whenever we let go of that which is holding us back or consuming our time and energy, we free ourselves and make room for abundance. Clearing out clutter in our minds and our lives is essential for our well-being. Clutter takes the space that our dreams and desires are waiting to fill. We all have some degree of clutter in our minds, our homes, and our lives. It takes discipline and awareness to choose simplicity, order, and harmony instead and to take steps toward them. This is simple abundance. This is freedom.

Anyone who has ever moved can attest that you always have much more "stuff" than you realized! Closets, corners, and attics hold both treasures and trash from years of living. Things get put away for "someday" and then forgotten. When the time of reckoning comes — as it always does sooner or later — the decision has to be made to keep or not to keep. We ended up making 11 trips to Goodwill with my husband's pickup full. I didn't count the large trash bags that were put on the curb, but there were plenty of those, as well. And just when we thought we were almost done — lo and behold, yet another closet to tackle! Yet another area to conquer! Yikes! It felt like a never ending process.

Here is the point: Getting rid of so much stuff was *amazing!* We felt like new creations! Our life transformed physically, mentally, and financially. We traded all that stuff, and a mortgage, for time, energy, money, and freedom. We realized that having more of *those* commodities was the key to abundance. Holding onto stuff and the belief that more is better keeps us from experiencing more *life*.

Our lives and our perspective are now forever changed, transformed by the experience of letting go, clearing out clutter, releasing the old, and embracing a new reality, a new way of living. When our time and energy are not held hostage by financial, emotional, and mental stress we are able to receive new ideas, creativity, healing, and abundance! It's our choice. It takes trust. Trust that we will be okay, that we will have everything we need, that we will be guided and strengthened. Embrace change and move through it step by step, and it will teach you what you need to learn. I've heard the phrase, "Anything worthwhile is uphill." I have experienced the climb, time and time again. It's hard. I feel like I have been climbing for years, but I now have a glorious view. I see more, I am stronger, and I've lightened my load. There will be more change ahead, more climbs; but when we learn to trust, breathe, and simplify, the journey becomes lighter and brighter.

Wind

One night we were sitting out on the back porch enjoying the cool breeze, and Art said, "You know, the trees need the wind." He went on to explain that when trees and other plant life were planted in a biosphere in Arizona as an experiment in creating a controlled living environment, the trees died. The scientists could not understand it until someone finally explained that the trees needed wind to grow and become strong.

That got me thinking about the analogy it holds for human life — for *spiritual* life. The wind is a form of pressure and movement that bends and strengthens us. What is the wind in our lives? It is any kind of challenge to which we must respond. If we are flexible we will not break, but we also need strong roots to keep us firmly in place. The wind helps the roots grow stronger, thus giving the tree a better foundation. The outer branches need to move with the wind or they will break. When a tree is full of leaves, the wind creates music as it blows through it. Therefore, what may appear to be painful or difficult can still bring music and beauty into our lives if we allow it to move through us and not break us.

What does it mean to stay grounded? To have strong roots? It means knowing who and what we are, beyond the human experience. It means having perspective in this life so that none of its challenges can overwhelm us. It means remembering, "This, too, shall pass," and it will probably make us stronger, deepen our roots, and deliver a gift. Life is full of wind, and we should welcome it. The wind comes in the form of loss, struggle, grief, illness, pain... you name it!

As we pass through the seasons of life, we have repeated opportunities to let go, release what is no longer helpful to us, and allow the life force within to heal us and move us to a place of renewal, rebirth, and growth. This is followed by fullness of life, but the spring and early summer bring storms that can bend us, almost to breaking. There are downpours of rain, cracks of thunder, streaks of lightning, and hailstones. Following even the most violent storm is the return of the sun, and often a rainbow. Hope, light, color, and beauty... as if to remind us that we are beyond the storm; *life* is beyond the storm. After a good rain the grass and all plant life flourishes, flowers bloom more vibrantly, and trees become lush.

Yes, the trees need the wind, and so do we.

ELISA JUAREZ

Lessons from the Garden: Attraction

> "Don't wait for someone to bring you flowers. Plant your
> own garden and decorate your own soul."
> — Luther Burbank

As the trees and flowers come into bloom and I choose what I want to plant this year, I consider how certain plants attract hummingbirds and butterflies. Trees and bird feeders attract birds, and once they have found these food sources, they return again and again. The birds and butterflies are around us, but when we plant seeds that attract them, they show up in our yard. They bring their beauty, grace, and music into our corner of the world. I used to sit on our back porch and watch them, listening to their songs.

Our lives are like this. We can create and attract beauty, wonder, and abundance by planting seeds of love, peace, gratitude, and generosity, and by feeding that which we want to increase in our lives. We give energy to whatever we think about, speak about, and act upon. We are the gardeners of our lives.

We used to have a hummingbird feeder on a 5 foot iron garden hook at the edge of our patio. The "nectar" that attracts the birds is a sugary liquid that you pour into the feeder. It attracted the hummingbirds all right. But the ants also discovered the yummy cocktail, crawling up the pole and onto the feeder for an ant garden party. They have a way of notifying all their friends that continues to

116

amaze me. It was tricky to get rid of them and prevent their return without spoiling things for the hummingbirds, but we managed to do so by spreading some oil or petroleum jelly on the pole, primarily at the base, so the ants could not advance!

Filling our minds with beautiful, positive thoughts is like that nectar; it attracts beauty and goodness into our lives. However, the world is full of pests, and they find their way into our minds and our lives, sometimes without notice until they have wreaked havoc. Gardening requires attention and discipline. The more we learn and grow spiritually, the more we realize we have yet to learn. Being alert to the little "invaders" in our minds — like anxiety, fear, resentment, jealousy, and judgment — is an ongoing task. If we can catch them at the door, so to speak, and turn them away, then they won't have a chance to multiply and take over our minds or our lives.

Belonging

This week has slipped by so fast, and much of it has been spent connecting with people. The value of such time is hard to measure, but we feel the benefits of it. We know that investing in people and relationships pays big dividends in our mental, emotional, spiritual, and physical health. Our family and friends give us a sense of belonging that is essential to our well-being.

Last Sunday I took my dad to church, picking him up at his assisted living place where he was engaged with some other residents and surprised to see me. He was glad, as always, to go to church, expressing his appreciation all the way there. When we sat in the pew, he said, "I am so glad to be here with you. This is where I belong."

Dad is a retired pastor who grew up going to church every Sunday. Despite his dementia, he still remembers the hymns, the Lord's Prayer, the Doxology, and the feeling of being in church. The experience connects him to his roots, his values, his identity, and his ministry. All this, woven together, creates a strong sense of belonging. It is comforting, affirming, inspiring, and reassuring, and it feels like home to his mind and spirit.

Belonging is a fundamental human need that starts at birth and continues throughout our lives. I am seeing it in my dad as he struggles with losing his memory and living without his wife. He makes frequent phone calls to family members "just to connect." He wants to hear our voices and know that we are there, that he belongs to us. In addition to our biological family (and in some cases in place of it), we need to belong to a community, to contribute to others in meaningful ways and develop a wider circle of relationships. When we engage with others in community service, social activities, or spiritual growth our lives become richer and deeper. Studies show that we also live longer, healthier lives as a result.

Gratitude is a magical attitude that activates grace in our lives, connecting us to Divine Love and the awareness of our belonging to God. Today consider where and how you belong to others, to your family, and your community. Give thanks for those relationships and opportunities, and reach out to someone who may need connection and support. There are many people around us who would love to feel welcome and "at home" in a community. We can each extend ourselves in ways that uplift others and bring more light, love, and joy into the world. Let's remember that we belong to each other.

Focus

> "The focusing power of attention never fails. It is the secret
> of success. Concentrate. Then go after what you want."
> — Paramahansa Yogananda

Friday arrived like an early house guest before the floors are vacuumed! Have you ever had that experience? Surely, we all have, in one way or another. This week has been full of preparations for a big event at my church this weekend, which I am helping to coordinate. My time and attention have been fully occupied by this project as the date quickly approaches.

The practice of being present is an ongoing lesson for me and for each of us as life seems to be spinning faster and faster. How do we hold on to that which we cherish when the world is continually changing? How do we stay present when there are numerous distractions all around us, clamoring for our attention? It can be exhausting, frustrating, and confusing!

Focus is a key word for me, as I realize how easily and often I get distracted. Can you relate? Focus is central to being present *and* feeling good, because what we focus on expands and increases in our lives. Being present requires focusing on the here and now and the beauty within it. There are "presents" in the "present," and "presence" is the gift. Wow! Think on that for a minute. The presence of God or Love

119

is ever present and everywhere present. It is *here* and *now*. When we are present, we become receptive to presence, which is love, joy, beauty, and peace.

I've noticed that the times I begin to feel anxious, my mind has shifted to some thought, concern, or discomfort of the past or future. As soon as I realize that, I can shift my attention back to the present, and the anxiety subsides. I have to choose to focus on gratitude, abundance, love, etc.

Try to become aware of your thoughts and feelings today and how they are connected. You are the captain of your thoughts. Keep those which increase your awareness of the *good* in your life and release those which cause anxiety, fear, or resentment. Remember that we were created to live joyfully and abundantly in the here and now. Joy, love, and laughter are infectious. Now go and spread some happy germs today by choosing to *focus* on the beautiful *presence* that is *present* within and around you.

Intention & Imagination

"Mental whispers develop dynamic powers to reshape matter into what you want. Whatever you intensely believe in your mind will materialize."
— Paramahansa Yogananda

One of my favorite and most influential spiritual teachers is Wayne Dyer. He taught the power of intention and visualization, saying, "Contemplate yourself surrounded by the conditions you wish to produce." Instead of focusing on the lack of what you need and desire, generate the image and energy of already having it. This is the principle of the Law of Attraction. When we have a strong desire and intention, and we imagine it to the point of seeing and feeling as if it already exists for us, then the energy of attraction is activated. Doing this consistently, faithfully, and patiently, with *gratitude and joy*, is the key to fulfillment.

"Whatever we plant in our subconscious mind and nourish
with repetition and emotion will one day become reality."
— Earl Nightingale

According to Napoleon Hill in *Think and Grow Rich*, our brains become magnetized with the dominating thoughts which we hold in our minds, and these "magnets" attract the forces, people, and circumstances in life which harmonize with the nature of our dominating thoughts. Wow! That's powerful! And it's true; it's a universal law.

"All thoughts which have been emotionalized (given feeling)
and mixed with faith begin immediately to translate
themselves into their physical equivalent or counterpart."
— Napoleon Hill, *Think and Grow Rich*

I have learned from experience that this does, indeed, work; however, since we are not all seeing and all knowing beings, it is wise to ask for "this or something better." I have had doors close and new ones open, revealing something that was better for me at the time than what I had imagined. This is why I trust in the Universe to support me and provide for me completely. I do my part and release any attachment to the outcome. That is where faith comes in.

ELISA JUAREZ

"Faith is the 'eternal elixir' which gives life, power, and
action to the impulse of thought."
— Napoleon Hill, *Think and Grow Rich*

Since "what we think about we bring about," I train my mind to align itself with my highest and best through the regular practice of meditation and affirmations. Here are a few of the statements that I use, thinking and speaking them with energy and conviction:

1. I attract people, resources, and opportunities that are in alignment with my interests, values, vision, passion, and purpose.

2. I receive guidance, wisdom, inspiration, and assistance from the Spirit within me.

3. I declare and claim divine order and abundance every day!

This is a powerful one that I found in *Science of Mind "Guide for Spiritual Living"* and adapted:

> *"I know love as absolute freedom in every area of my life. I*
> *release any sense of struggle, disappointment, failure, and*
> *wrongdoing. I live in an abundant universe where there is*
> *more than enough for all. I experience freedom in every*
> *moment by always having more than enough money,*
> *vibrant health, and loving relationships. I am rich, I am*
> *blessed, I am free!"*

When I truly believe in the work I am doing and stay *on purpose*, as Wayne talks about, I can trust the Universe to support me in every way. I remember that *feeling* good is instrumental in *attracting* good! I choose to be optimistic, accepting, and flexible. I see myself happy, healthy, and successful — regardless of my current circumstances. And

I continually give thanks. Gratitude unlocks the door to abundance, Divine Love, and generosity of spirit. When gratitude and giving become as natural as breathing, we experience an enlargement of love, health, and happiness, and a continual flow of beauty and grace in our lives. This expansion attracts joyous fulfillment and blesses the world in which we live.

Lemons

If you are caring for an elderly parent, as I am, you are experiencing the shift of roles and responsibilities and the inherent challenges. It is an opportunity to increase our capacity, our understanding, and our skills. It requires us to become more in response to the challenge, to grow in patience and compassion, to listen and learn, to reach deep down into our souls for strength and wisdom.

Whether you have this challenge or another one, it is full of potential for you and those around you. I have realized this sacred task gives me a new perspective from which to create, write, and speak. We have all heard the common expression, "If life gives you lemons, make lemonade." Challenge and adversity can be sour lemons. As a writer, I realize that I can squeeze that juice into a bowl, add sugar and water, and mix it into something refreshing and delicious, and so can you! What can you *add* to it to *create* something new and refreshing? Don't be passive in your current situation; don't just wait for it to go away or get better. You are *in it* because you have some special ingredients to add to it, and you can create something new out of it.

You have within you the presence of Divine Love which can transform anyone and anything. Sometimes we have to be squeezed for that love to be realized.

Take a closer look at where you are and what you are doing. Ask yourself, "What do I have to learn from this experience? What can I create in response to this challenge that will be sweet and refreshing to me and those around me? How can I use this to uplift and empower others who are in a similar situation?" These questions will lead you to the answers if you listen with an open heart and mind. Give thanks for the gift. Let your pitcher be filled love, beauty, and refreshment so that you can pour that out to others. It starts with lemons. Hold the lemons in your hands and feel the power you have to squeeze the juice from them and add your own special moxie.

If you are celebrating Holy Week, consider the power that was released out of extreme adversity through faith, surrender, and grace. When our lives are poured out for others, beauty arises from the ashes, and something new is called forth. Be still and listen. You are here now for a reason. Embrace the possibilities and taste the sweetness of life!

Holy Week

"If you have learned the art of understanding and tolerance, then you will suffer much less. Looking at living beings with compassionate eyes makes you feel wonderful. You do not change anything. You only practice seeing with the eyes of compassion, and suddenly you suffer much less."
— Thich Nhat Hanh, *Going Home*

This is Holy Week for Christians and Passover for the Jewish faith. For me it is a time to reflect on the story of Jesus, and his life and teachings that have shaped me and continue to guide me. At an early age I learned tolerance, and for that I am most grateful. I was taught to honor and respect other religions and practices and to be open to what I could learn from them. This is not a common attitude among Christians. However, for me it is the essence of my faith and consistent with how Jesus lived and loved. I saw it in both my grandmothers who treated everyone with equal respect and kindness. I never heard them speak ill of anyone. My parents also lived this way and showed me a love that was unconditional and embracing. It is very important to me, both as a person and a writer, to be open and affirming to others, to connect with people of diverse beliefs, cultures, and backgrounds, and to use inclusive language. That is why I use the term "Divine Love" interchangeably with "God." It is universal.

This week I have been doing meditations on gratitude and grace, and this quote spoke to me today:

ELISA JUAREZ

*"Love is such a deep gratitude. When you are truly in love
with life, every breath you take is gratitude."*
— Bryant McGill

I also read that when we learn to feel gratitude with a full heart, we are learning to love unconditionally. Living this Divine Love is living in grace. Jesus taught that the greatest commandment was to love God with all your heart, soul, mind, and strength, and to love each other. From that deep love which *is* God we are able to love others more fully. Jesus demonstrated this, living in a *radical* way by loving the "unlovable" and marginalized members of society.

We live in a time of considerable tension, fear, bigotry, judgment, and greed. All these elements were present in Jesus' day and he addressed them. He exemplified something different by challenging the cultural norms and making the religious and political leaders very uncomfortable. I can see many of our current religious and political leaders getting very uncomfortable with people and principles that threaten their power and privilege. I see many Christians hopping onto the fear and judgment bandwagon. Whatever our faith, we need to examine it and examine ourselves for the shades of darkness and denial that block Divine Love. What we think about and focus on will increase in our lives, so that is where we should begin.

Gratitude is the portal to Divine Love. When we spend time each day in the conscious awareness of this abiding love, we will absorb it into the very fiber of our being. It will begin to permeate all that we are and all that we say and do. If we all took just these two things from all the religious and spiritual teachings — *gratitude and love* — and really practiced them, we could change the world.

Why do we let specific issues and beliefs separate us? Why wrestle with and argue about who's *right* and who's *wrong?* Just allow *gratitude* and *love* to take hold of you and transform your life. Let them become your religion of choice. Such a religion excludes no one, hurts no one, judges no one, and fears nothing. Such a religion produces peace within and around us.

> *"Living in constant love and gratitude is the essence of spirituality."* — Akemi G

Herein lies the presence of grace and the path to wholeness.

Wildflower Wonder

> *"...To see the world in a grain of sand, and heaven in a wildflower, hold infinity in the palm of your hand, and eternity in an hour."* — William Blake

On a recent trip to the Texas Hill Country I was amazed by the bounty of wildflowers all along the highways and country roads, and across the fields and hillsides. According to a friend who lives there, the blooms were delayed by a lack of rain, and she was beginning to wonder if they would bloom this year at all. Then it came. Mother Nature saturated the earth with several inches of life giving water, and an abundance of wildflowers burst forth everywhere. I was in awe at the seemingly infinite display of color and beauty: bluebonnets, the queen of Texas wildflowers, plus coral, purple, yellow, white, and pink flowers lining every road and dancing on every field and hillside. It was glorious!

I longed to capture their beauty and take it with me. I wanted it to last forever. Then I realized that gazing with gratitude and awe would create an imprint on my mind and soul. So I consciously took in the beauty and wonder of it all, allowing it to permeate my being and fill me with rapture.

The same life force that created the flowers, the birds, and the sky also created you and me as expressions of divine energy and abundance. Is the world we see not a reflection of ourselves? "Beauty is in the eye of the beholder." Perhaps the ability to notice, behold, and appreciate beauty stems from an inner awareness of beauty and grace. When we are still and fully present in the moment, beauty arises within and around us.

Wildflowers represent renewal, carefree spirit, and abundance. Jesus taught and demonstrated these principles, and even used wildflowers as an example, saying not to be anxious about our lives, what we shall eat or drink, nor about our bodies, what we shall put on.

> "Consider the lilies of the field, how they grow; they neither
> toil nor spin; yet, I tell you, even Solomon in all his glory
> was not arrayed like one of these."
> — Matthew 7:25, 28-29

Wildflowers spring forth from the earth year after year as a gift of nature, revealing her glory, bounty, and renewing life. That same energy resides in us and seeks expression *through* us and *as* us. Imagine that glory and abundance abiding within you, just waiting for the rain of your attention and the sunlight of awareness to burst forth and bloom!

As the glorious gifts of springtime fill the world around us, take time to pause, be still, and absorb the beauty and wonder of it all. Rejoice, be glad, and give thanks. Love, laugh, and live well!

Smell to Live Well

Spring rains are soaking my herbs and flowers, helping them to grow in fullness and stature. I love the smell of rain! It is a time of renewal and refreshment all around us. Today I want to focus on the power of fragrance to heal, soothe, and inspire, and share some ideas for adding fresh, natural aromas to your home. Don't we all love to smell good, feel good, and live in a fragrant home? Sadly, most air fresheners and candles are made with synthetic fragrances which are *toxic*. *Gladly*, there are plenty of natural sources to discover, explore, and enjoy!

Sitting on my foyer table is a stunning and fragrant Easter lily which may last for a few more weeks. Herbs and flowers provide natural and sometimes intoxicating fragrances which carry wonderful health benefits. Essential oils are made by extracting and steam distilling the oils from plants, and they can be used for aromatherapy via diffusers and application to the skin. Some essential oils are food grade and can be taken internally. I have been using essential oils for many years, thanks to my mother who got into them and shared her oils and knowledge with me. They have been used for thousands of years for health and vitality, so they are not a passing fad! Once you start using them, you will realize how amazing they are and how *good* you feel!

This is a perfect time to plant your own herbs which is a sensory delight! Go to your local garden center and browse. Choose the herbs you will enjoy most for their beauty, flavor, and/or fragrance. Last year I discovered purple basil for the first time and had to buy it! This year I am growing rosemary, Italian oregano, English thyme, mint, lavender, and lemon balm. After buying and planting your herbs, you may want to visit the bookstore for a book about herbs, as I did. You can learn the many ways to use them in your cooking, household, and personal care.

> "The world around us possesses exquisite smells that can stir our memories, color our emotions, and transform our feelings and moods."
> — Sarah Ban Breathnach, *Simple Abundance*

The benefits of aromatherapy are mental, physical, emotional, and spiritual. Find what soothes and satisfies you, and what makes you feel happy and alive, and incorporate this into your daily life. It will increase your *wellness* and *wonder*, thereby helping you *live well!*

Wedding Week

It's "Wedding Week" at our house as we prepare for the wedding of Taylor's best friend, Madison. Taylor is the maid of honor, and I am honored to serve as the event coordinator. Since Maddie is like a daughter to us, this is a very special time. Our conversations about the wedding plans, pictures, flowers, guests, and festivities have triggered many memories of my own wedding. I even pulled out one of my wedding albums to show Maddie my flowers. Art and I have been married for 28 years next month and it has been quite a journey.

If you are married, take a few minutes to reflect on your wedding day. Can you remember how you *felt*? What were the highlights? Who was by your side as you got ready, and as you stood up to take your vows? If you are divorced or widowed, think about how you have honored and loved yourself since then. If you haven't done much for yourself, why not? What are you telling yourself? How would you like to be loved, honored, and celebrated? Find some ways to do this for yourself, either with friends and/or family members or alone! I suggest you write your thoughts, ideas, and feelings in your journal. That process will provide insight and healing.

If you are married, it would be fun and stimulating to bring out the photo album(s) and play some of the music from that time. Music takes us back to the feelings and experiences of our past. Sparking some memories from the time when you and your spouse were newly in love can awaken that passion within and between you. Even if it is just a spark, fan it into a flame! Marriage is a gift to be cherished, enjoyed, and celebrated. If yours is hum drum, it's time to shake it up! Don't settle for boredom and mediocrity! What we think about expands, so think about how you fell in love, what you used to do together, what you loved about him/her, and what you still love and appreciate about him/her! Write these things down and then find ways to communicate them to your partner!

Wherever you are in your relationships, let springtime renew your perspective, commitment, and love. First with yourself, and then with your partner, children, and friends. When we are refreshed, renewed, and authentic, we can give from a place of genuine love. We are also more magnetic to that which we desire. Renew your vows to yourself or make some new ones! Vow to be true to yourself, to love yourself in sickness and in health, to honor your mind, body, and spirit, to accept the abundance that life has to offer, and to always give thanks. Write down your vows to yourself and say them aloud! Then maybe you and your partner can renew your vows to each other, too!

Celebrate your life and relationships with gratitude and joy. Know you deserve the highest and best that life and love have to offer. Open your eyes, heart, and mind to receive it and say, "*Yes, I do!*"

The Sacred Art of Home Caring

After weeks of stormy weather, this week has brought some of the most beautiful spring days here in Texas. My herbs and flowers are filling their pots after all the rain! We cherish this time of year when we can enjoy being outside without melting! It's also a perfect time for spring cleaning since I can open the windows and refresh my home. I have increased my enjoyment and appreciation for home caring over the years as I have read and re-read *Simple Abundance* by Sarah Ban Breathnach.

> *"Today, no matter where or how you live, look upon your home through the eyes of Love. Walk around the rooms and offer thanks for the walls and roof that safely enclose*

you and yours. Pause for a moment to consider all the [people] who have lost their homes through death, divorce, debt, or disaster. Be grateful for the home you have, knowing that, at this moment, all you have is all you truly need."
– Sarah Ban Breathnach, *Simple Abundance*

As women have expanded their skills and influence in the workplace by pursuing careers and advanced degrees while juggling multiple roles and responsibilities, the sacred art of home caring has been diminished. Our lifestyles have changed, and we rush our meals, conversations, home caring, and self care. Over the years, I have had the privilege and opportunity to pursue a graduate degree, work in the non-profit sector, stay at home with my children, build a home based business, help open a restaurant, work in retail management, and volunteer in my church, my community, and our schools. Throughout all these different seasons of work, I found great joy and satisfaction in creating and maintaining a *home* that was a sanctuary of peace, joy, and *love* for my family and me.

There is too much of the world in and around us; we are bombarded daily with news, drama, conflict, and demands. We cannot always control what happens outside our four walls, but we *can* control, or at least impact, what happens *inside* those four walls. We all need a sanctuary, a refuge, a safe place in which to rest, relax, and renew our weary minds, bodies, and spirits. If our homes are not such a place for us, then we have some serious work to do. How can we operate at a high level as positive, productive people if we neglect caring for ourselves and our homes? What kind of environment are we creating for ourselves and our families? We must change the way we look at and approach this sacred task. As Sarah Ban Breathnach says, it starts with gratitude and awareness. Her book, *Simple Abundance*, is full of ideas and inspiration for living an authentic life and experiencing the sacred in the ordinary.

Housekeeping and home caring may seem too ordinary to appreciate and enjoy, but if approached with mindfulness can truly be an expression of your authenticity and creativity. I know that I have found a direct correlation between the state of my house and the state of my mind and spirit.

> *"Prayer and housekeeping—they go together. They have always gone together. We simply know that our daily round is how we live. When we clean and order our homes, we are somehow also cleaning and ordering ourselves."*
> — Gunilla Norris, *Being Home*

My home is an expression of my tastes, priorities, values, and experiences. It is also like a canvas for creativity, so I try to see it with fresh eyes and an open mind as I usher in each new season.

When I was growing up, I had a small bedroom with antique furniture (including a large, heavy dresser on wheels) which I used to rearrange every few months. I would move that furniture around all by myself to create a new perspective within the space. I have always enjoyed "playing" with my living space by experimenting with arrangement, color, design, and decor. What if you approached home caring as play? Just try it out! Take a few moments to pause and look around your home, walking through each room mindfully. Do you see a reflection of yourself? Give thanks for your home and all that it holds for you. Accept and bless your current circumstances, and then be open to new ideas and inspiration. Find new ways to organize your things, clear clutter, and add creative touches to each room. Think of your home as a canvas for your work of art, and an expression of the lives who share the space.

The six *Simple Abundance* principles are: *gratitude, simplicity, order, harmony, beauty, and joy.* Contemplate these things. What we think about and focus on will expand!

Fill 'er Up!

This morning I am sitting in my favorite café doing my writing and enjoying French Roast coffee and classical music. There is a fire in the fireplace that creates a warm and inviting atmosphere (even though it is very warm and humid outside)! This place feeds my soul in a way I can't explain. Whenever I come here to write I feel like I am giving myself a gift.

Living and giving from a full tank is a topic I am passionate about, as it is so crucial for women, in particular, and so hard to learn. We are wired to pour ourselves out for others all our lives. As times have changed and women are pursuing careers outside the home, we now have a greater challenge on our hands, especially if we have children. Our work does not end when we leave our job; it continues until we go to bed, and then we have the challenge of clearing and calming our minds so that we can sleep well. How many of you have still been folding laundry or putting things away when your hubby crawls into bed and falls asleep?

How can we fill our energy tanks each day so that our giving comes from the overflow? That is the best way to bless our families and our surroundings! Think about how you drive your car and pull into a gas station when your tank is low. Do you leave the car running while you try to fill the tank? No way! You have to *stop* the car, turn *off* the engine, and get *out* of the car to fill 'er up! Now apply this to yourself, your energy tank. We have to do the same thing for ourselves!

You know how great it feels when you have energy and joy and a good hair day! Things seem to flow with ease and the world smiles back at you! I believe this is how we were created to live – fully, freely, joyfully, abundantly. It doesn't mean that life will be easy, but that we can engage in life with a spirit of love, optimism, and gratitude. To maintain a healthy mind, body, and spirit, we need to figure out what we love, what fills us with energy and joy, and how to live from that fullness. We need to start the day by connecting to the power source, that which fills us with energy and light!

Writing in a journal is essential for my health and happiness. I highly recommend it for everyone because it's your personal conversation with yourself and God, or the wise and wonderful part of you. It's a way to connect and communicate with your soul. It's the best way to nurture yourself, process your experiences, and put things in perspective. Give yourself some time each day to read, write, reflect, and rest. Honor yourself as the creative and powerful being you are, and fill 'er up!

Morning Reflection

The other day I was listening to an audiobook by Mel Robbins, *The 5-Second Rule,* and learned that the first two to three hours in the morning are the best time of day for the brain. Therefore, you don't want to waste that time on meaningless, unproductive activities or distractions. I spend the first hour reading, meditating and writing in my journal. It sets me up for the day. I don't turn on the television because I want only positive, peaceful thoughts and images to fill my mind in the morning. Today I got up at 6:30 and had my quiet time for the first hour, then after Art left, I decided to use this "golden time" for writing. I am sitting in the armchair with my laptop, and the patio door open ajar to let in the morning air. It is a beautiful May morning after a refreshing rain overnight. The flowers are still damp, the air slightly cool.

As I sit here listening to beautiful piano music on Pandora, I see the sky darkening and hear a rumble of thunder. I can smell and feel the moisture in the air. I contemplate the absolute wonder and beauty of the universe and my place in it. I am blessed and humbled by the gift of this time and place in my life. When I pause and reflect on it, I realize that it is a respite after years of struggle, hard work, and sacrifice, of pouring myself out for my family, doing whatever was necessary and whatever we thought was best for our family. And all along the way I stayed deeply connected to the Spirit within, praying and receiving guidance, strength, wisdom, inspiration, hope, joy, and courage. I also practiced meditation and visualization by writing my goals and dreams and reviewing them daily, picturing and claiming a life of joyful service, creativity, health, vitality, purpose, and passion. I created it in my mind first, and now I am living in it.

Happiness is a choice, and I choose it each day. I remind myself that I went through a lot of pain, growth, personal development, stress, and sacrifice to get *here*. In a sense, I earned this; I imagined it, worked for it, and chose it. I co-created this. It's okay! It's wonderful!

It's not finished yet, as I continue to learn and grow, but instead of focusing on what's missing or on a sense of failure or inadequacy, I need to focus on and celebrate the abundant blessings in my life and the work I get to do. I know I was created for more, and I am working on myself every day. I want to help others do the same; I want to help them realize their beauty, passion, and gifts and bring them to the world. I want to uplift and empower people every day through my love, words, writing, actions, leadership, compassion, and life. This is my prayer and intention: "Take my life and let it be consecrated, Lord, to Thee. Take my moments and my days; let them flow in ceaseless praise."

Tree of Life

Nature holds an abundance of wisdom for us to gather and feast on like the squirrels gather nuts and seeds. I am always captivated by the *Planet Earth* programs which stir in me a sense of awe and wonder at the beauty and order in creation. Recently I watched the program about jungles, and one particular story resonated with me.

The plants in the jungle all have to fight for sunlight to grow, and because of the density of trees and plants, it is a struggle. They showed a particular tree that fights its way up to reach the sunlight, pushing through the growth of the forest until it is towering above the ground and soaking up the sunlight. This is what struck me: The tree then becomes home to many other plants, birds, and life forms. The narrator said the tree's growth gives life to many other plants. They showed ferns and other plants growing from the trunk and limbs of the tree. The life force that pushed the tree up and out and helped the tree fulfill its purpose now flows into the other plants, which are connected to the tree so that they can live and grow. If the tree had not grown to its stature, then the other plants could not have experienced its gifts, or its life.

What an amazing metaphor! Our growth is not just for us; it is necessary for others, too. It gives life and hope to those around us. I recently heard that struggle is a biological necessity. This was true for the tree, and it is true for each of us. It's not optional. It's how we were created. There is within each of us the same life force; it is a higher calling to grow and become more, to fulfill our purpose and our destiny. Staying safe, living small, and settling for less does not serve the world. We were created for growth, stature, and abundant life. So, focus on that light for which you were innately designed to reach up and out. As you grow you will absorb more light and love, and others will be drawn to you so that they may be a part of it, too. Don't be discouraged or defeated by the struggle; keep your eyes on your *why* and let the force within propel you forward, upward, and outward. As you stretch and reach for the light, the light will reach for you, too.

Your dreams were placed within you by your Creator, with everything necessary to make them come true. So be intentional about your growth. It will inspire and empower those around you to grow and become what they were designed to be. Let your light and your stature give life, light, and hope to the world.

Embracing Health & Wholeness

This week I attended a monthly caregiver support group sponsored by the local Alzheimer's Association. I'll admit that sometimes I leave there feeling worse, as the majority of the group members are caring for a spouse who is battling Alzheimer's or another form of dementia. Caring for a parent is hard enough, but a spouse is a whole other thing. The loss and grief are different; plans and dreams dissolve as the disease progresses; daily life changes dramatically, as well as the nature of the relationship. It has been deeply disturbing to realize the number of people who are being diagnosed between the ages of 58 - 68. Art and I are on the threshold of that age bracket, so this hits very close to home. My dad wasn't diagnosed until he was 84 years old.

This journey has driven me to study brain health to better understand the disease and perhaps protect my husband and myself from it. I have found many foods that are known to protect the brain, along with exercise and social engagement. The role of toxins is also critical, so any discussion about health needs to include that topic. Anything we do to improve our overall health and wellness is good for the brain. There are many factors that impact brain health and are still being researched, so a multi-pronged approach is necessary. For example, we have learned that the brain needs insulin, healthy fats, certain nutrients and antioxidants, and oxygen. Therefore, insulin resistance hurts the brain, as does a lack of healthy fat (and HDL cholesterol), nutrition, and oxygen. In addition to the physical aspects of brain health, there are mental and emotional factors. Our thoughts, emotions, and beliefs play a significant role in our overall health and cannot be ignored if we want to live with joy and vitality. It is a fascinating topic to study, and it affects all of us!

As with any disease, there is much to learn and understand, and our response to it will affect our experience and outcome. I am a firm believer in prevention, having studied nutrition and wellness for years. However, I also realize that there are things in this life and this world that we cannot control. When life throws us a curve ball, we have a choice to catch it and run with it or allow it to crush us. My mom taught me that knowledge is power and attitude is everything! Her determination to learn, understand, and overcome empowered her to make healthy choices in her approach to scleroderma. She tackled it with physical, mental, and spiritual armor which clearly extended her life. Empowerment also comes from sharing our experiences with others, listening to their stories, and accepting support and assistance.

At the end of the day I always come back to gratitude. In these past several years of caregiving I have made some amazing friends, developed a strong support network, and learned new skills. The journey has taught me to be more fully present and focus on the gifts I have been given. It has increased my patience and my capacity. It has given me new insights and deeper understanding. My confidence and compassion have been strengthened, as well as my trust in God's guidance and grace. I have moved from pain, grief, conflict, self-doubt, struggle, and exhaustion into healing, courage, forgiveness, peace, and wholeness.

Today I encourage you to look for the gifts and growth in your journey. Surely you, too, have experienced loss, grief, self-doubt, and pain, as they come with being human. When we embrace the *whole* of it, we become open to healing and hope. We discover a purpose in being who and where we are, which is empowering and enlightening.

> *"Have no fear, and trust that you are completely supported in all the good you are here to reveal. You are so loved by life. Life is here to support you. This, you can trust. Have faith in the process. Have faith in you. Fear not, for you are guided and directed always and in all ways."*
> — Eugene Holden

Infuse

One of the things I enjoy in the spring and summer is cold water infused with fresh fruit and herbs. I'll fill a pitcher with filtered water, then add slices of citrus fruit or cucumber, plus fresh herbs like mint and lemon balm. I once had an infuser water bottle, and I have seen drink dispensers and pitchers designed with built in infusers, as well. If you think about it, the infuser provides a valuable metaphor for our lives. Let's start with the definition of the word "infuse," which means, "*to introduce, as if by pouring; cause to penetrate; instill; to imbue or inspire; to seep or soak (e.g., leaves, bark, root, etc.) in a liquid, so as to extract the soluble properties or ingredients.*"

First, choose what goes into the infuser. Those ingredients will steep in the liquid and the flavors will be extracted into the water. Think of the water as your mind, body, and spirit. Whatever you hold in your mind will affect your whole being, physical, mental, and spiritual. If you don't like how you feel or what your life looks like, check your infuser. You may need to clean it out and put in some fresh ingredients. You may have some bitter herbs or sour fruit in there! Find what energizes and inspires you and refresh your infuser with it. Instill positive, uplifting, and inspiring thoughts, ideas, and practices. Your life is a reflection of the environment you create on the inside, so that's where you should begin if you want to change your outer world and relationships. Health, happiness, and vitality emerge from the inside and are reinforced by a healthy lifestyle on the outside.

Now let's look at the definition of the word "diffuse," which means, "to pour out and spread as a fluid; to spread out and scatter widely or thinly; disseminate."

Whether you realize it or not, you are diffusing whatever is on the inside. It is seeping into your home, your work, and your relationships. So this isn't just about you; your presence affects everyone around you! *You* are a diffuser! Refresh your mind, body, and spirit on a regular basis, and you will help create a healthy, happy world around you!

Mother's Day

> "Though we are grown, we never outgrow the need for
> someone special to hold us close, stroke our hair, tuck us
> into bed, and reassure us that tomorrow, all will be well.
> Perhaps we need to reacquaint ourselves with the maternal
> and deeply comforting dimension of Divinity in order to
> learn how to mother ourselves. The best way to start is to
> create, as an act of worship, a comfortable home that
> protects, nurtures, and sustains all who seek refuge within
> its walls." — Sarah Ban Breathnach, *Simple Abundance*

Mother's Day is an opportunity to remember, honor, and celebrate all the women in our lives who have left their imprint on our hearts and helped shape who we've become. It started with our mothers, of course, and the circle of women widened as we grew. Who were the women in your family that were a part of your growing up in addition to or in place of your mother?

Grandmothers often play a significant role in our lives, and sometimes aunts, sisters, and even cousins. I know my mother was a significant positive presence in the lives of her grandchildren as well as her own children. I remember when Taylor was born, and my mother came to stay with us for a week or so. Taylor was the first grandchild on both sides of the family, so it was a big deal. My mom said she never had any idea how amazing it would be to be a grandparent, that the magnitude of love she felt was beyond her expectations. She was very intentional about her relationship with each of her grandchildren, realizing that she had the opportunity to impact their development through unconditional love, creativity, and compassion.

Now that my mother has passed away, I have grown even closer to my Aunt Laurel who is my mother's closest sister. When I talk to her on the phone, I feel connected to my mother and her love. There is a golden thread within families that is woven into our relationships, even when they are difficult or strained. Sometimes we have to look closely to see it, but it is there. It is the gift of grace that holds us in its eternal embrace despite all the struggles of this life. Honor the women in your family by remembering their gifts and expressing your gratitude for their presence in your life, even if they are no longer living. Perhaps it will help you recognize and honor the imprint they left on your heart.

This Mother's Day take a wider look at the legacy of the women in your family and beyond. What can you learn about your ancestors and how they lived? What are the principles and values that have been passed down from generation to generation? Where and how do those show up in you and your immediate family? You are creating a legacy for your children and grandchildren that is connected by that golden thread to the women who have gone before you. What would they say to you now? What would you say to them?

Pour a glass of wine or champagne and raise a toast to motherhood, and all the amazing women who helped raise *you*. Celebrate the day and catch a shimmer of that golden thread of grace.

Writing connects us to our past and our inner wisdom. It is such a vital part of living for me, as it was for my mother. It is like breathing; it gives my mind and spirit oxygen. It is a biological and spiritual necessity and a way to "metabolize" my experiences. Much of my blog is an expression of things I learned from my mother, including authenticity and creativity. Reading my mother's writing connects me to her and reminds me of the legacy of love and passion she left for us. Her spirit lives on in my writing and my life.

I recently came across one of her writings entitled, *A Slice of Life*, about a time she was making her mother's chocolate chip cookie recipe, and it took her back in time to her childhood kitchen. It is a simple and precious reflection about her own mother who was in a nursing home at the time. I decided to include it in my book in honor of Mothers' Day and in memory of my mom and grandma.

A Slice of Life

By Janice Rand Tucker, my mother, who was a writer and artist. I found this story in one of her notebooks, and I share it in honor of her and my grandmother.

Today I want to make chocolate chip cookies; not just any recipe, but Mother's chocolate chip cookies with oatmeal and chopped pecans. I long to be with Mother, to close the 2,000 mile gap between Texas and New Hampshire where she sits in her corner of Birchwood Nursing Home, hooked up to oxygen.

Down deep I want to fold back the years, to be with Mother as she used to be. Mother, so sharp of mind, younger women prodded her memory for facts they couldn't recall. Mother, who dropped her work the minute the newspaper came to sit at the kitchen table with the crossword puzzle; whose zest for learning sent her scurrying for the *Rand McNally Atlas* whenever she heard of a place she didn't know. Mother, whose childlike spirit kept her alert all winter for a crust on the snow covered hill by our house, for a run on the "Flexible Flyer" sled her father gave her as a child.

This is the mother I ache to reach out and touch. I smile to myself as I stir her recipe, picturing Mother in her cotton print dress and fresh starched apron, stirring cookie batter while we kids hover around to snitch a taste. "Now run along before I forget what I'm doing! I don't know if I put the salt in or not!"

She stops stirring to check the wood stove. "I thought my oven was hotter than this!" She opens the oven door and slams it shut to jar the gauge for a more accurate reading, then opens the drafts, removes the stovetop lid and adds kindling from the wood box. A wave of black smoke erupts in her face. Mother has tended these fires since her marriage in 1929, never suspecting the "heartbeat" of her kitchen could be causing a gradual erosion of her lungs.

As my first batch comes out of the oven, I am thrust back in time. Once again I'm a school girl, running into our cozy kitchen, cookies just out of the oven spread to cool on the kitchen table. The aroma of melting chocolate chips in crisp golden cookies welcomes us. Mother has timed the treat for our homecoming.

Suddenly ripples of delight bubble up in me. I place a call to the nursing home.

"Hello?"

"Mother," I exclaim into the phone, "I'm making your chocolate chip cookies, your recipe with oatmeal, remember? Shut your eyes and picture them. Can you smell them?"

"Yum," she chuckles quietly, "I can taste them."

"Mother, you gave us such wonderful memories. I remember coming in after school just as you finished baking a batch of chocolate chip cookies, and the thrill of sitting down at the kitchen table for a cookie and a glass of cold milk. I'm so grateful for the good memories of home."

"Yes, I have good memories, too, and Dad is sitting here looking across the room at me from the dresser."

"I bet he's even closer than that! What's your weather like there?" Weather is one of Mother's favorite subjects.

"I don't know. I can't see out very well from my corner. What's your weather like?"

"We've had a warm day here, over 60 degrees. The sky is blue and the sun's shining."

"My, that sounds like summer."

"Yes, it was so warm I took a walk. Do you have snow?"

"Maybe a little. I can't see out the window very well."

"I hope they'll let you go to church tomorrow."

"Is tomorrow Sunday? What kind of weather are you having?"

Mother doesn't remember she just asked. "Oh, it's a beautiful day in Texas. The sun's shining and it's in the 60's."

"My, you like that, don't you."

"Can you tell me what you've done today?"

"Oh, the usual... word games in the activity room in the morning."

"You're good at those games, aren't you."

"Seem to be. Most of the time I just sit here with my crossword puzzles. I don't know what I'd do without them."

"You're fortunate to have such a sharp brain. Have you had company this week?"

"Marcia came one day. Maybe it was this week."

"Did she take you for a ride?"

"Yes."

"Did you get my letter with pictures?"

"I don't know, maybe. What were the pictures of?"

"Our family around the Christmas tree with one of me holding Lauren."

"How old is she?"

"Three and a half months."

"Oh, she's only a baby, isn't she."

"Well, I'd better go tend my cookies. Wish you were here to have a cup of tea and a cookie with me."

"That would be nice, but it's good to hear your voice."

"I'll eat a cookie for you, too. Here's a big hug." I grunt into the phone and she grunts back. We laugh and hang up.

I miss Mother. But it does feel like we've been together. For a few moments, her chocolate chip cookies help close the gap.

The Kitchen Table

There is no greater symbol of home and family life than the kitchen table. Here we share not only food and conversation, but the ingredients of daily life and learning. Here papers are spread out, homework is completed, ideas are exchanged, hands are held, prayers are lifted up, comfort is shared, and laughter bubbles over. At this table we start our day with nourishment, anticipation, and preparation, and at this table we gather at day's end to relax, release, and be fed.

My childhood kitchen was small, with a round table in the center. The meals were always nutritious and the conversation interesting. Most of the time we sat down as a family for dinner, and even breakfast. We started the meal with prayer, either spoken or sung. A drawing of Jesus hung on the wall right by our table, and I grew up feeling like I knew him, like he was always there with us. I sat next to my dad, which was great, because he would eat whatever I couldn't finish on my plate.

Mom would say, "Tom, you do not have to be a garbage disposal!"

On the contrary, he was always happy to help when it came to good food!

Cathy sat on my right. She brought many thoughts and issues to the table and wanted to discuss them. Most of the discussions took place between her and Dad, although Mom also participated. Randy and I would get bored with it and play "footsie" under the table. We wanted to have fun. He was about making people laugh, so whenever things got a little too serious, we could count on him to lighten things up. This often led to me giggling and laughing, sometimes uncontrollably.

I offered the family dramatic storytelling. I loved to recount my vivid dreams at the breakfast table, and the events of my day at the supper table. I would get out of my chair to act them out at times, and Dad would tell me that was not necessary. I don't recall either of my parents getting cross with us at the table — except maybe when Randy and I needed to be reined in from our silliness.

Mom was the expert on nutrition and manners, and she was very good at teaching us without ever nagging. She used the modeling method to teach good posture and manners, and she was intentional about it. When she would straighten up in her chair, we would all suddenly realize we were slouching! Wow, it worked without a word from her! When it came to nutritional information, she had a lot to share. She explained what each food had to offer, why it was good to eat, and how often we should eat it. I remember at least once asking if we could please eat it without the nutritional analysis, just this once!

After supper Dad usually had to head off to a meeting, and we would clean up the kitchen. This is the time Randy conveniently had to go to the bathroom for about 15 minutes. Whenever I washed the dishes, I would continually pour water over the clean ones in the drainer so they wouldn't dry on their own while he was gone, thus making his job of dish drying null and void! I intended to keep things fair, so they were still wet when he finally returned. Mom would stay and help us clean up until we started bickering. We learned early on that her help was conditional on us getting along and doing the work without complaining. That was the best incentive for us to keep our mouths shut. When we did the work cheerfully, Mom was quick to praise us. "Elisa, you are an *angel!* Thank you!" Or this one, "Thank you very much; you did a wonderful job!" which was actually a quote from a school patrol award ceremony at our elementary school in which a police officer said this line to each person as they received their award. It struck our funny bones at the time, so we kept using it.

The kitchen table was also important after school. I can remember many days when we came home to fresh baked bread cooling on racks on the table, and we would get a warm heel with butter and honey. I would sit there and talk to Mom about my day.

Now that I am grown and have a family of my own, I find that the kitchen table is still the hub of our family life. Since we do not have a dining room, the kitchen table is the only table at which we can eat, pray, share, and create. Our first kitchen table had a rectangle Formica top which was conducive to all kinds of activities. The girls could do arts and crafts there, play games, and make messes. Many memories were made on that table from the time Taylor was born until we moved out of our first house and sold it.

Then we were ready for a larger table made of wood to fit our new, more traditional style. Selecting the right table was very important and took a few months. This was again to be our only dining table, and a place for family activities to take place. When I first laid eyes on the Shaker style, rectangular wooden table that we now have, I knew it was the one. The color matched our kitchen cabinets, the chairs had cushioned seats and sturdy backs, the wood was beautiful and slightly distressed, and the size was perfect. It was nice enough for entertaining and casual enough for everyday family use.

During the years we have had it, it has become more distressed with numerous scratches and nicks from the kids, but it is still beautiful. Here we gather for nourishment, homework, creativity, and fun. I sit here often with the laptop to do my writing and computer activities. Windows surround our kitchen table with a view of the woods and our birdfeeders, so it is a lovely place to sit and relax. In the evening after supper, Art and I often linger at the table and talk over a glass of wine.

Our family mealtimes have become more comfortable over the years as the girls have grown and Art has learned to relax. When he was growing up, mealtime was just for eating. Children were not allowed to talk; it was adult time. It was not relaxed and open, so this concept was unfamiliar to him. After many years with me and our girls, he has learned that children will talk and giggle at the table and take their time eating. It is, after all, family time. It's the end of the day for all of us, and often our tiredness shows and our patience is thin. For the girls, and sometimes for me, it is a time of easy laughter when ordinary things can seem funny and it feels good to laugh. But this is only fun if Art and/or Lauren are not too tense or tired! Taylor is always about having fun, and her dramatics are often too much for us at that time of day. She has that piece of me, so I have more patience with her than the others do. Lauren always has a lot to share about her day, so between the two of them, Art and I do not get much airtime. He says very little during the meal but will talk with me afterward. Sometimes we all get into a good discussion about something of interest, like the girls' futures, their dreams and ideas, and our family's dreams. These are the best times and the girls thrive on them. Here, around the kitchen table, we share thoughts, explore ideas, and envision our dreams. Here we give each other attention, support, and love. For me, this is what family is about.

The food is also enjoyed and appreciated by our family. We all like a variety of foods, and I enjoy cooking and trying new recipes. Art is a good cook as well and will cook once or twice a week. Those nights are priceless, because we put on some good music, have a glass of wine, and work together in the kitchen. We are all fed by the love and joy of those mealtimes.

ELISA JUAREZ

We have had many meals with friends around this table, and it adds to the richness of our family and our home. Friends bring their own essence, warmth, and stories to the table. When others come and sit at our table, we have the opportunity to feed their bodies and their spirits. I see it as a joy and a privilege. When friends visit, we rarely sit in the more comfortable living room. Instead, we end up sitting for hours around the kitchen table talking and laughing. I know that our kitchen is warm and inviting, but it is more than that. It is the table. We come together around a table to share who we are and to be nourished in body, mind, and spirit. The table is the space where we connect most easily, where we are fed and blessed.

So many memories are created around the senses, and the kitchen is a place of aromas and tastes that become a part of our cellular memory. Food gives us comfort and strength and reminds us of our heritage. In this sacred space of connection and nourishment, our souls are revived.

Books

"If you have a garden and a library, you have everything you need." – Marcus Tullius Cicero

Good books are like salsa for the soul, adding flavor and nourishment to our lives, our perspective, and our understanding. We have much to learn from others' stories which can expand our world view and stimulate our thinking. Books are treasures, full of wisdom, ideas, experiences, stories, discoveries, lessons, and questions.

"Books help us understand who we are, and how we are to behave. They show us what community and friendship mean; they show us how to live and die."
— Anne Lamott, *Bird by Bird*

They can also transport us to different places and times, giving us a glimpse into other worlds and wonders. Whether or not we have the ability or resources to travel, we can always open a book and discover a new place, explore a different culture, and learn about history. As we read, we connect with the author and/or characters and incorporate their stories into our own consciousness. In our minds, questions and ideas arise, and we process these in the laboratory of our own lives. Then we experience new discoveries, opportunities, understanding, and awareness.

I've noticed that my deep love and gratitude for books has grown over the years as I have experienced more life. When I was a child it was hard for me to sit still long enough to do much reading, although I did enjoy books and read regularly. Being a slow reader, I stayed away from the large books that my sister devoured in a few afternoons. However, as I became a young adult I delved into personal development, spiritual growth, and the study of nutrition and wellness. I read books and listened to audio that focused on these topics and increased my hunger for more information and understanding. When I became pregnant, I added parenting books to my repertoire. When I got into business, I read and listened to books about leadership, professional development, and goals. At every step in my journey I have found books and audio to support me, stretch my mind, and feed my curiosity. They have been a vital part of my growth as a person, a communicator, and a writer. I've heard the phrase, "Readers are leaders, and leaders are readers." Leaders understand the importance of lifelong learning, of increasing their value and their skills by expanding their thinking.

> "Have a mind that is open to everything and attached to nothing." — Wayne Dyer

There is just so much to learn in this world, and books offer us an abundance of "salsa" for our mind, body, and soul! *When you expand your thinking, you expand your life!*

The Road Ahead

> "It's a long road to freedom, a-winding steep and high, but when you walk in love with the wind on your wing and cover the earth with the songs you sing, the miles fly by."
> — The Medical Mission Sisters

This past week, our family took a road trip from Texas to Indiana for our nephew's graduation and Lauren's return to Bloomington after a semester in Washington, D.C. We were driving two vehicles: a pickup truck packed with storage tubs and suitcases, and a Honda Civic that Lauren inherited from Taylor. The weather forecast for that day was ominous across the Midwest and all along our route. The day before there had been severe storms with flooding and tornadoes, and more were on the way.

I was nervous about it, so I lifted it up in prayer. First, I talked to my mother, knowing that if she were still alive, she would be worried for us. I just asked her to watch over us and guide us all the way. I believe she can do that from the other side, so it was comforting and reassuring to place the request in her hands. Then, of course, I prayed to the all-knowing, omnipresent, all powerful God in which I place my trust. So, no worries. We were in good hands!

We got up at 4:30 that morning and left at 5:00. No rain. As we got rolling on the freeway, I gave thanks and continued to pray. An inner voice said, "The way has been cleared for you. All is well." It seemed like more than my own affirmation; it felt like the calming and guiding presence of Spirit. It gave me peace. As we watched the weather radar on our phones, we could see that there were storms ahead of us and behind us. We came into some rain mid-morning for a few hours but nothing heavy. When it let up, we stopped at a lovely rest area to eat our picnic lunch. Radar showed heavy rain ahead in Indiana at the time we would be arriving. We got delayed by two traffic accidents, but when we got into Indiana there was no rain. We arrived safe and sound at 11:00 p.m. (Eastern time), exhausted but grateful.

I share that story because it got me thinking about how often we worry about the road ahead based on what we see, hear, or imagine. There is plenty of "bad" news coming at us every day, and it's easy to feel vulnerable. Life is bumpy and fleeting, and each day is uncertain. There is only so much we can control; the rest is out of our hands. My parents taught me, by example, to place my trust in a Higher Power that is all knowing, all loving, and everywhere present. That faith is my anchor and my compass. We can't ever see the road ahead, but if we knew the way had been prepared and cleared for us beforehand, then there would be no need to worry! The truth is that we choose what we think and believe, and that choice makes all the difference. We can't control what happens to us, but we *can* control our mindset, our perspective, and our actions.

As you look at your own journey, do you feel anxious about the road ahead? What is your fear? Consider the possibility that you are being divinely guided and protected. How does that feel? Turn on your GPS — your Guidance Protection System. How would it change your approach to life if you *knew* that a loving, guiding, protecting Presence was always with you and available to you? It is your choice to connect to it. You are in the driver's seat. You choose your direction, your focus, and your fuel. Your journey is uniquely yours, so follow your inner compass. Know that it is leading you to joy and surprises beyond what you can imagine.

SPRING RECIPES

Mom Tucker's Baked Mac & Cheese

This is the recipe my mother always used for macaroni and cheese while I was growing up. The recipe was adapted from her *Betty Crocker Cookbook*. We used to eat this favorite comfort food with ketchup.

- 4 cups hot drained boiled macaroni (8 oz uncooked)
- 2 tablespoons butter, cut up
- 1¼ cups sharp cheese, cubed
- 1 teaspoon salt
- ¼ teaspoon black pepper
- 2 eggs, beaten
- 3 cups milk
- Paprika

INSTRUCTIONS:

1. Combine beaten eggs, milk, butter, cheese, salt, pepper and pour over macaroni.
2. Sprinkle with paprika.
3. BAKE 40-50 minutes at 350 degrees until golden brown.
4. Garnish with parsley sprigs, pepper rings, and serve hot.

Black Bean Vinaigrette

By Elisa Juarez

- Two 15 oz cans black beans, rinsed and drained
- 4 green onions, chopped
- Red bell pepper, chopped
- ¼ cup chopped cilantro

DRESSING:

- ½ cup avocado oil
- 3 tablespoons red wine vinegar
- 2 tablespoons Dijon or coarse mustard
- 1 tablespoon finely chopped jalapenos (from a jar)
- ½ teaspoon sea salt

INSTRUCTIONS:

1. Mix salad ingredients together in a bowl, then toss in dressing.

Borracho Beans

This recipe was passed down to me by my mother-in-law.

- 2 cups dried pinto beans, sorted and rinsed well
- 1 – 2 cloves garlic
- 1 medium onion, chopped
- 1 tomato, chopped
- Handful of fresh cilantro, according to your taste
- 1 can or bottle (12 oz) of beer, room temperature
- Salt and pepper

INSTRUCTIONS:

1. Heat a large pot half full of water on high, almost to boiling.
2. Add beans and garlic.
3. Reduce heat to medium high and continue to cook for 2 hours, adding water as it cooks down and stirring occasionally.
4. Partially cover the pot to keep water from evaporating as quickly; but keep an eye on the beans!
5. When beans are almost soft, reduce heat to low, add remaining ingredients and stir.
6. Let simmer for an hour or two until done, or transfer to crock pot on low setting for 2-3 hours.
7. Add salt as needed.
8. Remove garlic cloves before serving, or break them up and mix in.

ELISA JUAREZ

Cabbage-Sausage-Potato Steamer

By Elisa Juarez

Adjust amounts according to how many people you will be serving. This recipe is good for two large servings. This is an easy, nutritious, one pot meal for a couple or a family. In addition to the cabbage and potatoes, you can add any vegetables and/or types of sausage you choose. This combination is what our family has enjoyed for years.

- Potatoes (2-3 medium or 4-6 small) cut into chunks
- ½ small to medium cabbage, cut into quarters
- 3 carrots, peeled and sliced and/or green beans
- ½ lb. smoked sausage, sliced

INSTRUCTIONS:

- Place potatoes and carrots in steamer basket in large pot; bring water to boil, cover and cook for 10 minutes on medium high.
- Add cabbage, green beans, and sausage and cook for an additional 10 minutes or until all vegetables are barely soft.
- Top with butter, sea salt, and seasoning of choice.
- Ranch dressing on the side or drizzled on top is also delicious.

Cilantro Lime Rice

- 2 cups water
- 1 cup brown rice, rinsed
- 1 tablespoon butter
- 1 teaspoon lime zest
- 2 teaspoons fresh lime juice
- ½ cup chopped cilantro

INSTRUCTIONS:

1. Bring 2 cups water to a boil.
2. Stir in butter and brown rice.
3. Cover, reduce heat to low, and simmer until the rice is tender, about 45 minutes.
4. Stir in lime zest, lime juice, and cilantro just before serving.

Makes 4 servings.

Enchiladas Verdes

The quantities for the ingredients depend on how many you want to make, but I prefer to buy a rotisserie chicken and use about half of it for a pan of 12-15 enchiladas. When I cook my own chicken, I use boneless, skinless breasts and/or thighs, drizzle with cooking oil, and season with garlic, sea salt, and freshly ground pepper. Smaller quantities can be heated in the microwave for 1-2 minutes.

- 3 cups shredded chicken
- 12-15 corn tortillas
- 2 cups Monterrey Jack cheese, shredded
- Tomatillo salsa (see recipe)

INSTRUCTIONS:

1. Heat oil in a large sauté pan and dip tortillas one at a time in oil for 10-15 seconds until they are soft enough to roll.
2. Fill tortillas with shredded chicken, roll and place in a rectangular baking dish.
3. Continue this process, lining up the enchiladas in the pan snugly so they do not open.
4. When the pan is full, pour salsa over the top, then cover with shredded cheese.
5. If chicken is pre-warmed, cover pan with foil and bake at 350 for 10 minutes. Remove foil and bake for another 10 minutes or so until cheese is melted and just starting to brown.
6. If chicken is cold, bake for 30 minutes (20 minutes covered, 10 minutes uncovered).

Tomatillo Salsa

This recipe was inspired by my sister-in-law, Deb Juarez, who is a successful personal chef in Ohio. This is how she taught me to make this type of salsa, and I absolutely love it!

- 8-10 fresh tomatillos
- 2 jalapenos, seeded
- 2-3 cloves garlic
- ½ onion

INSTRUCTIONS:

1. Peel tomatillos and onion and cut into quarters. Toss all ingredients in olive oil or avocado oil and spread onto baking pan.
2. Season with sea salt and fresh ground pepper.
3. Roast in 350 degree oven for approximately 20 minutes.
4. Let cool then blend with ½ cup. cilantro until creamy.

Makes approx. 3 ½ cups.

This recipe is mild to moderate heat depending on the jalapenos. For a hotter salsa, add more jalapeno. This one is delicious poured over chicken enchiladas or other Mexican dishes!

ELISA JUAREZ

Favorite Carrot Cake

This is my healthy version of a favorite carrot cake recipe.

- 1½ cups organic coconut oil
- 1¼ cups organic cane sugar
- 4 cage free eggs, well beaten
- 3 cups grated organic carrots
- 1 cup organic oat flour
- 1 cup unbleached flour
- ½ teaspoon sea salt
- 2 teaspoons soda
- 2 heaping teaspoons ground cinnamon
- 2 teaspoons ground allspice
- 1 cup chopped pecans or walnuts
- 1 teaspoon vanilla

INSTRUCTIONS:

1. Cream oil and sugar.
2. Add eggs and carrots; mix well.
3. Mix dry ingredients.
4. Add a small amount of flour mix to carrot mix at a time, beating well.
5. Add pecans and vanilla. (This mixture will fit into a Cuisinart processor.)
6. Pour into a 10 X 14" greased and sugared pan
7. Bake at 325 degrees for 1 hour.
8. Cool slightly before frosting.

FROSTING:

- ½ cup butter, melted
- 8 ounce pkg. cream cheese, softened
- 2 cups sifted, powdered sugar
- 1 teaspoon vanilla

INSTRUCTIONS:

1. Combine butter and cheese with sugar and beat well.
2. Add vanilla.
3. Mix well and spread on cooled cake.

ELISA JUAREZ

CHAPTER THREE: SUMMER

Summer

Sweet, refreshing springtime gradually gives way to the growing intensity of the sun as delicate blossoms are replaced by lush greenery. Growing things seem to multiply overnight, showing off their fruits, leaves, and flowers. Nature's song builds to a crescendo with the added choruses of birds, locusts, and tree frogs. It is a time of beauty and bounty.

Summertime brings a slower pace of life, more time to rest and play, and a sense of freedom and fun. These themes are woven into the summer essays along with reflections and recipes from the garden, and invitations to listen, linger, and let go. Simple pleasures that soothe and sweeten our souls are bumped to the top of the priority list.

> "Summer, after all, is a time when wonderful things can happen to quiet people. For those few months, you're not required to be who everyone thinks you are, and that cut-grass smell in the air and the chance to dive into the deep end of a pool give you a courage you don't have the rest of the year. You can be grateful and easy, with no eyes on you, and no past. Summer just opens the door and lets you out." — Deb Caletti, Honey, Baby, Sweetheart

Summertime: Fresh & Fun

My favorite theme for summertime is "Fresh and Fun," and I like to apply it to every area of my life. The truth is, we *all* need to refresh from time to time, and summer is perfect for that! It's a great time to bring more *fun* into our daily routine, both at work and at home. As we get older this can become more of a challenge, so we may have to consciously choose or create it. Sometimes it just takes a shift in attitude and perspective to open our minds and spirits to something fresh and fun that will help us relax and release old ways of thinking and being.

Start by letting the summertime vibe get into your veins. It seems to arrive with the month of June as school lets out and routines change. Hot days cause us to move slower, grab cold drinks, and look for ways to cool off and relax. Farmers markets come alive with garden fresh produce, farm fresh eggs, herbs, and handmade foods and crafts. There are plenty of outdoor activities to enjoy, as long as there is shade and a breeze! In Texas, the most popular summer spots are water parks, lakes, and swimming pools!

The idea is to find refreshment and have fun, so be creative this summer and look for something *new* to see, learn, and do. Every time we experience something *new*, we expand our perspective and become more open to the abundance that is all around us.

ELISA JUAREZ

Most of us tend to do the same things, go to the same places, and eat the same foods over and over. We get comfortable with the familiar. We may not even realize we are in a rut until we start feeling sluggish, irritable, and bored. It doesn't take a major change to create an energy shift and refresh our minds, bodies, and spirits. We can all find places in our communities that we have never visited, like a museum, gallery, park, market, winery, restaurant, etc.

Just last week I met a client for lunch at a coffee and sandwich shop located in a large, old house with a wrap around porch. I had never been there and was delighted to discover it! Not only was the shop a great find, but so is this client who is becoming a good friend. It's a perfect example of keeping life fresh and fun. When we stay open and receptive to new people, places, and experiences, our life is fresh, full, and fun.

How can you keep things fresh and fun this summer? Well, it is truly a season of abundance, so try a *taste* of fresh foods, fresh air, and fresh ideas. Try some new recipes and activities. Meet some new people! Step out of your comfort zone and let the Universe surprise you! Let this summer be a time of healing, happiness, and hoorays for you!

The Tune for June

"What's your tune?" Have you heard that expression? I'm sitting here thinking of words that rhyme with June, and that came to mind. We can choose our tune each day; it's like our attitude, right? Maybe it's also our focus, our "theme," and our mojo. So, what's your tune for June?

My "fresh and fun" theme is my favorite tune for this season which is overflowing with fresh flowers, fruits, veggies, herbs, cold drinks, and *fun*. I'll be singing my tune this weekend as I travel to the Gulf Coast for a quick day trip and a visit to the fresh seafood market! Then I'll be humming my happy tune on a visit to our favorite spot in the Texas Hill Country! I'll carry my tune into my writing, cooking, and creating. Perhaps it will help me to stay curious, playful, relaxed, and present.

Find a tune that's in harmony with *you*. Choose or create it consciously, write it down, and then live it with intention and enthusiasm! Don't just coast along without one; the days of summer are brimming with possibilities! Maybe even put it on a Post-It note on your mirror. Choose a tune that will uplift you and those around you. Choose a tune that will raise your awareness and creativity. Choose a tune and invite others to sing it with you by sharing in your activities, your ideas, and your joy! Think of it as your motif, attitude, focus, and essence! Then play it with all your heart!

Garden Goodness

*"We might think we are nurturing our garden, but of
course it's our garden that is really nurturing us."*
— Jenny Uglow

What are you growing in your garden this summer? Do you have a backyard garden or potted plants? I have a container garden on my third floor balcony with several pots of herbs and flowers! I enjoy the greenery of my mini-garden and the courtyard below. The elevated perspective allows me to see over the Spanish tile rooftops and watch the sky.

If you grow vegetables, that is a wonderful thing. I look forward to having a vegetable garden when we build our next house so that we can enjoy *really fresh* produce! I grew up in a mid-size city, and we had a small vegetable garden in the backyard plus a flower garden surrounding the perimeter of the house. I can remember the morning glories, hydrangeas, lily of the valley, iris, and tulips, as well as the cucumbers, lettuce, tomatoes, and green beans we grew.

Whenever I think about gardens, I consider the metaphors that nature provides for our lives. My mother used to say that our minds are like gardens, and we should be careful what we plant in them. We plant seeds with our thoughts and words. If we don't like what we see growing in our lives, then we may need to examine what we've planted, and what we continue to feed and water! We all need to take care of our inner gardens with loving attention and intention! Weeds can grow in any garden and must be pulled regularly so they don't take over.

> "Weed out disappointments, frustrations, diminished ambitions, unfulfilled expectations, and anger about what has gone before, or what has not yet come. These emotional weeds only choke your creativity. Let an unfettered imagination sow the seeds of possibility in the rich soil of your soul. Then let passion tend the garden with patience and perseverance. For, as Frances Hodgeson Burnett (author of The Secret Garden) discovered, 'When you have a garden, you have a future, and when you have a future, you are alive.'"
> — Sarah Ban Breathnach, Simple Abundance

Gardens can bring us an abundant harvest when they get the light and water they need, plus regular weeding and tending. Our thoughts, words, intentions, and actions can also bring abundance into our lives. Take some time this summer to examine and tend your inner garden. Write your thoughts, observations, and dreams in a journal so you can be conscious of what you plant and grow. We truly are the gardeners of our lives, working together with nature to create beauty, nourishment, and joy. Sometimes we need to put our gloves on and dig in the dirt, but it's well worth it!

ELISA JUAREZ

Swings & Homemade Ice Cream

"The most fortunate are those who have the capacity to appreciate again and again, freshly and naively, the basic goods of life, with awe, pleasure, wonder, and even ecstasy." — Abraham Maslow

I have a sweet and funny memory from a visit to my parents' home when the girls were young. We were sitting outside on the back patio eating homemade ice cream under the canopy of the giant shade tree. The ice cream was soft to begin with, and melting quickly as we topped it with warm chocolate sauce and pecans. Still, we had to capture the moment with a picture, so Dad went in at Mom's request to get the camera. I love the idea of having that picture, but in that moment, I just wanted to relish the ice cream before it melted away!

Dad took the picture, then his battery died. Mom wanted to get another picture with Dad in it. One is never enough in my family. We have to get everybody, and when the larger family is there, we *also* have to get a shot with everyone's camera! "Oh, would you take one on *my* camera, too?" is heard whenever someone gets a great shot. I offered to use my camera for another picture, but Dad was already inside hunting for batteries as his ice cream turned into vanilla milk. We both emerged with our cameras and took a few more pictures after more ice cream was enjoyed.

After the ice cream came the pleasure of swinging with glee under the trees in the woods. Lauren and I ran to the swings and swung high in the air, touching the trees with our feet. As I love to do, I leaned all the way back as I swung forward and felt the rush from head to toe as I came back up. It filled my chest, and I let out a squeal and uncontainable laughter. Swinging is a childhood pleasure that I still enjoy. Inside I feel the same. The swing is not as comfortable now that I am bigger, but I still experience the same joy when swinging with my daughter (maybe more).

I've realized as I get older that as life changes us in some ways and creates more challenges for us, it also brings us new joys and discoveries. These are not gifts from the outer world but from our inner life. If we are open to that process, we will grow older in body but deeper and wiser in spirit. At the same time, we can enjoy the simplicity of childhood with and through our children. We still have those joys in our cell memory; we can love, laugh, and swing with glee, and it all comes back. God is in everything. All is gift.

Father's Day Fare

Father's Day is a time to remember and celebrate our dads, grandfathers, and husbands! If these men are no longer in your life, what are you carrying in your heart and mind as a result of their presence in your life? What is or was their legacy?

I realize that I am fortunate to have an abundance of happy memories of my father, and he is still in my life in a big way at nearly 90 years of age. I have found that those cherished memories are bittersweet, filling me with a blend of gratitude and sadness. I often share some of them with him, and he chuckles and says, "Oh, my! I don't have any recollection of that!"

At times I am surprised at what he *does* remember. I am most grateful that he still remembers me. He knows not only that I am his daughter but that I am here for him whenever he feels lost or confused. I have the sacred opportunity to give back to him through loving care and attention, as he gave to me so freely throughout my life.

If your memories of your father are not so happy, perhaps you can find a way to metabolize those memories through writing. We may have had a better relationship with a stepfather, grandfather, or other male figure growing up. It can be difficult to accept some of the people and circumstances that were hurtful to us. It may take a lot of inner work to overcome obstacles and find peace. Even though I had a happy childhood, I have spent my entire adult life doing inner work to overcome my many limitations, struggles, and challenges. We can choose to carry only that which serves and empowers us, and that is the way to freedom and healing.

Whatever Father's Day brings up in you, give it your loving attention and do something creative with it. Celebrate your life and the gifts you received from your father that helped shape who you have become. Give thanks to *all* the men in your life who have loved and cared for you, believed in you, and supported your dreams. Let go of anything that may be blocking the flow of Divine Love within you. Know that that Divine Love is your birthright and your very essence; it is seeking you and seeking expression through you. It is neither male nor female—or perhaps, it is both—and it gave birth to you. It is still within and around you to hold, uplift, nurture, and guide you. That is something to celebrate!

Presence

"There is nothing more significant and more humble than being who you really are." — Deepak Chopra

My childhood home sat on a hill overlooking a busy street. Two large maple trees, one on each side of the house, created a giant, leafy umbrella over the front yard. I have a fond summertime memory of my dad and me sitting under that canopy at dusk as he sang the evening hymn, *Now the Day is Over.* I can still feel the cool grass beneath us and the evening breeze caressing the leaves above us. I hear my dad's gentle, soothing voice and recall the sense of comfort and calm that it brought me. He said and did many things that taught me to enjoy and appreciate life, but it was who he was and how he lived that really made the difference. It was his presence.

When I became a parent, I was determined to get it right, to do it well, to be the best mom I could be. During my pregnancy I read *What to Expect While You're Expecting,* I meditated and exercised regularly, and did all that I could to prepare for our child. I quit my job to be home with her that first year (which turned into 18 years) and focused my time and energy on that sacred and challenging task. After a few years, we had our second daughter and I continued to try to *do* all the right things. Time, experience, and spiritual growth helped me to realize that who I was carried more weight than what I did. I learned to look at things in new ways, let go of my striving for perfection, and accept myself as I was. I realized the importance of presence.

Now I stand between my father, who gave me such a rich legacy of love, and my young adult daughters, who continue to give me immeasurable joy. My father's world is getting much smaller as his memory crumbles. My daughters' worlds continue to expand as they pursue their dreams. What remains constant is the abiding presence of love, which gives our lives meaning, value, and joy. Presence arises from within us as the truest expression of who we really are. It has the power to transform situations and relationships. There is nothing we can *do* that carries more significance than our presence.

Think about those people in your life who have a positive, powerful, and peaceful presence. How do you feel when you are around them? How do they affect the environment? Are you aware of how your own presence affects those around you? When you hold the intention of peace for yourself and others, you will attract peace and all that comes with it. This is how you really make a difference in the world. Presence is the greatest gift we can give to others, and the most valuable gift we can receive. It is worth our time and attention to practice being present and bringing more light and love into the world.

Packing for the Big Trip

Summertime is in full swing and July is just around the corner! When I was growing up, this was the time when our family was preparing for vacation. My dad was a pastor, and every summer he got a full month off work. We would pack the car for a long road trip that included exploring state parks, camping, and visiting family and friends. I have a treasure trove of memories from those trips, and a deep appreciation for the natural wonders that we got to see and experience.

Preparing for a month long vacation in a four door sedan with five people is quite a task. Thankfully my dad was a former Boy Scout (along with his dad and brothers) and had lots of skill and experience with traveling, packing, camping, and other outdoor adventures.

Here's how it went. The day before departure, each of us kids packed our own suitcase and took it to the garage where Dad had a large tarp laid out on the floor. He was the Master Packer. In addition to the trunk, we had a "top box" that was attached to the roof of the car. He had to pack camping equipment, bedding, beach towels, food, and other necessities into those two compartments. It was like a puzzle for him, and he was very strategic about fitting everything perfectly with little room to spare. It was something to watch!

My mom was in charge of the food, and she prepared sandwiches, snacks, and homemade cookies for the road, plus non-perishable items which she packed in a cardboard box for our camping time. I'll never forget the giant bag of cheese puffs that we would get for the trip – the kind that make your fingers and lips turn orange – as it was the only time all year we got to have those! I can also still remember the smell of ripe bananas that lingered in the car.

Each of us were responsible for part of the preparation, but it was Dad who pulled it all together. I got to thinking about this as a metaphor for our lives. Are we not each responsible for what we pack and carry on this journey? We have to make choices, organize our things, manage our time and space, and work with others.

A trip such as that would have been easier with just one or two people, but we had five. We had to share the space in the trunk and inside the car. I'm sure we had to leave some things behind reluctantly. It can be a challenge to pack less and travel light. We all tend to hold onto things—physical, mental, and emotional—that are unnecessary and weigh us down.

Finally, I think about how we packed our bags and then laid them down on the tarp, leaving the rest to Dad. We did our part and then let go of the rest. Never did I question my dad's ability to accomplish his task—even though it looked doubtful at times! When we pursue a goal or dream with a destination in mind, it is our job to do the work and then let go of the results. We often try to control how things fit together or turn out in our lives, not seeing or understanding the big picture. My dad mapped out our trip in advance, knowing where we were going and what we would need. He put it all together; we were free to let go and trust the process.

> *"Someone who loves you unconditionally is at the helm.*
> *Divine Love sustains you, surrounds you, enfolds you,*
> *protects you. Go in peace. You're as ready as you will ever*
> *be, well equipped for the adventures awaiting..."*
> — Sarah Ban Breathnach, *Simple Abundance*

So, pack wisely, travel light, and stay curious!

Morning Glory

*"It is in the early morning hour that the unseen is seen,
and that the far-off beauty and glory, vanquishing all their
vagueness, move down upon us 'til they stand clear as
crystal, close over against the soul."* — Sarah Smiley

I love how the day begins gently and quietly. The sun rises slowly, not with a sudden blast. If you get up early enough you experience this glorious awakening of the day. I highly recommend it. Embrace the early morning gifts of peace and comfort. Let the beauty and the stillness be absorbed into your being and they will accompany you throughout the day.

The early morning holds treasures that can transform our lives day by day if we open our eyes and ears to receive them. The outside world is ready to bombard us as soon as we turn on the television, the computer, or our cell phones, but *wait.* You will be thrust into the world soon enough; guard your heart and mind as you begin the new day. Allow the Spirit within and around you to fill you with peace, gratitude and wisdom. It's like plugging in to the power source or filling your tank with fuel. It's vital and necessary.

Learn to notice more. To be fully alive we need to be fully conscious. Notice the little things around you, pause and pay attention. Notice your inner world; your thoughts, ideas and feelings. When we have an awareness and experience of the life within us and in all creation, we can truly say, "Life is good." Therein lies the *glory* of each new day. It starts within, and we can honor it or ignore it.

ELISA JUAREZ

Carve out time at the beginning of the day and allow the Light to arise in you as the sun arises over the world. Then let that Light illuminate your path as you step into the day. It will empower you and transform your experience, your relationships, and all that you do.

The Flow

"Going with the flow is responding to cues from the universe. When you go with the flow, you're surfing life force. It's about wakeful trust and total collaboration with what's showing up for you." — Danielle LaPorte

You've probably heard the phrase "in the flow," which indicates smooth sailing, energy and creativity, confidence and effortless ease. Hopefully you have had this experience at one time or another and know how great it feels! It's that "good hair day" or "divine order day." It's when life just seems to flow smoothly with ease and grace, and you smile at everyone you meet.

"Whenever we experience the Flow, we experience a luminous liftoff: we're alert, soaring, unselfconscious, authentic, moving at the peak of our abilities. Obstacles dissolve in the Flow. Toxic emotions, anxieties, and depression disappear. We're in this world, but certainly not of it..." — Sarah Ban Breathnach, Simple Abundance

Sarah says that this state is most often attained with simple pleasures, including work, *"when we bring the right attitude and attention to our tasks."* It is being fully present and focused.

William Kenower talks about the Flow in writing, saying that this is where the magic happens:

> "When you're in the Flow, you always feel good, because you are exerting no effort, and all of your attention is focused on something about which you are very curious.... No experience can be separate from the Flow, for this would suggest that some experiences are apart from the loving, compassionate, creative, cooperative, friendly flow of life." — William Kenower, *Fearless Writing*

He emphasizes that the Flow is life itself, and always available to us; it just takes some awareness and attention on our part. The Flow is always available to us; it just takes some awareness and attention on our part. Think about a garden hose that is connected to a water source. You go out to water your garden and you turn it on. As you drag the hose across the yard, you notice the water isn't coming out the other end! You examine the hose and find a kink which is blocking the flow of water. We can turn on the "water" in our lives by asking to invoke the flow, but if we are holding onto anger, resentment, fear, or any other toxic emotions or limiting beliefs, then we are blocking the flow of energy, creativity, joy, and love. It is there, but we are not fully open to it.

Today, choose to let go and enter the Flow. Know that it is the presence of Divine Love awaiting your invitation and openness. Just be willing to ask, trust, and believe in it.

> "If you can believe in the Flow when you're out of it, you can begin to find it on purpose. It's there because it's you, and the moment you believe again in the Flow, you also

restore faith in yourself."
— William Kenower, *Fearless Writing*

You can live fully and freely; just relax, rejoice, and go with the flow!

Body Language

"To pay close attention to and mostly accept your life, inside and out and around your body, is to be halfway home." — Anne Lamott, *Almost Everything*

In all our efforts to love ourselves a little more, I think giving love to our bodies may be the thing we avoid or ignore most. We tend to be critical of our bodies with every glance in the mirror, every ache and pain, limitation, and reminder that we are getting older. We may compare our bodies to others, to an ideal, or to an earlier time in our lives as we see what has changed, what we've gained and lost, or what remains as an unwelcome part of ourselves. Listening to the critical voice in our heads, and any negative thoughts about our physical selves, is a rejection of the Love that created us for health and vitality. We need to change our *body language*, that is, the way we communicate with our bodies.

One way I overcome that critical voice and any anxiety about my health is to speak words of life and love to my body. I usually do this in the shower. I speak to the different parts, thanking them for serving me so well, telling them that I love them, and affirming that every cell and organ is functioning beautifully.

"Every thought we think is accompanied by an emotion— each of which has a distinct biochemistry associated with it. Thoughts of empowerment, love, and support feel good and result in an increase in immunity and a decrease in stress hormones that create wear and tear on the physical body. Thoughts of revenge, sadness, or anger feel bad. . . . And held over time, they are associated with chemicals in the body that cause cellular inflammation—the root cause of most degenerative disease. . . A thought that is repeated over and over becomes a belief. And beliefs held over time become our biology. Our beliefs have the power to affect our genetic expression."

— Christiane Northrup, M.D., *Making Life Easy*

Therefore, the practice of thinking and speaking life and love to our bodies has actual physical benefits, especially when we add the energy of feeling to our words.

The other component of body language is *listening*. When we learn to love, respect, and trust our bodies to support us, we will become more receptive to the intuitive and physical messages they are sending us each day. Ask your body what it needs and wait for a signal, a prompting. Maintain an attitude of acceptance as your body communicates to you, even when that message comes as pain and discomfort. Your body is the temple of your soul, and it is the only one you get in this life.

*"The Soul brings us into our bodies, and our bodies are
where the Soul work gets done. The Soul speaks to us
through our bodies. And its lessons come through our bodies
in many ways, including pain and illness."*
— Christiane Northrup, M.D., *Making Life Easy*

As we consciously look and listen within for wisdom and guidance, we will expand our awareness and improve our body language.

You can change your beliefs by choosing new thoughts and speaking life to every cell of your body. Do it until it becomes easy and natural for you, and you will experience a renewal of healing energy. As we develop a healthy belief system with positive, empowering body language, we will become more effective at creating and maintaining a vibrant, healthy lifestyle. If you are battling a chronic illness or disease, then it is essential to give your body extra love and compassion. Let it be your teacher; ask your soul to reveal the lesson it has for you. Choose to face each day with relentless optimism and courage. As you give your body the love and support it needs on every level, it will support you in discovering and living your best life.

Thoughts on Health & Happiness

"No matter what you are doing, keep the undercurrent of happiness, the secret river of joy, flowing beneath the sands of your various thoughts and the rocky soil of your hard trials. Learn to be secretly happy within your heart in spite of all circumstances."
— Paramahansa Yogananda

As much as I believe in the importance of good nutrition and a healthy, active lifestyle, I also believe that true health and happiness is an inside job. The healing energy of love and joy is more powerful than anything in the outer world. We benefit from *all* of it, of course. Eating well and exercising regularly improve our blood flow, energy, endorphins, brain function, etc.; it's all connected. Happy cells are healthy cells. The benefits of a loving relationship are immeasurable, as is a life of passion and purpose.

I've read and heard stories of people who were diagnosed with a terminal illness and decided to start doing the things they loved most and really making the most of each day, and they outlived the prognosis. They connected to a part of themselves that is invisible and eternal; they found their inner wellspring of joy, energy, and life! When we connect to our life force, our passion, and Divine Love, we experience renewal, healing, creativity, and power. We connect to something beyond the physical which created the physical, which heals and transforms us. This is the secret to health and happiness, vim and vigor, agelessness, and vitality. This is "salsa" for the soul!

So, I embrace the daily simple joys, like morning quiet as the sun rises and casts its rays across the tile rooftops, coffee, good books, doves on my balcony, and the love of my life. I give thanks for the beauty and wonder of life within and around me. I give thanks for writing, reading, and learning every day. All is gift. Life is good, and the more we open ourselves to receive its bounty, the more health and happiness we will experience.

Come and See My Garden!

"Study the cycles of Mother Nature, the garden whispers,
for they correspond with the cycles of your soul's growth.
Quiet your mind. Rope in the restlessness. Be here. Learn
to labor. Learn to wait. Learn to wait expectantly."
— Sarah Ban Breathnach, *Simple Abundance*

When I was in my early 20's my parents lived in Evansville, IN, and my mother had a large garden in the backyard which brought her great delight and satisfaction. Her own mother had a magnificent garden in New Hampshire, full of beautiful flowers, vegetables, and raspberries. Visiting either of these avid gardeners always included a stroll through the garden to take in all the beauty, aroma, growth, and good eats.

I will always remember arriving at my parents' house when it was already near dark outside, and Mom saying, "Come see the garden!"

She couldn't wait until morning when daylight would have happily glorified its beauty.

I said, "But Mom, it's almost dark! I can't really see it that well!"

It didn't matter; it was about her eagerness to share something she loved with her daughter. Now I catch myself doing the same thing with my 20-something daughters when they come home. When I had a garden, I was eager to show them what I was growing. Now that we are in an apartment, the pots on the patio don't get the attention the garden did in those first moments of homecoming. However, I always have other goodies that I am eager to share, as my girls will attest to. It's my latest good find from the grocery store or market that I know they will enjoy and appreciate. I did it last night when we arrived home from Indiana with Lauren, whom we hadn't seen in five months. We were all tired from the 14-hour drive, but nevertheless, I had some goodies to show her! She chuckled, and I immediately realized that I was doing my mom's thing. Ha!

Now my mom is gone, and there are so many things I wish I could share with her. We used to share almost everything with each other. I don't know if it happens like this with sons, as I only have daughters, but I sure am grateful for their presence in my life. Our relationship as adults is so enriching; I continue to learn from them and observe how their lives have blossomed out of the environment my husband and I created. A family is like a garden that needs the warmth of the sun, the refreshing rain, and the nourishment of many nutrients in the soil. A legacy of love keeps the plants and flowers coming back year after year, producing more fruit and beauty and dropping more seeds. I see the legacy of love from my grandparents and my parents manifesting in my life and my family.

Whether or not your children are at home or grown (or both!), you are still gardening. You are creating your legacy of love which will produce fruit for generations to come. This is a most precious and sacred task; embrace it with gratitude and joy. If you are experiencing grief, loss, or struggle, realize that these hardships can enlarge your capacity and deepen your faith. Open your heart, mind, and spirit to receive the gifts that are available to you, and you will soon notice butterflies and hummingbirds coming to drink your nectar. Beauty and grace are ever present in all our relationships and experiences — but only when we are open and willing to see and receive them. *Come and see!*

Freedom

"For to be free is not merely to cast off one's chains, but to live in a way that respects and enhances the freedom of others." — Nelson Mandela

The week of July 4th brings up many happy childhood memories and good feelings for me. My family would spend the holiday cooking out, swimming, lighting sparklers, and walking to the park to see the annual fireworks display at the fairgrounds. We lived near a beautiful park with a large hill that overlooked the fairgrounds a few miles away. Every July 4th they did a grand fireworks display, and people from the surrounding neighborhoods gathered on the hill to watch. I will always remember the unified chorus of "ooh" and "ahh" in response to each burst of colorful lights in the night sky. It made us giggle with delight at times.

The Fourth of July was about family, fun, and freedom. It still is, but my understanding of freedom has evolved over the years. We each have our own definition and experience of freedom. I think it is the most important value in our country and our world, and certainly in our personal lives. I look at it from many angles, considering what it means and how it feels. There are freedoms I have now and others I am working toward, like financial freedom. I believe, as our founders did, that freedom is a right, not a privilege. Freedom can also be gained and lost through our opportunities, choices, and actions, and the actions of others. We need to be mindful and merciful regarding human rights and freedoms, as many people in our country do not have them. Others use their personal freedom to threaten and destroy life. We have a responsibility to our human family to speak out against injustice and violence, stand up for equality, and treat every person with dignity and respect. Freedom in that sense is not just a noun but a verb. I know that I want to live in a country that upholds that value for everyone. However, when our personal freedoms impinge on the safety, welfare, and freedom of others we need to be held accountable.

Freedom takes on new meaning for us whenever it is threatened or taken away. This week our dear friend Kim went into the hospital in great pain, had tests run and surgery done, and received a cancer diagnosis. She was on the verge of a new beginning, a move back to Texas, and a new teaching position here. Now her world has turned upside down. She has, at least temporarily, lost her freedom.

However, we always have the freedom to choose our thoughts, attitude, and perspective on life, and no one can take that away. Our mental and spiritual freedom transcend physical limitations and conditions. Kim is a brave, courageous, and positive person with faith and fortitude. She will get through this, but right now the sky is dark and ominous. It is a harsh reminder of how precious life is and how quickly it can change.

This week as you celebrate the Fourth, consider what freedom means to you. What does it look like? How do you use it? As you raise the American flag, raise your awareness of those in our country who do not have the freedoms that you have. Raise your level of compassion and empathy. Raise your thoughts to imagine an America that is united, not divided. Create a vision of America in which people work together, listen to each other, and call forth the best in each other. It starts with you and me. It takes intention, effort, and commitment to bring liberty and justice for all. Have a Happy 4th!

Keep on Singing

When life delivers an unexpected blow, it alters our consciousness, and our experience of time. This one started with a phone call from Kim on a Sunday afternoon. Kim is one of my closest friends — more like a sister, really — and our families are like family to each other. We met as new moms to two year old daughters. They lived around the block from us in our first home. We shared that most precious experience of raising children, each having a second child within two years of when we met.

Now our kids are grown and we are empty-nesters, beginning yet another new season of our lives with hopes and dreams and adventures to be had. Her husband, Jay, is about to retire from the Army, and they plan to move back to Texas. She was just here interviewing for teaching positions, but she had been battling some health issues for about a month.

Eager to hear any news about job offers, I texted her for updates. She said she had been ill and ended up the hospital, as she was unable to recover from the illness and was unsure what it was. That Sunday morning in church I prayed silently for her, and afterward I let her know. She said she needed those prayers and asked when she could call. She said that Art would want to listen in on the conversation.

We were intrigued. News! Hopefully, happy news!

When she called, I said, "I sure hope this is a *good news* call and not a *bad news* call!"

There was silence on the other end, then, "Uh...well, are you sitting down?"

A wave of dread came over us as we sat on the couch. "Oh, dear. What is it?"

Kim sounded drugged. She began to tell us the story of how she ended up in the hospital for the second time in the past week, this time in Florida where they went to see their daughter graduate. As difficult as it was for her to speak, she wanted to share the whole story. In a nutshell, her abdominal pain led to a CT scan which revealed a mass, so surgery was done that morning. The doctors sent it off for a biopsy, but they were fairly certain it was cancer, and lesions on the scan indicated that it had possibly spread to her liver.

The news hit us like a brick. Tears filled our throats and our eyes. When would they have the results? In a few days. Oh boy. It clearly didn't look good, but the test would tell more. She promised to let us know as soon as she got the results. For three days we waited, carrying sadness and anxiety, living in sharpened awareness of life and the realization that a painful and difficult road lay ahead. Our conversations kept coming back to Kim, all day every day. We moved through the day and the tasks before us with heavy, aching hearts. Each day involved waiting. Waiting for news, waiting for updates, waiting for another conversation, waiting for a ray of light and hope. We may be waiting awhile for that. We find comfort in each other's presence and the shared love and deep concern for our precious friend.

As she lay in a hospital bed sucking on ice cubes and waiting for the biopsy results, her life hung in the balance, everything turned upside down. Her devoted husband sat at her side, wrestling with his own inner agony and holding onto hope. All his military training and experience could not have prepared him for this... this moment in time like no other, so fragile and uncertain, the love of his life threatened by an ominous unknown lurking like a dark shadow across the room.

Together we waited. Together we prayed, leaning into the Everlasting Arms, trying to push back the anxiety and fear. Even though cancer is no longer a death sentence, the standard treatment is devastating. It's long and hard and the effects are profound.

Finally, on the morning of July 4th the call came. She had just gotten the results. Metastatic colorectal adenocarcinoma. Stage 4. It has spread to the liver and the abdomen. I broke down in sobs. Art came into the bedroom where I sat on the bed in disbelief. His eyes filled with tears. In the waiting time the doctors had talked with them about deciding where to do treatment, so she and Jay were considering the options. She needed to recover from surgery first, which could take 4 to 6 weeks. They can wait that long to start chemo? They say they can. There is also paperwork to be done, and preparation for a move and transfer to another facility if she decides to come to Texas. Time to make a transition. I pray that she has time.

Kim got out of the hospital on Saturday, one week after being admitted, and is staying with her in-laws in the area as she continues her recovery. She is looking into cancer treatment centers in Texas. So, the journey has begun. I pray it is a healing journey. A heroine's journey that will require every ounce of courage she has in her brave and beautiful soul.

Many little things throughout the day bring me to tears; I close my eyes and feel the sadness, moving through it consciously. I have moments in which my breath is taken away and I almost have to gasp for air. At times I just break down and sob. A friendship this deep and lasting involves sharing our tears, fears, and struggles, as well as our love, laughter, and victories. We've walked hand in hand, heart to heart, side by side, carrying each other's burdens, lifting each other's spirits, and believing in and for each other to the very end, but praying that the end is nowhere near, that we will have many more memories to make together.

It's hard to be here when I want so much to be there with her. Time is so crucial at this stage; she is recovering from major surgery while cancer is growing in her body. We wait with hope, dread, and anxiety. We wait in prayer, trying to let go and lean into our faith. But what will waiting bring? She has today; that is all. That is all any of us have.

ELISA JUAREZ

Grace and peace surround us, holding our tender hearts and shining light on the path ahead. Whatever lies before us is nothing compared with that which lies within us. We step into the unknown together, holding onto hope, faith, and unbounded love.

I listen to the angelic, ethereal voice of Enya to soothe my soul and accompany my tears. I call to my mother on the other side, knowing her spirit abides with me in this hour of deep concern and sadness. This song has always been meaningful to me, and today I meditate on its lyrics.

How Can I Keep from Singing?
By Enya

My life goes on in endless song
Above earth´s lamentations,
I hear the real, though far off hymn
That hails a new creation.
Through all the tumult and the strife,
I hear its music ringing.
It sounds an echo in my soul.
How can I keep from singing?
While though the tempest loudly roars,
I hear the truth, it liveth.
And though the darkness 'round me close,
Songs in the night it giveth.
No storm can shake my inmost calm,
While to that rock I´m clinging.
Since love is lord of heaven and earth,
How can I keep from singing?

198

When tyrants tremble in their fear
And hear their death knell ringing,
When friends rejoice both far and near,
How can I keep from singing?
In prison cell and dungeon vile,
Our thoughts to them are winging.
When friends by shame are undefiled,
How can I keep from singing?

It lifts me above the tumult in this world and the sadness in my own heart. Again, I am reminded of the delicate balance that life offers, taking us from joy to pain, from strength to weakness, from brokenness to wholeness, from despair to deliverance. I am reminded to move gently through each day, holding my dreams lightly, allowing them to inspire me while releasing my attachment to them. Nothing is certain but the abiding presence of Divine Love, and that is enough. That is what sustains, comforts, strengthens, guides, and protects us along this twisting, climbing path. Nothing can separate us from it — ever. It is our source, our substance, our reality, and our Home. It is in this awareness that we can rise above the tumult and the strife to let go of fear and keep singing. All we really have is this very moment, as the present is all there is.

I listen to the music, and the dryer running. I see the sunlight outside the windows and dark clouds moving in. I realize the afternoon has arrived and the time is slipping by. Time cannot be stopped, and our experience of it is dependent on our awareness and attention.

ELISA JUAREZ

If I received a diagnosis that threatened my life, what would I do? How would I keep on singing? I would have to write, and write, and write my heart out until I die so that I don't leave this earth with my music still in me, as Wayne Dyer used to say.

"Don't die with your music still in you." – Wayne Dyer

Keep on playing to the very end. I have a book to write and publish this year. It is important that I get it done. None of us have a guarantee of long life. We don't know what's around the next bend. We are here to discover and express who we really are. Each challenge is an opportunity to reach deeper into our souls and draw out the moxie of our authentic selves. We are stronger than we realize. We have creative, healing, restorative power within us, waiting to be tapped. So how can we keep from singing?

Music Memories

"I think I should have no other mortal wants, if I could always have plenty of music. It seems to infuse strength into my limbs and ideas into my brain. Life seems to go on without effort, when I am filled with music."
— George Eliot

Today as I was singing in church with my dad, I was filled with gratitude for his singing and the joy and love that he continues to express through song. I have many happy music memories from my childhood, like singing funny camp songs that Dad taught us on long road trips, singing mealtime prayers and evening prayers, praise songs and hymns, and lying on the front lawn with my dad at dusk as he sang *Now the Day is Over* under the giant maple trees. Hearing him sing now stirs feelings of security, warmth, and affection within me as I connect to those memories. His voice has always been soothing, comforting, caring, cheerful and uplifting.

As I was growing up, our house was always filled with music. My parents enjoyed Broadway musicals, classical, jazz, big band, gospel and religious music. My dad was a fan of Harry Belafonte, and I have many of his songs memorized. I used to dress up and dance to Herb Alpert and the Tijuana Brass! During the Christmas season we listened to holiday music every day and our home was filled with joy. Each of us kids played at least one musical instrument, and often practiced at the same time! For my sister it was harp and viola, for my brother the trombone, and for me, piano and flute. Quite a cacophony of sounds when we practiced in different rooms simultaneously!

Just as I grew up singing, dancing, and playing instruments, so did my two daughters. Ours was a musical household, and the girls both learned to play guitar and piano. It started at an early age with lullabies, silly songs, Bible songs, and other fun kids' music. As the girls grew, they began to enjoy a wide variety that included rock and roll, soul, jazz, praise songs, and Broadway musicals. Art and I would often cook together on the weekend and put on a concert DVD like U2 or other '80s bands. These are cherished memories for all of us.

Music becomes stored in our cells and our brains in significant ways, stimulating our creativity, emotions, and memories. Today at age 87 my father has lost much of his memory, but he remembers music lyrics like nothing else. He sings every day and blesses everyone in his presence with his joy. I hired a music therapist to work with him once a week, and she has him play a bongo drum, sing old tunes, and talk about the memories they trigger. I think love songs are his favorite, and he speaks often of my mother and the life they shared before she passed away. In addition to his songs, the word he says most frequently is "grateful." Maybe that's why he is still singing.

I know I am grateful for a life filled with music, movement, and happy memories! Music stirs and soothes my soul in every season of my life, connecting me to something larger than myself. It uplifts, inspires, motivates, heals, and energizes me at every level of my being. It connects me to myself, my past, my present, and my hopes and dreams. It can make me laugh, cry, sing, dance, rejoice, and relax. Music is magic to me, and an ongoing source of energy and joy.

Storytelling

"Our uniqueness is what gives us value and meaning. Yet in the telling of stories we also learn what makes us similar, what connects us all, what helps us transcend the isolation that separates us from each other and from ourselves."
— Dean Ornish, M.D.

One of the simple pleasures of summer is getting lost in a good book! We each have a favorite genre for summer reading, whether it's a steamy romance, a suspense thriller, a biography, or something inspirational. For me it can be hard to choose, so I end up starting more than one and going back and forth between them depending on my mood. As a writer, I love to read descriptive novels and nonfiction that inspire and improve my storytelling skills. The best writing is that which draws us in, connects to our emotions, and engages our senses. I think of how I felt when I read *Eat, Pray, Love* by Elizabeth Gilbert. She took me to the vibrant streets and cafes of Italy, an austere monastery in India, and the lush, coastal terrain of Bali. I could almost taste the food, see the sights, and feel the excitement. That is the kind of book I love in summertime – one that takes me to another world!

Have you thought about writing your own stories? As I have said before, you do *not* have to be good at it. Do it to remember and reflect on your life experience. Draw out as much sensory detail as you can – even if this means embellishing it! The story can be *based on* or *inspired by* a real experience. Pick something or someone from your life and just start writing. As author William Kenower says, writing is all about *feeling*, so connect to your senses as you write. For example, instead of writing about the *fact* that it is raining, write about how it *feels* to stand in the rain. Use your imagination to recall the sensory experience of the story you are telling and describe it. Kenower also emphasizes that writing should *feel good*, so relax into it and enjoy the process without expectations. Let it flow from you without concern for grammar, spelling, or sentence structure. Just write. See what comes and where it takes you.

> *"The specific details are what make it universal, what make it sing. Life is made up of these mosaic moments, seemingly meaningless details that tug on your sleeve to get*

your attention." — Anne Lamott, *Almost Everything*

Why is it valuable to write our stories? As we get older, we gain perspective on ourselves and our lives. Writing can increase our self-awareness and understanding. Sharing our stories can help others accept and appreciate their own experiences and realize they are not alone. Looking back on our lives gives us a sense of wonder and gratitude as we reflect on the path we have traveled, the people who have influenced us, and the experiences that have shaped who we are. This process will bring up all kinds of feelings and writing them is therapeutic and enlightening. Remind yourself that we are *all* artists of our own lives, and creative energy is within each of us. Harness this to write your story. Believe in it and allow it to happen through you. No one is going to judge you. Let all that go.

"You will find your confidence and begin to write fearlessly
when you stop caring about what anyone else thinks."
— William Kenower, *Fearless Writing*

I highly recommend these two books for writing tips and inspiration: *The Right to Write* by Julia Cameron, and *Fearless Writing* by William Kenower, as well as anything by Anne Lamott, Sue Monk Kidd, Mary Anne Radmacher, and Elizabeth Gilbert. Those are some of my personal favorites, but there are so many more!

Let this be another way to keep your life fresh and fun. Read, write, relax, reflect, and let your story be told. We all share a universal human experience and telling our stories connects us and reminds us that we are part of something greater than ourselves.

Kitchen Wisdom for Body & Soul

Salsa for the soul is found in the kitchen while making salsa for the body. Preparing food is an activity that centers us and feeds our inner longing to create and connect. Preparing fresh food gives us a connection to the earth, and the beauty, flavor, and nourishment of its fruits. Sharing a meal connects us to others and nourishes the relationships that give our lives meaning, purpose, and joy.

> *"The table is a meeting place, a gathering ground, the source of sustenance and nourishment, festivity, safety, and satisfaction."* — Laurie Colwin

When we prepare food, we are touching the four elements of the universe: earth, water, air and fire.

> *"You mix it with your love and emotions to create magic. Through cooking, you raise your spiritual level and balance yourself in a world that is materialistic."*
> — Laura Esquivel, *Like Water for Chocolate*

I have grown into a deeper appreciation for the art of cooking as I have raised a family, read some enlightening books, learned to practice mindfulness, and continued to quench my curiosity about food, nutrition, and living well. Bringing the fruits of the earth into my kitchen for creative play and nourishment is deeply satisfying and often therapeutic.

ELISA JUAREZ

Author Sarah Ban Breathnach and others have helped me savor life more fully, recognize the sacred in the ordinary, and celebrate simple pleasures.

> *"Do not discount the fire that burns in your soul, the water of your sweat and tears, the earthiness of perseverance, and every breath you take as you struggle to master the art and unravel the mystery of an authentic life."*
> — Sarah Ban Breathnach, *Simple Abundance*

As I pick fresh herbs, chop vegetables, and combine them with olive oil and seasonings in a sauté pan, salad or salsa bowl, my mind and spirit are focused and calm. I am centered in the energy of Love that is the source of all life. The sense of struggle and weariness that the outer world bestows upon me is replaced by a sense of gratitude, delight, and fulfillment. No matter what is happening "out there," I can create a haven of peace and nourishment "in here," my kitchen, my home, and my soul. We still need to eat. Day in and day out, our bodies, minds, and spirits need to be fed. We choose what goes in, and we choose how to prepare it. When we make that task important and sacred, we will give it the time and energy it deserves — and that *we* deserve. The result is a greater sense of well-being, which will spill over into everything we do, every relationship we have, and every aspect of our lives.

When I cook, I am also connected to my mother who taught me how to cook, eat well, and grow a family around the kitchen table. We prepared the meal together, sat down and prayed together, then ate while we talked to each other, sharing our thoughts, ideas, and experiences. It was a time of nourishment and connection, gratitude and satisfaction. I learned much about life as well as food in that creative and sacred space. Those nuggets of wisdom and nutrition laid the foundation for a healthy, happy life.

The Art of Cooking

"The kitchen actually reminds me a lot of the garden. You put your hands to work and tend to it, and when the harvest comes, it gives back to you a hundredfold. There is a reward that come from working with your hands - whether it's in your home, garden, or kitchen. We can choose to view the everyday tasks of life as either chores or gifts. It's powerful how just a slight change in perspective can transform something that you dreaded into something you look forward to. For me, this whole cooking thing has become one of the things I look forward to most and I wouldn't trade my time in the kitchen for anything."
— Joanna Gaines, *Magnolia Table*

Do you realize that you are an artist? I bet you underestimate this truth. As it turns out, we are all artists, artists of the everyday and artists of our own lives. Artists have many different forms of expression: writing, painting, cooking, throwing pots (not cooking pots, haha!), designing, decorating, gardening, and photography, just to name a few! So, think about it, what is your art? What kind of work or craft do you do with your hands and your heart?

You may enjoy multiple forms of art. However, your life is your #1 artform. How do you create, design, and develop your life?

One universal element of our lives is *food*. Cooking is an art, whether you recognize it as that or not. Maybe you believe that in *your* kitchen it is anything *but* art, but let's take a look at that. In *Simple Abundance*, Sarah Ban Breathnach says a paring knife can be as creative as a paintbrush!

> *"Whenever I don't know what to do — whether it's writing or living — I seek discoveries in the kitchen, such as trying to recreate a great dish I enjoyed somewhere else."*
> — Sarah Ban Breathnach, *Simple Abundance*

Can you relate? Do you see cooking as work or fun? Mundane or creative? It's up to you, really. When I designed my blog, *Spoonful of Salsa*, I chose to incorporate food through recipes and nutrition nuggets. Food is central and fundamental — not only to survive but to thrive and to live well. Food brings people together; it feeds not only our bodies but our souls. It is through cooking that I have learned to discover the sacred and beautiful in the ordinary.

My appreciation for the art of cooking has increased through reading, trying new recipes, and occasionally watching cooking shows. The more I learn, the more fun and interesting cooking and eating become! The joy of preparing food starts with mindfulness . . . being present, paying attention, and enjoying the colors, textures, flavors, and aromas of the ingredients. As you learn to be present and grateful in the process, you will discover the art of cooking. You will connect with the artist within and new ideas will begin to flow.

You've heard the phrase, "It's all in the sauce!" My husband and I are saucy. Yep, we love sauces. It is true that a flavorful sauce can take a dish from good to magnificent! I encourage you to try a new sauce this week and see how it transforms your meal. Most sauces are simple to make and yet easy to forget. If cooking is not your forte, start with sauce. Learn to make a few simple and delicious sauces and see how your meal is elevated! It may inspire you to take another step, to try something else new.

Summer is a wonderful time to find new, simple recipes using garden fresh ingredients. Find your inner artist and satisfy your hunger for creativity and fulfillment. Visit my blog: www.spoonfulofsalsa.com and perhaps find a new cookbook that inspires you, as well. Whatever you do, keep it fresh and fun and *live well!*

Salads & Sauces

Summer is halfway through; are you wilting? Here in Texas we are having triple digit heat every day this week and next, so we are definitely wilting, as are my poor plants on the balcony. I keep telling myself, "This, too, shall pass!" Each season peaks and passes. We can be assured of that. In the meantime, what can we do to enjoy it and reap the fruits of this season, literally and figuratively?

Fresh fruits and veggies are one of the best features of summertime, so I hope you are taking advantage of this bounty! Fresh, in season produce is not expensive, and can be easily found and enjoyed. It may be too hot to do much cooking, but there are so many simple and nutritious ways to create good meals! Think outside the box of what you always buy, eat, and prepare, and try something new each week.

Salads are one of the most creative concoctions you can make in the kitchen, next to soups. You can put all kinds of greens, veggies, nuts, and berries into a salad! They say we should "eat the rainbow," means to get a variety of colors in every meal. Salads are a great way to do this! You can even "hide" some things in there that your family members don't really like by chopping them really small! I do this with a variety of greens so that the salad isn't just plain romaine lettuce. Be creative and add as many superfoods to your salads as you can!

Sauces are a simple, delicious addition to... everything! But since we're talking about fresh veggies, this is another way to "dress up" your veggies and make them even more yummy. Naturally, you want to be careful what you put into your sauces, choosing only the healthy oils (olive, avocado, walnut, organic butter, and expeller pressed oils), fresh herbs (whenever possible), sea salt, etc. Sauces and salad dressings are simple to make and much healthier than buying them packaged or bottled. I'm including a few recipes for you to play with and make your own! Keep things fresh and fun, be curious and open minded, and squeeze the juices out of summertime so it can be a season of refreshment!

The Sacred Art of Play

*"Forget not that the earth delights to feel your bare feet,
and the wind longs to play with your hair."*
— Kahlil Gibran

Do you play more in the summer than other times of the year? Why or why not? When we were children, summertime meant a vacation from school and a break from routine. It was the season to relax and play! I'm sure you can remember that sense of freedom and fun. What were some of your favorite activities? For me it was swimming! We had a large city park with a pool just a few blocks away, and we swam regularly. As I grew, I moved from the wading pool to the big pool, from the shallow end to the deep end, and finally to the diving boards! I went from taking swim lessons to becoming a lifeguard and *teaching* swim lessons!

Think about how you played as you grew into a teen and then young adult. Was play a regular part of your life? Some forms of play we outgrow, while others continue into adulthood. If you married and had children, you were drawn back into childhood play, wonder, creativity, and delight. I enjoyed watching Disney movies, making puzzles, playing games, and swinging with my daughters. I still do, and they're grown!

Unfortunately, we may forget how to play as we get older. Our society tells us to work the days away to get ahead or just to keep up and make ends meet. We may tell ourselves that play is a waste of time, or play is for children, or play is a luxury we cannot afford.

> *"Play is learning how to wait, how to applaud someone else's success, how to let others go first. It's reciprocity and laughter. It's very simple and it brings us deeply into the Now, and, just for a while, maybe for the rest of the day, you don't have to judge yourself or kill anyone."*
> — Anne Lamott, *Almost Everything*

What have you told yourself about play? Perhaps you play well, and if so, I commend you. My dad is a great example of someone who has never forgotten how to play. He worked hard as we were growing up, but he also played with us. As a grandpa, he enjoyed taking the

211

kids to the playground and pushing them on the swings and the merry-go-round. At the age of 86, he slid down the bannister into the lobby of his retirement home, did a forward roll, and stood up proudly, receiving applause and laughter. That just encouraged him! The next time he pulled that trick, he fell and broke a bone in his foot. It was a tough lesson, but it didn't dampen his youthful spirit.

> *"Play, if it is anything, is a sensual fiesta. It means being*
> *alive in this world—to exude playfulness squarely in the*
> *sights, sounds, smells, and tastes of this day."*
> – Mary Anne Radmacher, *Lean Forward into Your Life*

It's about savoring simple pleasures, being present, laughing easily, and letting go. Radmacher acknowledges that we may need to retrain our eyes or our minds to appreciate the simple things, awaken to them, and be open, available, and curious.

I believe play is a sacred necessity for our souls and our authentic selves. The spirit within us is ageless, as I see in my now almost 90 year old dad. Many people are numb to that part of themselves, but we can awaken it and engage it through love, laughter, and play. Just be willing to quiet the negative voice in your head and let go of your resistance.

> *"Delight in your friends. Practice the art of doing nothing.*
> *Embrace moments of grace. Give the child in you a wide*
> *sky. Understand that laughter is prayer."*
> – Mary Anne Radmacher, *Lean Forward into Your Life*

Life is good, and it is meant to be shared and savored. Now go out and have some fun! It's summertime!

String of Pearls

"Expect your every need to be met, expect the answer to every problem, expect abundance on every level, expect to grow spiritually." — Eileen Caddy

Have you ever had a day that started as an uphill climb and ended as a refreshing oasis? Precious moments, sweet surprises, and little boosts throughout the day are evidence of grace. I call this being supported by the Universe, or God. Whatever you call it, it is the all-encompassing presence of Divine Love. It just *is*. It doesn't matter what name you give to it, only that you recognize, honor, and appreciate it. The more you do, the more you will see and experience grace, goodness, and gratitude. I continue to learn that it is all about presence: being present, really noticing the little things and savoring them.

I had one of those days last week after a restless night. The lack of sleep made me even more vulnerable; I felt the tears in my head and heart. I felt them in my stomach and throat, as well. They are so close these days, just below the surface, ready to leak out at any moment. I moved through it slowly and gently, feeling tired and fragile. My eyes and my heart were open, and the road rose to meet me at every step.

I got a coffee and a blueberry scone at Starbucks and found a shaded park bench, where I sat to savor it all. The scone boasted fresh, plump blueberries that seemed larger than usual. Yum! I drank in the

ELISA JUAREZ

beauty of nature all around me which soothed my soul. I rested in the moment.

From there, I went for my annual Well Woman exam and opened up to my doctor about Kim's cancer. More tears. She put her arms around me with empathy and compassion. She recommended a few books for my Kim and for me. I felt supported.

Later that afternoon I got a call from one of my besties, asking if I'd like to meet her at the neighborhood wine bar for a glass of wine. *Yes!* The day turned out to be like a string of pearls, one glimmering gem after another on the frayed strand of my being.

Life is like this if we are open and receptive to its gifts. I read in my morning devotional, *Jesus Calling*, today that people "crawl through their lives cursing the darkness, but all the while I am shining brightly." It's easy to see and feel the pain and suffering in our world. Empathy and compassion connect us to humanity and to the Divine Love that created us all. The fact is life is hard. It carves a deep well within us, increasing our capacity and our courage.

> "Move out or grow in any dimension and pain as well as
> joy will be your reward. A full life will be full of pain. But
> the only alternative is not to live fully or not to live at all."
> — M. Scott Peck, *The Road Less Traveled*

The older we get, the more we learn to accept life as it is. I guess this is some of the wisdom that comes with age. We also discover the "pearls" of beauty, grace, wisdom, wonder, and delight, and value them more than diamonds. When the strand of our being feels frayed and fragile, we can strengthen it by connecting to our friends, family, and faith. We can choose to believe that the Universe is supporting us, and evidence will show up at every turn. So, embrace your life and move through it openly. When tears of joy or sadness fill your throat and your eyes, let them come.

> *"Tears will bathe, baptize, and hydrate you, and the seeds*
> *beneath the surface of the ground on which you walk."*
> — Anne Lamott, *Almost Everything*

They will cleanse your soul and water that which is dry. They will make your pearls shimmer in the light.

Attention

Attention is a high commodity these days, and it seems that everyone is clamoring for it! We get bombarded with attention grabbing ads in the media, and nearly everywhere we go our attention gets pulled in many directions! Our cell phones captivate a great deal of our attention and keep us from focusing for long on anything else! We are easily distracted, and our attention is fragmented. I think we now have more adults with Attention Deficit Disorder than ever before! I struggle with this myself, so I'm speaking from experience!

Mindfulness is a worthwhile practice that helps us focus our attention on what we are doing and where we are. Here's an example that I bet you can relate to: You're talking on your cell phone in the car (hopefully hands free) while pulling into a store parking lot. You get out of the car, lock it, and walk into the store, still on the phone. When you come out of the store, you can't remember where you parked. Well, of course you can't! You weren't paying *attention* to where you parked! That can happen even if we are not on the phone; we are so often distracted that we miss important cues and connections around us. And yes, this has happened to me. But only once! After that, I made sure not to do it again.

Mindfulness is really as simple as it sounds, but not easy. It's all about attention. Pay attention and be fully present with what you are doing in every moment. Pay attention to the people around you. Keep your mind fully present, not scattered! When you are tempted to divert your attention to your cell phone or something else grabbing for your attention when you are in the middle of a task or a conversation, consciously choose to ignore it for the moment. Trust that it can wait a few minutes at least while you finish what you are doing. When you are driving, *please* practice this! Keep your eyes on the road and your mind on your driving! Practice. Practice. Practice. That's what it takes. Practice and discipline. Focus. This practice will result in greater peace of mind, productivity, focus, and awareness. You will be safer and saner because you are not distracted!

This week notice how your attention hops around. Notice what grabs it and how it affects you. Notice what you do to get others' attention, and how it feels when someone you're talking to is not giving you their full attention. Practice giving your full attention to the people in your life, and to anyone who is talking to you. Make eye contact and give attention to people when you are out and about; show kindness and caring. Attention is a gift when it is used wisely and given to the present moment. It also opens our eyes and ears to receive the beauty and abundance that is all around us, thereby increasing our awareness and gratitude.

Back-to-School Shopping

August is "Back to School" shopping time as teachers are get ready to return to work and the end of summer is in sight! If you're like me, you hit those school supply sales even though you no longer have kids in school! I like to take advantage of the great deals on supplies I use year round, and also buy supplies for the kids who can't afford them. You may do this as well; there are many organizations and retailers that assist in providing school supplies to under privileged children. This is one of the simplest ways to make a difference since school supplies are inexpensive right now and the need is significant!

Our church has adopted a local elementary school that has a high population of children living in poverty. One of our members is a teacher there, so we have a connection. I bet you know a teacher somewhere, too! Teachers are angels, often going above and beyond to support and assist their students. If you don't already have a way to give supplies to a local school, then find a teacher you know and ask. This is a good time to consider ways in which you can support a teacher, school, or family this school year with simple donations and acts of kindness. Invite some friends, a social group you belong to, or your church (if they don't already do this) and find a way to give.

I am quite sure that every teacher and student in America is carrying some level of anxiety about returning to school, considering the increase in school shootings these past few years. If you are a parent whose children are still in school then you, too, are affected. There are many complicated factors that contribute to this frightening epidemic, and the solutions are equally complex. However, I do know that we can all show love, support, and appreciation to teachers, students, and school staff. Together we can build stronger communities and safer schools. Consider what you have to give and who you know that would join you. Good thoughts, prayers and actions have a ripple effect! Enjoy the rest of your summer and go school supply shopping!

Porch Time

"Time can be slowed if you live deliberately. If you stop and watch sunsets. If you spend time sitting on porches listening to the woods. If you give in to the reality of the seasons." — Thomas Christopher Greene

My childhood home in South Dakota had a screened porch in the back where we spent many happy hours and enjoyed summer meals on the wooden drop leaf table. There was a pass thru window from the kitchen which made mealtime a breeze — literally! The porch was a comfortable spot to read, play games, visit, and listen to the evening song of crickets and cicadas. My mom planted morning glories in the garden alongside the porch, attaching strings from stakes in the ground to the gutter along the porch roof. The plants climbed up along the strings, creating a curtain of bright blue flowers that bloomed each morning and closed in the evening.

There is something so special about porches and the time we spend there, I've come to believe our souls need them. We just returned from a wonderful weekend with friends in the Texas Hill

Country, and they have a large porch with a panoramic view of the hills and trees. Although the days were around 100 degrees, there was a refreshing breeze on that back porch that made it comfortable to sit out there for hours. We started and ended each day on the porch, allowing nature and friendship to nurture and inspire us.

Porches are designed for sitting, rocking, relaxing, visiting, dreaming, and sipping. Since they are outside, they remove us from inside distractions, like television and housework. They help us connect to nature and each other, to be more fully present and alive. We hear the earth's music, feel the breeze, and watch the birds and wildlife. Porches give us a different perspective. They give us pause. In our last house, I loved sitting out on the back porch at night listening to the symphony of crickets, cicadas, and tree frogs. It started out low and increased in volume as the darkness set in. It filled me with awe and soothed my soul at the end of day.

If you don't have a porch where you live, find one in your community. We have a local coffee and sandwich shop that took up residence in a large, old house with a wraparound porch. It is an ideal space for visiting, reading, or writing! Wicker furniture and bistro tables give people seating options, and it is a popular neighborhood lunch spot. Many restaurants and coffee shops have patios which are the next best thing to a porch. Seek and ye shall find! Your mind, body, and soul need some porch time.

Life can take the wind out of us. It can spin us around and make us dizzy and anxious. Porches call to us, inviting us to come and rest awhile, rock and reflect, pause for perspective, and unplug from the world. We need this to keep from going numb. All our senses get overstimulated in a world that is always on, and porch time gives us space to breathe, unwind, wiggle our toes, tune into nature, and calm down. Carve out some porch time at least once a week as a necessity for your well-being. Stay awhile. Savor the simplicity of just *being* there and let it fill you with peace, gratitude, and joy.

Listen Well to Live Well

> "Listening is a gift of spiritual significance that you can learn to give to others. When you listen, you give one a sense of importance, hope and love that he or she may not receive any other way. Through listening, we nurture and validate the feelings one has, especially when he or she experiences difficulties in life." — H. Norman Wright

Anyone who knows me knows that I love to talk. The "gift of gab" came with me into the world, and over the years I've learned that it is not always a gift. That was pointed out to me by some of my schoolteachers as well as my parents. On my path of higher education in psychology and social work, I learned how to ask questions and listen with focused attention. As a counselor, this is extremely important, and my time in that role gave me plenty of practice. In my personal relationships, I have found that listening intently without judgment creates an opening for deeper trust, understanding, and acceptance. Although my girlfriends and I can talk for hours, I have made it my intention to listen *more* and listen *well*. When I do, I learn more and develop rich, supportive relationships.

> "Listening is much more than allowing another to talk while waiting for a chance to respond. Listening is paying

full attention to others and welcoming them into our very beings. The beauty of listening is that those who are listened to start feeling accepted, start taking their words more seriously and discovering their own true selves. Listening is a form of spiritual hospitality by which you invite strangers to become friends, to get to know their inner selves more fully, and even to dare to be silent with you." — Henri J.M. Nouwen

So often we listen with our minds going in other directions or planning what we're going to say next. We are a distracted society with rampant attention deficit disorder. Learning to be still and listen is a discipline that goes against the tide, but the benefits are significant. For me, it has helped to start with my inner space and learn to quiet my busy brain. The practice of getting still, meditating, and connecting to my inner wisdom prepares me to be a better listener with others. In fact, I believe it is a necessary first step in creating the space for listening and receiving. It also puts us in tune with our own bodies and souls which will tell us what they need. As long as our minds are cluttered and noisy, we cannot listen fully to others *or* to our authentic selves.

Listening is a form of love and respect that we give to ourselves and others. It takes intention, practice, and discipline to stay focused and resist the temptation to interrupt, but the rewards are priceless.

"Listen with curiosity. Speak with honesty. Act with integrity. The greatest problem with communication is we don't listen to understand. We listen to reply. When we listen with curiosity, we don't listen with the intent to

reply. We listen for what's behind the words."
— Roy T. Bennett, *The Light in the Heart*

The more we listen to our authentic selves with an open heart, the greater will be our awareness of how we listen to others. It starts there.

"Always listen to your soul and feel the purity of that moment, no matter how sad or joyful, because it will speak to you further... a healing, an understanding, a perspective or more will come out of it. Only because you listened."
— Angie Karan

Opening to Happiness

"That we are designed for joy is exhilarating, within reach, now or perhaps later today, after a nap, as long as we do not mistake excitement for joy. Joy is good cheer. My partner says joy and curiosity are the same thing. Joy is always a surprise and often a decision. Joy is portable. Joy is a habit, and these days, it can be a radical act... so for now let's define joy as a slightly giddy appreciation, an inquisitive stirring, as when you see the first crocuses, the earliest struggling, stunted emergence of color in late winter, cream or gold against the tans and browns."
— Anne Lamott, *Almost Everything*

It's Labor Day weekend, the threshold to a new season, and I'm ready! As you enjoy the last weekend of summer, savor your favorite seasonal pleasures, and the memories you made over the past few months. Celebrate the gifts of simple abundance in nature, friendship, family, and food. We are truly surrounded by seasonal bounty, a smorgasbord of good things, so relax, rejoice, and give thanks!

To notice and enjoy this bounty, we need to open our senses as well as our hearts and minds. You've heard that happiness is a choice; well, to really be happy, you need to be open. Sometimes we're not aware of how and where we are closed because it has become so normal and natural to us. Here are a few questions to ask yourself that will help you to determine if your inner "doors" are open or closed: Are you willing to try new things (foods, experiences, places), meet new people, and listen to views that are different from your own? Are you curious about life and people? Are you a lifelong learner? Take a look at yourself and your life and answer these honestly.

Here is what I've noticed about being open. Openness attracts beauty, wonder, and joy — no matter what my circumstances may be. Some of the most difficult times in my life have carved a deep well within me that holds more love than I ever imagined. Living with openness brings a lightness of being, energy, vitality, curiosity, and continual discovery. Openness helps us notice and accept our feelings and failures with a little less judgment. Judgment is our critical voice which tags along in our shadow like a grumpy uncle who won't be quiet or go away. I've noticed that as I learn to stop judging myself, I judge others less, as well. The uncle's voice fades when I stop listening to it.

Choosing happiness involves letting go of judgment. The two are not compatible, and I'd rather have the companionship of happiness.

Gratitude gives oxygen to happiness, and happiness naturally reciprocates by creating more to be thankful for. And so it goes and grows. How good we feel has a direct impact on — well, everything! Our attitude, our work, and our relationships. By choosing happiness we are choosing to feel good and serve humanity. The choice has a ripple effect and multiplies as it spreads. Haven't you noticed how well your day goes when you feel good? You have energy, you smile more, you open doors for people, say thank you more easily, and give a helping hand or cheerful greeting wherever you go! It's magical. By choosing happiness and openness, we attract abundance and become a force for good in the world.

This doesn't mean that you always *feel* happy, but when you are *open,* you can stay connected to the presence and power of Love. The deeper and stronger your awareness of Love, the closer you will always be to joy and peace. They abide in your deep inner sanctuary and rise to meet you wherever you are. This is the key to the "good life," to living well.

So, as you say farewell to summer, take a look at what else you can bid farewell to and experience more happiness, energy, and abundance. Imagine packing a suitcase with all your negative thoughts, resentment, judgment, and hurt, and sending it out the door with that grumpy uncle! The "good life" is within reach as soon as your hands and heart are open and ready.

Dig the Detours!

"Life is either a daring adventure or nothing. To keep our faces toward change and behave like free spirits in the presence of fate is strength undefeatable." — Helen Keller

Back in the '60s and '70s there was a hip expression, "Dig it!" To "dig" something meant to like it or think it was cool. I don't hear that anymore, but it came to me today as I was thinking about this message.

We've all heard the phrase, "Life is what happens while we're making other plans!" The longer we live the more we experience this truth! We set out with our own plans and intentions, which is fine and dandy, but often get redirected by an unexpected event, circumstance, or communication. It feels like a detour, and it's usually uncomfortable and unsettling. Sometimes it is significant, painful, or even tragic. Other times it is a bump in the road, a swerve in a different direction — a detour, nonetheless, but, *not* the end of the road. It may *feel* like the end of the world, and sometimes our world does get turned upside down! Life isn't a straight and smooth road; it is a steep, winding, rocky path that stretches us, turns us around, and cracks us wide open. However, detours are a part of life, so we might as well stop resisting and reacting. I believe we can even learn to "dig" detours! Start by changing your belief that detours shouldn't happen, that they are somehow "bad" or "wrong." Accept that they are part of life.

225

ELISA JUAREZ

I learned this simple but profound lesson from a wise professor on a college study program overseas. Every day he would tell the group, "Expect the unexpected!" It was his motto. His many years of travel experience had taught him to be adaptable, to go with the flow. Detours are "the unexpected," right? So what if we learn to *expect* that life will take us on a grand adventure that we cannot plan, control, or foresee, and to *trust* that, all the while, the Universe has our back? Can you dig *that*?

This adventure will open our eyes and our hearts to something we haven't seen or experienced before. It will increase our capacity, our wisdom, and our strength. Detours can take us away from something that might harm us or distract us from our purpose. They can take us toward a new discovery or opportunity. They can lead us to our authentic selves. Therefore, even without knowing why or how, we can give thanks and trust that we are headed toward our highest good. Perspective and attitude are everything. They are always in our control and will determine how we navigate the detours. When we face life as a daring adventure and expect the unexpected, we will find that the flow of life and love carries us, guides us, and blesses us abundantly!

Start by accepting the little interruptions in your day with flexibility and gratitude. Be open and receptive to unexpected surprises. Notice what you tell yourself when things don't work out as you had hoped or planned. Be willing to let go and let God. This adventure is full of twists, turns, detours, and discoveries. Stay curious and alert so you don't miss the road signs that are there to guide you. And all along the way, love, laugh, and expect great things! The journey is not meant to harm you, but to bring you to your highest good. Dig it!

Some Days

There are days when life shifts our vehicle into neutral — or even reverse — and all our best laid plans get put on hold. All our conditioning will kick up the dust of resistance, but to no avail.

This, too, is opportunity. It is life teaching us to let go and accept ourselves right *where* we are, *as* we are. Some days are for *being*, not *doing*, and our value remains the same. Some lessons are best learned when we stop long enough to rest, listen, observe, and surrender. If we pay attention to the small detours and rest stops of our lives, we may avert a crushing blow — or even a complete breakdown. Learning to bend can keep us from breaking when storms come.

Wherever you are, keep your heart open. Divine Love is ever present. It abides, guides, and protects you. Some days are about learning to trust that and lean into it. There is no judgment, only the opportunity to listen, learn, and love a little more.

Life Lessons from "Yoga with Adriene"

The practice of yoga is a physical and mental discipline with a spiritual foundation. It aims to bring mind, body and spirit into balance and alignment. I have been doing yoga for most of my adult life and find that it reduces stress, increases flexibility, improves balance, and builds strength.

Several years ago, Taylor introduced me to *Yoga with Adriene* on YouTube, and I began to follow and participate in her programs. Incidentally, Adriene graduated from the theatre program at St. Edward's University in Austin, TX, as did Taylor. Adriene brings the Austin vibe (and occasional theatrics) to her routines, which makes her program authentic, creative, and fun. She meets you where you are and welcomes you to the mat, sharing her thoughts and ideas for a healthy, happy life, along with the movements and postures. I have embraced her philosophy in my daily life, and well beyond the yoga mat. Here are some examples:

1. Show up for yourself on the mat. Take time for yourself. Sometimes that is the hardest part.
2. Find what feels good. Listen to your body; don't push or force it.
3. Make it your own. Find something new each time.
4. If you fall, no worries.
5. Breathe, and move with the breath. Inhale, lots of love in; exhale, lots of love out.
6. Remember that you're not in this alone. There is a community of people doing this with you, all over the world.

Every one of these yoga guidelines can be applied to other areas of my life. They can help reduce stress, increase flexibility, improve balance, and build strength. It truly is a holistic practice that brings us into higher awareness and acceptance of our own mind and body. Adriene continually reminds me that:

1. By showing up on the mat, I have accomplished the biggest step.

2. Each person is unique, and I can trust and honor my body by paying attention to what it's telling me. It's okay to do what feels good; I don't have to experience pain in order to gain. There are always *options*, and I should choose the ones that work best for *me*.

3. It helps to have examples and guidelines, but ultimately this is my program, my body, and my life. To honor my authentic self, I need to learn to trust it and make my life my own!

4. Don't be afraid of falling or failing; it's all part of the process. Be willing to try new things, stretch yourself, and stumble along the way. If I keep showing up and doing the work, I will wake up one day and see how far I've come. I will discover that I am stronger and more flexible than when I started.

5. Breathing consciously keeps me aware and relaxed. It helps me focus and move more easily.

6. I am part of a wider global community of people who are living, moving, and breathing with awareness and intention. My efforts add energy to the movement for health and happiness for all humanity.

Those are some simple yet powerful lessons for living fully and freely, for finding balance and wholeness. Yoga takes discipline, practice, patience, and trust, just like everything else in life. As I learn to accept myself where I am, as I am, and make this path my own, I experience a sense of freedom and flexibility. I become more open to new steps and stretches. I increase my compassion for myself and others. I allow more love in, and more love out. Thank you, Adriene,

ELISA JUAREZ

for showing up on the mat and in our world at this turbulent time on our planet. Thank you for helping us to breathe, relax, trust, focus, and find balance. Thank you for helping us to live with greater awareness, flexibility, and silliness. You are helping to heal the world.

A Spoonful of Solitude

"When we consecrate a time to listen to the still, small voices, we remember the root of inner wisdom that makes work fruitful. We remember from where we are most deeply nourished and see more clearly the shape and texture of the people and things before us." — Wayne Muller, *Sabbath*

It's not always easy to hit the pause button in our busy lives, go into our room and close the door. We may *want* to do it throughout the day, but it's easier said than done! When I was a child, my mother made this a daily practice for herself and each of us. If my siblings and I were playing outside with the neighbor kids, she would call us in. *Ugh*. No one else had to go in for quiet time; why did we? It was kind of embarrassing. Just for 30 minutes, but still! Yes, *still*. We each had to go into our own rooms and spend half an hour by ourselves, quiet. When I became a young adult, my mom explained that she did that so we would learn to value time alone (and so she could rest). *Brilliant.* It worked! Each of us grew into adults who carve out time alone to read, write, and reflect on a regular basis.

This becomes a significant challenge when we are immersed in a career and/or raising a family. The demands upon us increase, and just going to the bathroom without interruptions is a small miracle!

230

Having a regular practice of solitude develops and strengthens us from the inside out, thereby transforming our lives at every level. Day by day we step into the unknown and into a crazy, volatile world. This can cause us much anxiety. It takes immense trust to keep our spirits strong and steady.

For me, time alone to read, write, pray, meditate, and observe nature is essential to my well-being. It grounds me and helps me keep things in perspective. It calms my soul.

> *"Deliberately seeking solitude–quality time spent away*
> *from family and friends–may seem selfish. It is not.*
> *Solitude is as necessary for our creative spirits to develop*
> *and flourish as are sleep and food for our bodies to*
> *survive."* — Sarah Ban Breathnach, *Simple Abundance*

Sarah says that solitude *"cracks open the door that separates two worlds: the life we lead today, and the life we yearn for so deeply."* To discover and inspire our authentic selves, we must carve out time to be alone without interruptions or distractions, including our electronic devices. As our connection to our true self deepens, "the life we yearn for" will unfold through us. Our relationships and work will take on a richer quality, a vibrancy that can only come from within. Also, the stronger our inner core, the steadier and secure we will feel in the world.

> *"...the bigger, more real, and friendlier the world inside me*
> *becomes, the safer I feel in the outside world. As above, so*
> *below; as inside, so before us."*
> — Anne Lamott, *Almost Everything*

I've noticed that people who nurture an inner life tend to have creative and fulfilling outer lives, as well. They tend to be happier, more relaxed, secure, and peaceful than those who focus primarily on the outer physical world. They also live from a sense of purpose, which gives their lives meaning and value.

As we age, our mind and body may weaken and break, but our spirit is ageless. We all know elderly people with a vibrant spirit that shines through their physical body. I have seen this in my dad whose youthful optimism and loving demeanor have persisted, even as his memory crumbles. On the other hand, my mother-in-law has never nurtured an inner life, and her outer life lacks joy, energy, and purpose. She tends to feel insecure, lonely, bored, anxious, and unhappy. The difference is remarkable.

Our souls are the eternal part of us, the *real* us, which is one with the divine. Solitude and silence open us to a wider and deeper inner reality that awakens and transforms us. It is not just about being alone; it is about making conscious contact with your higher self and turning your attention inward for a time. Even Jesus referred to this when speaking to his disciples.

> *"When you pray, go into your room and shut the door..."*
> — Matthew 6:6

To discover the divine within you, pause your busy life, turn off your cell phone, and turn your face inward. Be still and listen to the inner voice of wisdom.

> *"There are voices which we hear in solitude, but they grow*
> *faint and inaudible as we enter the world."*
> — Ralph Waldo Emerson

The investment you make in your inner life will not only impact your life and relationships *now*; it will develop a beautiful spirit within you that will carry you through anything life brings.

The Power of Plants

My daughter, Lauren, is a pescatarian, meaning that she does not eat meat, other than occasionally seafood. She chose this in response to what she learned in some of her college classes about the negative social and environmental impact of the meat industry.

In our family we have always enjoyed a wide variety of foods, and Art has made it very clear that he will never give up eating meat. Well, no one asked him to give up meat, but I am all about eating less meat and more plant based foods. When Lauren is home, I get creative with meal planning! Thankfully Art is not a picky eater and doesn't need or want meat every night. As we see many people in our age bracket battling chronic and serious health issues, I continue to be committed to eating and living consciously.

I recently read an article from *Consumer Reports* about the benefits of eating a plant based diet. They used the term "flexitarian" to

ELISA JUAREZ

describe people "who make plant foods the star of their diet, with meat, fish, dairy, and eggs playing a supporting role." That's me! Wherever you are on the continuum, consider how you can increase your plant based foods and decrease your meat intake. The article gives some valuable information and ideas. For my blog, *Spoonful of Salsa,* I have written many Nutrition Nuggets about vegetables, fruits, and herbs, and delicious recipes featuring plant based foods. The people I know who are eating plant based foods exclusively or primarily are seeing significant health benefits. Nutrition experts have long said that we should "eat the rainbow" by making 75% of our diet whole grains, fruits and vegetables, and only 25% meat and dairy. We can all make changes, little by little, toward healthier eating, and thereby increase our energy, vitality, mental sharpness, and overall well-being. It's hard to imagine any food that is worth more than that!

SUMMER RECIPES

Favorite Potato Salad

This is my Grammie Rand's recipe and has always been one of my favorites! I especially like using Yukon Gold potatoes which have a wonderful buttery flavor, or red skinned potatoes. I leave a little skin on the potatoes, but that's up to you!

- 6 medium potatoes, cooked and cubed
- ½ small onion, diced
- 4 - 5 sprigs parsley, chopped
- ¼ cup vinegar
- ¼ cup salad oil
- 1 teaspoon salt
- 1 teaspoon pepper
- ½ cup mayonnaise
- 1 cup celery, diced
- 4 hard cooked eggs, chopped
- 2 large dill pickles, minced

INSTRUCTIONS:

1. Combine warm potatoes with onion and parsley.
2. Combine vinegar, oil, salt, and pepper. Pour over potatoes.
3. Toss lightly with a fork. Chill for 2 hours or longer.

4. Add remaining ingredients. Mix gently.

5. Add ¾ teaspoon mustard to mayonnaise for tangy flavor.

Makes 12 servings.

Fresh Garden Salsa

- ¼ small to medium red onion
- 2 medium tomatoes
- 1½ serrano peppers
- 1/3 cup cilantro
- Juice of 1 lime
- 5 yellow cocktail tomatoes
- 1 garlic clove
- Sea salt
- ¼ vine ripened tomato
- 4 colorful cocktail tomatoes, quartered

INSTRUCTIONS

1. Combine red onion, 2 medium tomatoes, 1½ serrano peppers (remove seeds for milder version), cilantro, juice of 1 lime, 5 yellow cocktail tomatoes, and 1 garlic clove in food processor.
2. Chop well.
3. Pour into bowl.
4. Add sea salt, coarsely chopped tomatoes, ¼ vine ripened tomato, and 4 cocktail tomatoes, quartered.

Southwest Grain Medley

This recipe came from my Aunt Laurel who made it one summer when we were visiting her in Maine.

- 1 cup sweet corn (fresh or frozen)
- 2 cups cooked quinoa
- 1 cup cooked brown rice
- 1 can black beans
- 1-2 cups chopped bell peppers or celery
- 1 cup chopped cucumber
- 4 tablespoons sliced green onions
- 4 tablespoons lime juice
- Fresh cilantro
- Salt and pepper
- Olive or avocado oil

INSTRUCTIONS

1. Roast corn in olive oil in skillet over medium heat. Stir until browned; put in bowl.
2. Add black beans, quinoa, rice, peppers/celery, cucumbers, green onions, lime juice, 2 tablespoons oil, cilantro, salt, and pepper. Mix together.

Blueberry Muffins

This recipe was adapted from the *Fanny Farmer Cookbook* which my mother used throughout my childhood, and I have been using all my adult life!

- 2 cups flour (reserve ¼ cup, sprinkle over blueberries)
- 3 teaspoons baking powder
- ½ teaspoon salt
- ¼ cup sugar
- 1 egg, slightly beaten
- 1 cup milk
- ¼ cup melted butter
- 1 cup blueberries

INSTRUCTIONS

1. Preheat oven to 375 degrees.
2. Butter muffin pans.
3. Mix 1 ¾ cups flour, baking powder, salt, and sugar in a large bowl.
4. Add the egg, milk, and butter, stirring only enough to dampen the flour. The batter should *not* be smooth.
5. Sprinkle blueberries with remaining ¼ cup of flour.
6. Stir blueberries into batter.
7. Spoon batter into muffin pans, filling each cup 2/3 full.
8. Bake for 20-25 minutes.

ELISA JUAREZ

Blueberry Buckle

Adapted from the *Betty Crocker Cookbook*, which my mother used faithfully throughout my childhood and beyond!

- ¾ cup sugar
- ¼ cup soft butter
- 1 egg
- ½ cup milk
- 2 cups unbleached flour
- 2 teaspoons baking powder
- ½ teaspoon salt
- 2 cups well drained blueberries
- ½ teaspoon cinnamon

CRUMB MIXTURE:

- ½ cup sugar
- 1/3 cup sifted flour
- ½ teaspoon cinnamon
- ¼ cup soft butter

INSTRUCTIONS

1. Mix crumb topping and sprinkle over batter.
2. Bake 45 – 50 minutes.
3. Serve warm, fresh from the oven.

Creamy Italian Dressing

- 1 cup mayonnaise
- ½ small onion or 1 shallot
- 2 tablespoons red wine vinegar
- 1 tablespoon sugar
- ¾ teaspoon Italian seasoning (or a few springs fresh Italian herbs such as basil and oregano)
- ¼ teaspoon salt
- ¼ teaspoon garlic salt or powder
- 1/8 teaspoon fresh ground pepper

INSTRUCTIONS:

1. Place all ingredients in blender; cover and blend on medium speed 15 seconds or until smooth.
2. Cover and chill.

Makes 1¼ cup.

Garden Pasta Salad

Pasta salad is like a work of art and color! Have fun with it, change it up, add whatever you like! Here is one of my versions.

- 16 oz package uncooked tricolor pasta
- 2 stalks celery, chopped
- 1 cup chopped sweet bell peppers (red, orange, yellow)
- 1 pint grape tomatoes, halved
- 1 zucchini, chopped or thin sliced and cut into half moons
- ½ cup chopped green onion
- Two 15 oz cans cannellini beans
- 4 Mozzarella cheese sticks, cut into ½" pieces (or cut ½" cubes from a block of cheese, approximately ¾ cup)
- ¼ cup Mezzetta mild pepper rings
- 16 oz bottle Italian dressing

INSTRUCTIONS

1. Cook pasta according to package directions until al dente.
2. Rinse under cold water and drain.
3. Mix celery, bell peppers, tomatoes, zucchini, and green onion together in large bowl.
4. Add beans, mozzarella, pepper rings, and cooled pasta.
5. Pour dressing over the mixture and mix well.
6. Chill before serving.

Makes 8-10 servings.

Sauce Recipes

From *The Joy of Cooking*, by Irma S. Rombauer and Marion Rombauer Becker

White Sauce or Bechamel

- 2 tablespoons butter
- ½ to 2 tablespoons flour
- 1 cup milk
- 1 small onion studded with 2 or 3 whole cloves
- ½ small bay leaf
- Nutmeg

INSTRUCTIONS

1. Preheat oven to 350 degrees.
2. Melt butter over low heat.
3. Add and blend 1½ to 2 tablespoons flour for 3 to 5 minutes
4. Slowly stir in 1 cup milk
5. Add 1 small onion studded with 2 or 3 whole cloves and ½ small bay leaf.
6. Cook and stir the sauce with a wire whisk or wooden spoon until thickened and smooth.
7. Place in a 350-degree oven for 20 minutes.
8. Strain the sauce.
9. Season to taste.
10. Add a grating of nutmeg and serve.

For better consistency, you may scald the milk beforehand; but be sure that the roux is cool when you add it to avoid lumping. For creamed dishes, use half as much as solids.

Makes 1 cup

Florentine Sauce

- 1 cup White Sauce
- A dash of hot pepper sauce
- 2 drops Worcestershire sauce
- 1 cup finely chopped spinach
- A fresh grating of nutmeg
- 1 tablespoon finely chopped parsley.

INSTRUCTIONS:

1. Combine 1 cup White Sauce, a dash of hot pepper sauce, 2 drops Worcestershire sauce, 1 cup finely chopped spinach, fresh grating of nutmeg, 1 tablespoon finely chopped parsley.
2. If using the sauce cold for fish, do not thin. If using it hot, you may thin with cream or dry white wine.

Makes about 2 cups

Cheese Sauce

- 1 cup White Sauce
- 1 cup or less mild grated cheese
- ½ teaspoon salt
- 1/8 teaspoon paprika
- A few grains cayenne
- ½ teaspoon dry mustard

INSTRUCTIONS:
1. Prepare White Sauce until smooth.
2. Reduce the heat and stir in grated cheese.
3. Season with salt, paprika, cayenne, and dry mustard.
4. Stir until cheese is melted.

Makes about 2 cups

ELISA JUAREZ

CHAPTER FOUR: AUTUMN

Autumn

"*Earthly souls ebb and flow in sorrow and joy according to the seasons of emotion, just as the seasons of the natural world move through the cycle of life, death, and rebirth. These are the days to be grateful for the harvest of the heart, however humble it might be, and to prepare for the coming of the year's closure. Even now, the season of daylight diminishes, and the time of darkness increases. But the true light is never extinguished in the natural world, and it is the same with your soul. Embrace the ebb... and do not fear the darkness. For as night follows day, the Light will return.*"
— Sarah Ban Breathnach, *Simple Abundance*

Autumn is a time of harvest, hearth, and home. We gather the fruits of the earth, gather with family and friends, and give thanks. Nature is a master teacher, and this is the season of radiance and release. Radiance is demonstrated in the vibrant foliage as it changes colors. Release comes afterward as the trees drop their leaves, exposing bare branches for the winter months.

We, too, carry the life force that created us and continues to shape us through each season of our lives. Radiance and release are the natural order of things, both within and around us. As humans we tend to dim or block our own radiance by failing to release old hurt, beliefs, resentment, and attachments. It is like a tree retaining its leaves as they turn brown, dry up and die. The life force within the tree will send out new shoots and buds in the spring, but if the old leaves are still attached they block the new growth.

Have you ever really noticed the way the leaves dance in the streets when the autumn winds blow? They are free and the trees remain a bold expression of continuity amid change. Life is movement, and we are all designed to be vessels of Creative Energy, allowing the continual flow of life and love to move in and through us. When we block it by our own fear, distrust, anger, resentment, etc., we become stagnant and our lives lack radiance. We were made to dance, to create, and to grow.

As you savor autumn, embrace the lessons nature has to teach you. Take time to observe, listen, and learn. Open your heart and just be willing to let go of that which is no longer radiant. Tune in to the music within and around you and be willing to move, to dance, to release. This is your season. Allow the beauty and radiance of your own colors to shine, and you shall indeed live well.

Autumn themes include seasonal cooking, change, patience, gratitude, giving, anticipation, and holidays.

ELISA JUAREZ

Threshold to a New Season

Today I feel like I am approaching the end of a path with a doorway ahead. The week is coming to end, and so is the summer season. Lauren has been home for the past few weeks before going to Spain for her study abroad program this fall. We have cherished every day and every moment with her. Now we are at the threshold of a doorway that opens into something new for each of us. There is a mixture of excitement, anticipation, and anxiety as we approach the new and unknown — and isn't that every day of life? What does the new day hold? What does the new *season* hold? We cannot know until we step into it.

Labor Day is like a threshold that we cross from summer into autumn, from lazy days into crazy days. Suddenly the holidays are in our face every time we enter a store or turn on the TV. We realize the pace has increased and the expectations for ourselves and others are ramping up. We live in a society that covets work and material success, so it is easy to measure ourselves and our success on that superficial scale. When I first read Sarah Ban Breathnach's definition of "authentic success" in *Simple Abundance*, it was truly an "Aha!" moment. It changed the way I looked at my life and work from then on. I have written about her ideas and principles as I have incorporated them into my daily life.

As an empty nest mom with young adult daughters, the topic of success is very relevant. I think about what they have learned and observed from Art and me. I consider the values they carry as a lantern

250

to guide their footsteps and inform their choices. I recognize and honor their unique gifts. I envision authentic success for each of them and our family, based on our ideas, dreams, and endeavors. I celebrate the way we share these with each other and encourage each other, and I am learning to accept that some of the ideas, hopes and dreams we have for them may look different than the ones they choose.

As you approach the new season, savor your summer treasures and give thanks. Choose to travel lightly, to bless and release any circumstances or relationships that no longer serve your highest good. Accept responsibility for your own life, your health, happiness, and authentic success. This life is yours to create, contribute, and celebrate. Cross the threshold with glad anticipation of the new experiences that await you.

Being with Dad

The other day I went to visit my dad in his assisted living facility. I'm thankful for all that he has there; friends, meals, activities, and support, as his disease progresses gradually. He still knows all of us, but gets mixed up sometimes about how he is related to different members of the family. He calls me when he gets confused and needs some gentle help and reassurance to put him back on track for the time being.

Dad is the most cheerful, fun loving man you will ever meet. His optimism and good humor have made this road much brighter for him and all of us. However, as his confusion increases, he has times of frustration and irritability. This particular day was one of those times. He was involved in a word search puzzle when I arrived. In the process of preparing to sign a birthday card for my nephew, Alec, he became confused and upset when trying to make sense of his notes about Alec's age and birth date. Then he stalled and stared at the card before finally writing something (since we don't just sign our names in this family). It was a struggle for him, and as soon as it was over he returned to his puzzle.

I have learned that these word search puzzles are a great way to calm and focus his mind. Although we sometimes play a game of Scrabble when I visit, this time I met him where he was, slipping quietly into his world. I opened another word search book and began working, then put on some of his favorite music. He began to relax, chuckle, and comment on the music, saying over and over how much he enjoyed hearing it. Both of us kept our attention on our puzzles, but we were together.

I thought about how it must feel to him to realize that his brain isn't working. He knows it. He made a comment this morning that his mind wasn't working. I sensed his frustration and felt sadness and compassion for him. I see how he has tried so hard to keep everything straight, remember, understand, and hold on. He writes notes on his calendar and in his address book, sometimes going over and over the writing with his pen as if that will etch it into his memory. I just want to wrap my arms around him and tell him how much I love him. I've tried this, and although he still enjoys and appreciates a good hug, something has changed. At least he knows that I am there for him with love, support, and encouragement whenever he feels confused or unsure of himself.

On days like today I realize that my presence is enough. He is not alone. I am walking beside him through this fog, holding his hand as he held mine so many times, speaking to him gently and lovingly as he did to me throughout my life.

Although it is natural to want to bring people into our world, to draw them into our sphere, sometimes the most supportive and compassionate thing we can do is to tune in to where they are and step into their reality. We don't need to fix anything; our presence is enough. We can be a comfort and a source of peace and strength for others when we are in a place of acceptance and awareness.

Perhaps this week you will find an opportunity to do this. In one of my devotionals is a message I have carried with me for years: "It's not what you *do* but what you *are* that makes the difference." Bring your light and love into your relationships with others. Perhaps you can become a better listener and observer in the process. That is my intention, and I find that life gives me more and more opportunities to practice.

The Joy of Seasonal Cooking

This is my favorite time of year to cook! As the weather cools down, my kitchen heats up! Seasonal herbs and spices add a rich aroma to my home and trigger many memories from my childhood. My favorite things to make are soups, crockpot dinners, and baked goods. In preparation for this seasonal cooking, I have created a list of staples to keep on hand so that I can throw together a delicious, nutritious meal easily!

Naturally, you will want to craft your own list according to your unique diet and delights! But these are some basics to make shopping and cooking easier and more enjoyable! Once you stock your kitchen with the essentials for the season, you will save yourself time and money each week! Your grocery list will be shorter and you'll be more likely to cook if you're prepared!

You may think you don't have time to make this list and fill it, but I have given you a guideline to simplify the process, and I assure you that it will be well worth it! A little planning and preparation go a long way! I have not been the best at this, so I am doing it for myself, as well! I'd like to spend less time and energy trying to figure out what to make for dinner during the week and making extra trips to the grocery store because I am missing one or two essential ingredients! Can you relate?

My suggestion is to edit the list, print copies, and put one on your refrigerator so you can keep track of what you need as you use things up. It will serve you well when you are making your grocery list each week, and help you keep track of what you already have in the pantry so that you don't overbuy certain items (I have this problem!). If cooking is not your favorite thing, then this is even more important, and here's why: *By stocking your kitchen with the essentials, you will spend less time and energy in the kitchen.* Choose a day to make one or two recipes for the week that you can divide up or maybe freeze and have meals *done* ahead of time. Get more mileage out of your cooking by making enough for at least two meals. While you're cooking, put on your favorite music, pour a glass of wine or tea, and pay attention to the abundance of flavors, textures, aromas, and colors around you. Pretend it is your *favorite* thing to do, and you just might find more enjoyment in it!

Also, hooray for you if you have fresh herbs growing inside or out! Those are the *best!* I like to grow basil, thyme, sage, rosemary, and mint. I keep them alive for as long as I can into autumn and winter!

This is truly the season of simple abundance. Savor it and give thanks. Feed your spirit as well as your body! Keep things fresh and fun and live well!

"Essentials" Shopping List

PRODUCE:

- Onions/shallots
- Garlic
- Celery
- Carrots
- Parsley and/or cilantro
- Winter squash
- Sweet potatoes
- Potatoes

PANTRY:

- Organic broths and stocks: chicken, beef, and vegetable
- Canned tomatoes: crushed, petite diced, and sauce
- Canned beans: pinto, black, cannellini, kidney
- Rice: brown, basmati/jasmine, etc.
- Pasta (several varieties)

SPICE CABINET:

- Dried herbs
- Bay leaf
- Seasonings
- Garlic salt
- Cinnamon

- Ginger
- Allspice
- Cloves
- Pumpkin pie spice
- Sea salts
- Cooking wines
- Vinegars

BAKING:

- Whole grain flour, gluten free oat flour, and brown rice flour
- Organic, unbleached, all-purpose flour
- Sugars: organic cane sugar, brown sugar, confectioners' sugar
- Vanilla
- Almond extract
- Semi-sweet or dark chocolate baking chips
- White chocolate baking chips
- Dried cranberries and/or raisins
- Walnuts and/or pecans

Recipe for a Colorful Life

This week I tried some colorful fingerling potatoes, including red and purple which I hadn't had before. I was curious and eager to try purple potatoes, having heard that they were very nutritious, so I bought a bag of multicolored fingerlings. I cut them in half, tossed them in olive oil, sprinkled them with sea salt, pepper, and herbs, and baked them in the oven along with a few chicken thighs. It was a delicious meal!

To have a well-balanced diet, we need to eat a variety of fresh and colorful foods. If you grew up like I did, then eating lots of fresh vegetables and fruits is natural for you. However, we all need to be intentional about it since it can take a little extra time and effort to shop for and prepare fresh whole foods, instead of taking shortcuts and grabbing packaged convenience foods.

Lately I've been thinking about how a varied and colorful diet gives us the physical nourishment that our bodies need, and how that nourishment can also be a metaphor for the rest of our lives. Take a look at what is on your "plate" in terms of activities, relationships, and experiences. What fills your life? How do you feed your mind and spirit? What makes for a rich and colorful life? It can be easy to get into a rut, going through the motions day after day, feeling uninspired, dull, and even discouraged. This is a sign that we are not getting enough nourishment, variety, and inspiration in our lives!

I often encourage people to stay curious, keep things fresh and fun, and live well. This is a motto for me. This is how I keep my life from getting dull and uninteresting. I seek to learn and grow, to inspire and be inspired, to get out of my comfort zone, try new things, and to discover more about myself and others. I keep an open and curious mind and enjoy listening to people's stories. We have so much to learn and experience here! Do you have purple potatoes in your pantry? Do you regularly make new recipes, meet new people, visit new places, read books, and ask questions? This is a recipe for a colorful life!

Keep your eyes, ears, and heart open. Be willing to do things differently. Listen to people and seek to learn. Dance around your living room once in a while or do as my friend Sue does and take a dance class! The more color, flavor, and texture you have in your life; the more you will add to others. Taste and see that life is good, and make this season rich and vibrant!

Live Well, Eat Well (Part One)

The art of living and eating well is one of my favorite topics, and the theme of *Soul Salsa*. Each season brings its own materials to the table of design and delight, and what we do with them is our art. Living well is perhaps the highest art, and one that we can all learn to master. It requires conscious attention and intention more than any particular skillset. Thankfully it does *not* require a large bank account, but you'll need a heart and mind that are open to gratitude and simple abundance.

ELISA JUAREZ

Where do you find ideas and inspiration for your life? I have mentioned several authors and spiritual teachers who demonstrate the art of living well e.g., Sarah Ban Breathnach, Dr. Christiane Northrup, Wayne Dyer, and Eckhart Tolle, to name a few. They are my inspiration. They have shown me how to find the sacred in the ordinary and savor simple gifts and pleasures. Learning something new each day increases my well-being and expands my mind and heart.

Have you noticed that stretching your body helps release tension and build flexibility? It's the same with your mind. Be willing to stretch your thinking and experiment with new ideas to redesign your home, your cooking, and your life.

Cooking and eating well is fundamental to living well. If you think or say, "I don't cook," I challenge you to change that. Start by changing the thought to: "I haven't gotten into cooking yet, but since I like to eat, I am open to it." Seriously, we all need to eat, and if we want to live well, then we need to look at our relationship with food. We may need to stretch our palate by trying new foods and recipes. Variety is the spice of life, and we need it in our eating as much as anything! It starts with loving ourselves enough to treat our bodies with the respect they deserve.

Choosing and preparing whole, fresh, clean, nutritious food is one of the most basic and essential practices for a healthy, happy life. Nowadays there is so much information available about nutrition and wellness, there is no excuse for putting garbage into our bodies. My blog, *Spoonful of Salsa* has Nutrition Nuggets to help you choose your foods and ingredients wisely (www.spoonfulofsalsa.com/nutrition).

You can also find recipes on the blog, and on Pinterest, cooking websites, and traditional cookbooks.

Simplify your meal prep by stocking your pantry with good staples and keeping a shopping list on the fridge for your fresh and refrigerated foods. Cooking with a crockpot will also save you time, energy, and money! The prep can be done the night before, then you fill the pot with fresh veggies, meat, and spices in the morning and let it cook on low all day. Easy peasy! You'll come home to a house that smells amazing, and a meal that is ready to eat! If you're cooking for just one or two, then you can share the extra, eat it throughout the week, or freeze some for another time.

'Tis the season for simply abundant cooking, eating, and living! An investment of time, attention, and energy in the kitchen will pay high dividends to your health and well-being. *You* are worth it!

Live Well, Eat Well (Part Two)

Living and eating well starts in our minds with our thoughts and beliefs about ourselves, our world, and what it means to "live well." Take a few minutes to jot down what "living well" looks like and feels like to you. Does that description match your real life? Why or why not?

We can change what we eat every day of the week, but if we hold onto beliefs that do not support our health and well-being, then we will still find ourselves falling short of "the good life." Our lives reflect our beliefs and attitudes. So that is the starting point for creating a life of wellness, joy, and vitality.

This morning I read this quote in my daily devotional:

> *"I believe we have the freedom to be happy, to be well, and to be prosperous... We live in a universe the nature of which is so extravagantly abundant and so abundantly extravagant."* — Ernest Holmes

Do you believe that? If you really did, your life would demonstrate it! I don't mean *perfect*, as changing our thoughts, attitudes, and beliefs can take time and discipline, but it is well worth the investment.

While you are working on that, take a closer look at what you are putting into your grocery cart. In this fast food, microwave culture we have gotten into some poor habits by cutting corners where we should instead be sowing seeds of wellness. To live well, we need to understand the importance of clean, whole foods and the critical role our diet plays in our quality of life. One step in the right direction is buying fresh, organic foods. Since these tend to cost a little more, it helps to start with the "Dirty Dozen" shopping list from Environmental Working Group (www.ewg.org). They provide a list of the produce that carries the most pesticides (the "Dirty Dozen") and those that are the "cleanest." Avoiding these toxins is so important that it is well worth spending a little more and buying a bottle of veggie wash to clean *all* your produce. You can usually find this in the produce section of the grocery store. Toxins such as pesticides and herbicides can lead to cancer, hormone imbalances, and many other diseases.

Although organic produce and dairy products may cost more than the alternatives, you'll find that the more fresh, whole foods you have in your cart, as opposed to packaged and processed foods, the lower your grocery bill will be — not to mention your healthcare expenses! Cheap food is just that — cheap. It offers nothing of value to your body and may even induce harm. Foods like brown rice, quinoa, produce, and cage free eggs are not expensive and provide excellent nutritional value. If this is not your standard shopping list, then try switching out one or two processed/packaged foods each week for a healthy alternative. Pay more attention to the labels. The longer the ingredient list the more questionable it is. My mom used to tell me, "If you can't pronounce an ingredient, you probably shouldn't be eating it!" Know your ingredients and go for the foods with no preservatives or additives.

One of my favorite ways to eat and live well is by adding healthy fats to my diet. Fats have gotten such a bad rap over the years, and so much of our population is overweight that we tend to avoid the good fats and consume the cheaper, damaging fats. There will always be controversy and mixed information about fats, but I will share what I have learned through my own research and conversations with my doctors.

Who doesn't love real butter? It's the good stuff! Stay *away* from butter substitutes, spreads, margarine, etc. These contain damaging fats which can even hurt your brain. Go for the real deal, and once in a while spring for the *best* — pasture raised butter! Think *pure, real, whole foods.*

Be willing to try something new each week, expand your palate, and take steps toward a healthier, happier *you.* Eating well is

263

affordable if you learn how to shop, and the rewards are plentiful! The more fresh, whole foods you buy in place of packaged and processed foods, the less you will spend and the better you'll *feel!* Treat your body like the sacred temple that it is by giving it quality food, exercise, and rest. Living well stems from loving yourself and your life, finding joy and beauty in the simple things, and practicing gratitude. Have your fill of this good life!

The Beauty and Wonder of Change

Are you someone who dreads change or embraces it? Maybe you're somewhere in between, just accepting what comes with mixed feelings and hoping for the best. The longer we live the more we learn that change is indeed a mixed bag of blessings and challenges. What comes as hardship and loss may end up delivering profound growth and transformation. Nature demonstrates the beauty and wonder of change as it moves through each season, giving us clues and jewels of wisdom for our own lives.

Just as the natural world was created to move through seasons, so were we. As much as we would like to hold onto our favorite season — the season of abundance, warmth, and vitality — we recognize that this season would not be possible without all the others. It brings me comfort, assurance, and hope to watch nature's rhythm through each season. I am reminded that there is an order within creation and an energy that renews and restores life. Watching *Planet Earth* and other nature programs is a wonderful way to put your life and the world into perspective. We are truly part of a grand and mysterious creation that has innate intelligence, wisdom, and beauty.

As we see in nature, some seasons are long, harsh, and intense, bringing storms and extreme conditions. Growing up in South Dakota, it was the winter. Now, living in Texas, it is the summer. Just as the arrival of spring in South Dakota was a joyous occasion, so is the arrival of autumn in Texas. Going through any season of discomfort helps us recognize and appreciate the relief and refreshment that a new season brings.

Although winter looks stark and barren, it is a time of deep and significant growth underground. In a season of dormancy and rest, growth takes place beneath the surface. When we go through a time that appears dormant, unproductive, or difficult, we can grow our root system by shifting our focus inward and strengthening our connection to God. When we feel parched and weary, refreshment can be found at the well within. Life continually renews itself in and through us when we allow its natural rhythm and flow.

Autumn is arriving in all her glory, bringing a transformation of the landscape. This is the colorful prelude to winter, a time of seasonal delights and celebrations. Each season offers precious gifts, lessons, and discoveries. Wherever you are, accept and bless this chapter of your life. Remember that it is only a season. Move through it mindfully with gratitude, openness, and trust. Be willing to let go of the past and anything that is blocking that flow of life. Use this time to plant and water the seeds you'd like to grow in your own life and in the world. What you do with this season will determine what the next one looks like.

Authentic Success

*"Authentic success is living each day with a heart
overflowing."*
— Sarah Ban Breathnach, *Simple Abundance*

Why is "success" such a loaded word? It carries expectations, measures, judgments, comparisons, cheers, and sighs. We strive for it our whole lives, and yet, *are we clear on what it means?* We are continually fed images of material success in the media and we gobble them up! How yummy it is to taste success when it looks so enticing, attractive, and exciting! We imagine having all the goods, services, and experiences that wealth can afford. We buy into the whole belief system that measures success quantitatively, externally, and financially. In our society success in the form of wealth and power is coveted, and countless and often significant sacrifices are made to achieve it.

*"Most of us were not taught that there are two kinds of
success: worldly and authentic. But in order to live happy
and fulfilled lives, we need to know the difference between
what's Real and what's not, because success is part of Life
University's required curriculum."*
— Sarah Ban Breathnach, *Simple Abundance*

As Sarah says, there is nothing wrong with the pursuit of worldly success and financial independence, but authentic success is much more. It is living by your own lights. I have discovered that it is about creating a life from the design that was instilled in me by my Creator, and that is authentic. It is a fullness and richness of life, a tapestry woven with love, beauty, compassion, joy, creativity, courage, faith, wonder, and grace. It is learning to live fully and freely in the present, to forgive ourselves and others, to see the good in people and situations, to trust the Life and Love that is God, to find joy and beauty in every experience and every day, to know who we are, and to be comfortable and happy in our own skin while continuing to stretch, reach, and grow stronger.

The definition of authentic success given by Sarah Ban Breathnach in *Simple Abundance* has impacted my life significantly, transforming my perspective on my life and work.

> *"Failure and success are the yin and yang of achievement,*
> *the two forces in the Universe over which we have*
> *absolutely no control. We keep forgetting that all we can*
> *control is our response to failure and success."*
> — Sarah Ban Breathnach, *Simple Abundance*

John C. Maxwell has a book entitled *Failing Forward* in which he explains how the experiences we may deem as failures are actually valuable growth opportunities for us, preparing us for something greater. As Sarah says, our response is our business and will determine what we gain from the experience. Learning to reframe our circumstances in light of these ideas can shift our energy and attention from discouragement and disappointment to encouragement and optimism. We may not understand why things didn't turn out the way we had hoped, but we can use the experience as a springboard to something new.

I have had many business endeavors that looked and felt like failures. Each time, I asked myself why I continued to struggle without "success." I thought I was following both my instincts and the guidance and support provided by others. So, why did I fail?

Each experience taught me something that I needed to learn about business and myself that I would not otherwise have learned. Each one brought people into my life who were teachers, mentors, and sometimes even friends. By each one I was led into another experience that was new and different. I had to get out of my comfort zone over and over again. The more I got out of my comfort zone, the wider that zone became, and the more capable and confident I felt. I know that would not have happened if everything had been smooth, easy, and comfortable for me. Recently I heard someone say, "Struggle is a biological necessity." For anything or anyone to grow, struggle is necessary.

The other valuable component to our growth is perspective. Time and experience help us develop perspective, without which life can seem random and meaningless. I can see now that each of my life experiences helped shape me, prepare me, and provide a solid foundation for my life's work. They have broadened my view and given me wisdom, understanding, and resilience. Authentic success is a matter of perspective, and it is different for everyone. How we look upon ourselves and our circumstances is up to us.

"Comparison is the thief of joy." — Theodore Roosevelt

It is too easy to draw comparisons as we look at what and how others are doing as a measuring stick for our success. I must continually remind myself that this is irrelevant to me.

*"I know that what is mine will claim me, know me, rush to
me. I accept the gift of Life for myself and for everyone
else."* — Ernest Holmes, *This Thing Called You*

This passage from *Simple Abundance* is so exquisite that I decided
to share it in its entirety:

*"Authentic success is having time enough to pursue
personal pursuits that bring you pleasure, time enough to
make the loving gestures for your family you long to do,
time enough to care for your home, tend your garden,
nurture your soul. Authentic success is never having to tell
yourself or those you love, 'maybe next year.' Authentic
success is knowing that if today were your last day on
Earth, you could leave without regret. Authentic success is
feeling focused and serene when you work, not fragmented.
It's knowing that you've done the best that you possibly
can, no matter what circumstances you faced; it's knowing
in your soul that the best you can do is all you can do, and
that the best you can do is always enough.*

*Authentic success is accepting your limitations, making
peace with your past, and reveling in your passions so that
your future may unfold according to a Divine Plan. It's
discovering and calling forth your gifts and offering them to
the world to help heal its ravaged heart. It's making a
difference in other lives and believing that if you can do
that for just one person each day, through a smile, a shared
laugh, a caress, a kind word, or a helping hand, blessed are
you among women.*

*Authentic success is not just money in the bank but a
contented heart and peace of mind. It's earning what you*

feel you deserve for the work you do and knowing that you're worth it. Authentic success is paying your bills with ease, taking care of all your needs and the needs of those you love, indulging some wants, and having enough left over to save and share. Authentic success is not about accumulating but letting go, because all you have is all you truly need. Authentic success is feeling good about who you are, appreciating where you've been, celebrating your achievements, and honoring the distance you've already come. Authentic success is reaching the point where being is as important as doing. It's the steady pursuit of a dream. It's realizing that no matter how much time it takes for a dream to come true in the physical world, no day is ever wasted. It's valuing inner, as well as outer, labor – both your own and others'. It's elevating labor to a craft and craft to an art by bestowing Love on every task you undertake.

Authentic success is knowing how simply abundant your life is exactly how it is today. Authentic success is being so grateful for the many blessings bestowed on you and yours that you can share your portion with others. Authentic success is living each day with a heart overflowing."
– Sarah Ban Breathnach

Perhaps these words resonate with you as they do with me, opening your eyes, mind, and heart to a deeper understanding and acceptance of your authentic path. I hope they will inspire you and even ignite your passions.

This life is ours to embrace, create, and experience fully. We have brought with us a unique design and purpose that is ours alone. Our work is to turn within to find it, connect with it, and then live it boldly and beautifully. Decide for yourself what true success looks like and feels like for *you*. Your purpose here is unique to you, and only you can fulfill it. Find what inspires, energizes, and fills you with joy. Pursue this with your whole heart and soul, living and giving it to a dry and thirsty world like a fountain of cool water. Therein lies your success, satisfaction, and *soul salsa*, which will have a ripple effect for the generations that follow.

Serenity

"God, grant me the serenity to accept the things I cannot change, courage to change the things I can, and wisdom to know the difference." — Reinhold Niebuhr

It is one thing to accept and embrace change in our lives, for change is inevitable. Learning to be flexible and adaptable helps us to bend without breaking, and ultimately to experience more peace and joy. We don't have to understand it, but we can choose to allow life to unfold without resistance. We can look for and focus on the good, the gifts, in each situation and maintain a positive expectancy.

It is yet another thing to have the courage to change the things we can change, stand up for what we believe and know to be true, stand up for those who cannot defend themselves, and stand for the principles and values that give our lives meaning and purpose. This takes wisdom and courage. Some things we accept, others we don't. Sometimes it's not clear which is which, so we seek wisdom and guidance from within. We look to our principles and values to guide us. We act accordingly and then learn to release the outcome. That is perhaps the greatest challenge of all... letting go of our attachment to a particular outcome. When we are passionate about our goals, intentions, and principles, it can be difficult to let go of the results of our actions and trust that things will work out somehow — regardless of appearances. We think things should go a certain way, and when they don't we may feel frustrated, angry, worried, or discouraged. We must remember that our sight is limited and there is a bigger picture we cannot see. Our actions may be impacting others in ways we cannot see or generating a shift, and we may never know. It may take time for results to show up, and we need to be patient and trust that all things are working together for good. We can live our lives according to our principles and values without concern about the outcome. That is freedom. Let the results take care of themselves; we are *not* in control of that. We may or may not like or agree with certain outcomes, but we *can* learn to let go.

So, during this season of change and release, notice what is happening in nature, allow your colors to come through vibrantly, and then let go when it's time, as the leaves turn brilliant colors before falling from the trees. It's all part of the amazing and mysterious cycle of nature, and our lives. When the trees are bare, the life force still flows within them and the roots continue to grow deeper and stronger. In times of rest and dormancy, life continues as growth takes place within. Each season passes into the next and life goes on. Keep this perspective so you can remain calm, confident, and at peace through all the seasons, all the changes, and all the joys and disappointments of your life.

Mindful Mornings

"If there is joy in the labor of your hands... it is more than simply 'work.' If there is value in the difficult experience... it becomes more than just 'loss.' If there is enthusiasm at the beginning of the day... it is not just 'ordinary.' We lift ourselves up on the wings of our own vision and hope."
— Mary Anne Radmacher

What does "good morning" mean to you? What makes for a good morning? Do you have a mindful morning ritual that fills your tank for the day?

Early morning is a mystical interlude between darkness and dawn, a sacred time before the outside world comes crashing in through electronic entryways. To preserve my sanity and serenity, I begin and end each day with a golden gap of stillness. I turn off the noise and distractions that can captivate my attention.

My morning starts with making the bed, stepping back, and saying, "Ah, nice!" I give thanks for the new day, refill the diffuser with essential oils, and brew a pot of coffee. These are "feel good" aromas for me. I get in a few good stretches before settling in my armchair to read, write, and reflect. This is how I fill my tank and prepare myself to step into the unknown.

I connect to the power source, to Divine Life and Love, which I call God. This unchanging and abiding Presence becomes more evident when I am still, and I open my mind and heart to experience it. Writing helps me clear my head of clutter and listen to that inner voice of Love. I am centered in the present moment, which helps dissolve the remnants of anxiety, weariness, or grief that tend to linger in the shadows.

The morning ritual we choose can make or break the day for us. It can wake us up to what we need for the day, like providing gear and water for a hike. You wouldn't want to skip that!

We're all noticing how crazy and scary things look and feel right now, and we need something solid to hold on to. We need protective clothing, an oxygen mask, and a built in navigation system! Thankfully signs of hope keep showing up everywhere, like blades of green grass pushing through cracks in the sidewalk. I believe there is a transformation and an awakening happening — even if you have to squint your eyes or pull out the binoculars to see it!

The light shines behind layers of dark, stormy clouds. It seeps through narrow openings, pushing the clouds apart, creating unexpected rainbows and streams of bright light. There is no doubt that it's there, making some kind of progress, even as the storms produce thunder, lightning, and twisters on a daily basis.

As much as I enjoy watching weather and forecasts, there is always a degree of uncertainty. It's reassuring that the sun doesn't die or give up; it just can't, because it is, after all, the *sun*. Dark clouds and storms pass, but the sun keeps on shining because that is what it *is* and what it *does*. For now, we just have to wear our raincoats and carry our umbrellas and emergency kits with us everywhere. That's how this time in our history looks and feels very turbulent and upsetting, raising the continual questions of what to do and how to respond. It can be hard to see clearly when rain is pelting your glasses or your windshield. It can be hard to understand and navigate this passage, which is why the morning and evening times are so crucial. Too much turbulence can make us nauseous and dizzy! We need shelter, a time and space for rest, reflection, and renewal where we connect to the Light and Love within us. That's our built in navigation system and our charging station.

Stay the course — no matter the weather. It starts with morning, which is your launchpad. Listen to your intuition and sweep anxiety to the curb. *This, too, shall pass*, and we will be okay. We have to know on some level that we are spiritual beings having a temporary human experience. There is more to life than what we see, and more to us that we can *be*. The world needs us to contribute more light, love, calm strength, wisdom, and compassion. Love will show us the way. Wake up to beauty, wonder, and grace. Wake up to the power and courage within you. What you look for you will find. Carry your binoculars and your sunglasses and make it a *good morning!*

Living on Our Own Terms

"The insistent and universal desire for self-expression is the Divine Urge within us, even God Himself 'tapping at the walls of our heart,' urging us on to a fuller life."
— Ernest Holmes, *Know Yourself*

This morning as I was taking a shower and thinking about 21 year old Lauren, this thought came to me: *She's living life on her own terms.* It really struck a chord in me! That's it exactly! She is navigating her life and relationships as a responsible and thoughtful young adult, making new choices and decisions that are not always simple. She is learning to live in the now and release her anxiety about the future. She is also realizing that her perspectives, beliefs, and values are not always the same as her peers, and that's okay. She is developing her own terms based on who she is and how she chooses to experience life.

I remember when Taylor was this age and going through the same process. I'm grateful for the close relationship I have with each of them, and the amazing experience of witnessing the butterfly emerge from the cocoon. The nest of home and family was the cocoon, and it provided safety, warmth, security, and support. I would say that they started breaking through it before they left home for sure, and once they were out on their own, the wings came out! When we're raising our kids, we do it on our terms. They live and learn within our belief system, our values, perspective, and boundaries. We create the environment of the cocoon. We have some control. As they get older, the boundaries often get stretched to accommodate their growing independence and maturity. We begin to loosen the controls and give them more space and freedom. We try to prepare them to take flight and navigate their own lives responsibly. Then they leave the nest!

If they go to college, then they are still partially dependent on us while they learn to make their own decisions and establish their own terms. This can be both exciting and painful for us as parents. They may struggle, fall, or get hurt. They may try things we never tried, choose partners we wouldn't choose for them, or question the faith and values we instilled in them. It is crucial for young adults to build their lives on their own terms, exert their independence and spread their wings. Despite how uncomfortable it can be at times for those close to them, it's much healthier than living their lives on someone else's terms and missing their own calling. Their terms will evolve as they continue their adult journey, but they may need to shake them up in the beginning to see what sticks and what doesn't. They are still learning to be authentic, trust their own instincts, and navigate adulthood. It's no small task!

During this turbulent process, it is tempting to reimpose *our* terms, pull them back in a little, and just remind them of that wonderful cocoon that nurtured them into adulthood. If we can let go and be patient, we will see them find their own way. We may also realize that their terms are a reflection of the ones we provided for them. They look different now that they are doing life out in the world, but the fact that they are thriving and making responsible, thoughtful decisions is something to be celebrated.

Art struggled with this most of his early life and into young adulthood. He was smart and talented in high school and wanted to go to college, but his oppressive and critical father got in the way. Sadly, he didn't push his limits and continued to live life on his father's terms for several years, until he met me and moved away. It still took time for him to figure out his own terms and who he was apart from his dad. He didn't know what he wanted to do for a career, so he stayed in the default lane for years, doing what he knew and longing for something more.

Thankfully, as we raised our daughters, he was very clear with them that they could follow their dreams and go to college. We both worked hard to provide many enriching opportunities that would set them up for success and broaden their perspective. By the time they each left home for college, they had tools, resources, experiences, and faith that provided provide a firm foundation, and a vision for those butterfly wings. They've had to test those wings without the most confidence to realize they had what they needed. They both moved through their fears, including separation anxiety and self doubt, to get onto the ground of their own terms.

Now that the nest is empty, I am beginning to live life on my own terms, as well. No longer focused on the significant task of raising children into young adults, I can shift my attention and energy to recreating my life and myself.

I have been surprised by the continued challenge of overcoming self doubt and judgment. We carry self imposed standards and expectations, along with societal and family expectations, and these affect our thoughts, ideas, and behaviors more than we realize. You would think that by mid-life we would be past these obstacles, but they rear their heads even still, giving us more opportunities to rise above them and into a new realm of freedom. Freedom! Don't we all want freedom? To live an authentic life is true freedom. Freedom to do and be, to live fully with love, laughter, joy, and peace of mind. When we learn to be fully present in the *now*, we find freedom from the past and the future!

Living on our own terms is essentially what it means to live an authentic life. It is our creation and our expression of who we are. It is our joy, our essence, and our gift. We do it by finding and embracing our authentic selves, letting go of external measures of value and success. Those externals can be like a cocoon that keeps us from becoming all that we were created to be. When we use our inner wisdom and strength to break out of that cocoon, we will discover the light of who we truly are. We will find it easier to relax more, stress less, laugh more, complain less, and give expression to our unique gifts. Along the way, we must learn to trust ourselves and listen to the inner voice of wisdom that is ever present. When we get comfortable in our own skin, accept ourselves as we are, and learn to not take ourselves so seriously, we will feel lighter, have more energy, and experience more peace. If we can stop comparing ourselves and our lives to others, freedom and joy will be our reward. We will be healthier and happier! And without even trying we will inspire others to do the same.

Wherever you are in your life journey, come to terms with yourself. Take responsibility for creating, developing, and expressing an authentic life. It is your path to the discovery of wholeness and holiness.

Resilience

When I think about resilience, I remember the words of my father when I was going through a tough time: "You'll bounce back. You always do." He also frequently passed down his mother's phrase, "It'll all work out," which reassured me even when it was hard to imagine how that was possible. Over time I developed resilience, optimism, and faith in something greater than me and my circumstances. When others have confidence in us it is a little easier to develop confidence in ourselves, but it still takes time, practice, and adversity. How can we find our own strength and resilience if we never struggle? Adversity is essential for us to find our inner resources and discover the power within us.

ELISA JUAREZ

Life has taught me that my thoughts create my reality, and every challenge presents a choice and a gift. When I choose resilience, optimism, and faith, I am empowered to move through the experience with greater flexibility and strength. That choice also unlocks the unexpected gift. Those times reinforce my belief in myself to bounce back, and in the Power within that guides and sustains me.

You may know about the amazing giant Sequoia trees which can live up to 3,000 years. Periodic forest fires clear away everything that threatens the trees' survival while ensuring their growth and regeneration. It is the intense heat that causes the Sequoia cones to open and release their seeds. Without the clearing force of fire, the seedlings would be overcrowded by competing shade trees and not have enough sunlight to grow. We can understand the value of pruning when it comes to trees and other plants, but forest fires are extreme! It is hard to imagine anything good coming from something so destructive! And yet the phenomenal creation of the giant Sequoia tree depends on such adversity in order to survive and thrive. What if we could face the challenges and "fires" in our own lives with a perspective that empowers us and increases our resilience? What would be the gift for us? What if resilience is the key that unlocks adversity to a treasure that will transform us?

Each one of us is a phenomenal creation, carrying seeds of greatness and beauty. Our gifts are like the cones of the Sequoia tree; only heat will open them so the seeds can be released! Welcome the fire and the clearing of old habits, beliefs, and obstacles. Nature is a wise teacher, always demonstrating the creative power of the Universe and the life force in all living things. You were created to thrive, to nourish others, and to discover and develop your gifts. The fires will come, but not to destroy you. Choose resilience, optimism, and faith. Let the fires in your life ignite your inner fire, releasing your amazing potential and power.

Hen Party

"The circles of women around us weave invisible nets of love that carry us when we are weak and sing with us when we are strong." — Sark

This week I had coffee with my friend Jan, and she was telling me about the upcoming women's reunion in her family. I've known about this for as long as I've known her, and it amazes me still. They call this gathering "The Hen Party," and they have been doing it every year for the past 29 years! In that time, as the family has grown, attendance has increased from 30 women to 60, and it stretches as far as seventh cousins. She told me how significant this group of women has been to her over the years, saying that she draws strength and courage from their presence and support. She shared a few of their stories with me, and I was moved by the legacy these women are creating and living as they encourage, empower, and hold one another. What a remarkable gift to all of them and their families!

This got me thinking about my own family and the women who have gone before me. I did some writing and reflecting about my maternal grandmother whose birthday is this month, and my mother who has been gone now for almost 4 years. Thankfully my mother wrote about her mother's life, and her grandmother who lived with them for many years while she was growing up. On my father's side there were some amazing women (and men) as well, planting seeds that continue to grow and blossom many generations later. There is a treasure trove of memories and a legacy of love, strength, and courage, that make up the foundation of our lives.

There are parts of who we are that we may not understand, and perhaps those are strands of DNA from our ancestors. It is a mystery, which can be awe inspiring if we take the time to consider it. You've probably heard it said that if you go back far enough in any lineage, we are all related somehow. I think it is helpful in this day and age to accept such a notion. How would you view others differently if you considered them to be your family? How would you treat people you barely know? How would you feel when someone is mistreated, violated, or killed? These are big thoughts, but our minds and hearts are capable of holding much more than we realize. Perhaps we can learn to hold each other and the world with more compassion.

Who are your female heroes, the "hens" of influence in your family (or outside it)? Are they still living? Consider how they have impacted your life and who you have become. I encourage you to write about these women and the legacy they left behind or continue to create.

Among my top picks are each of my grandmothers. My maternal grandmother was a humble, simple, hardworking woman who never complained and never spoke ill of anyone. I noticed that she treated everyone with kindness and respect. That left an impact on me.

My paternal grandmother was a warm, loving, and encouraging woman whose nickname was "Happy." My dad remembers and often repeats her saying, "It'll all work out." She would tell her children that sometimes in life you have to be patient and trust, but things work out in the end. This philosophy shaped his optimistic outlook, and he passed it onto me. I remember playing games with her as a child, and whenever any of us had a "win," she would say, "Goodie for you!" She was always cheering us on.

I could write much more about my grandmothers and the treasures they left for us, and I will. But for now, I would invite you to carve out some time to do this for yourself. It is important for us to remember. Writing and sharing these stories helps to embed them in our consciousness and encourage us to carry the legacy forward. As the leaves change and the weather cools down, pause to reflect on the vibrant colors in your life, those relationships which have shaped and strengthened you, and the seasons you have been through. Together they add depth, color, and texture to who you are and how you live. This is one reason you are much stronger and wiser than you know. You carry the strength and wisdom of your ancestors within you. Imagine having your own "hen party" with these women. What would they say to you? What would you share with them? Recognize the colorful strands of their unique gifts woven into who you are and smile. Cluck, cluck!

Spoonful of Spice

What spices and aromas do you associate with fall? For me its cinnamon! I love using cinnamon year round, but it is an aroma that is especially prevalent in fall and winter. You've heard that we have smell memories, right? Our cells store memories connected to certain aromas, and those memories are triggered when we encounter those scents. Think about the spices and aromas you remember from childhood and the images and feelings that come up.

Perhaps it is no accident that herbs and spices, which are gifts from nature, carry many medicinal healing properties. They have been valued as such for thousands of years. They are available to us in various forms such as essential oils, leaves, teas, and ground spices. Whenever we use them, we connect to the life force that is present in nature and in us. We access that healing energy while also accessing the memories we may have in our cells. Think about that for a minute! What aromas can we fill our homes with that bring comfort, healing, and connection to ourselves, our past, and our rich present?

When we find nourishment and encouragement for our bodies, our minds, and our spirits, our lives will reflect that "spice" as vitality, energy, and wholeness. Your authentic self has been designed to seek and fulfill your passion and your purpose. The spice of your life will be different than someone else's. That is what makes it spice! Your life would be flat and flavorless without the presence of your authentic gifts – the spices of who you are!

So, as you bring seasonal spices into your kitchen, your living space, and your entire home, pay attention to what comes into your heart and mind. Honor your connection to nature and your true self. Honor your memories, the building blocks of who you are, and the potential for healing and vitality here and now. Enjoy the rich, fragrant, and delicious gifts of the season on every level of your being.

The Thing About Soup

It has been a week of letting go, pulling focus, and giving thanks. I've learned that it's easier to give thanks when my attention is on the present moment. I tend to get restless and anxious when I let my thoughts take me backward to the past or forward to the future. So, I continue to practice present moment awareness and realize how rich my life really is, here and now.

This week I made lentil soup in the crockpot. This is one of my favorite soups, and I hadn't made it in a long time. One thing I remembered about making lentil soup, or any bean soup, was that it can take several hours for the beans to cook fully. In addition, the carrots, celery, and potatoes take just about as long to become tender. I started peeling and chopping mid-morning, putting everything in the pot around 10:30, adding a few springs of fresh thyme from my container garden. Making soup is so satisfying and fun for me. It's a bit like working in an art studio; I prepare vegetables of different colors and textures, peeling, slicing, chopping, dicing, and putting it all together. Soup is truly a creative and colorful endeavor, as you can throw in all kinds of ingredients without messing it up.

Life is a lot like making soup! We can add a wide variety of ingredients (e.g., experiences, relationships, endeavors), using our imaginations, intentions, and resources to create a rich, colorful life. Have you noticed that some people choose to play it safe and use the same few ingredients over and over? They are afraid to experiment, try something new, add a new herb or spice, or toss in a few extra veggies. Perhaps that sounds like you? It's never too late to "kick it up a notch," as celebrity chef Emeril Lagasse likes to say. "BAM!" *You are the chef of your life!*

The thing about soup is the time it takes to make it. In the past I have underestimated the cooking time for beans, disappointed to discover that they were still not ready to eat when I thought they would be. This is a lot like my life. The timer for my dreams and desires to be served up often has to be adjusted. *What? More time? Really?* Like those beans that need to simmer for hours, some dreams take months or years to be fully cooked and ready to eat! The Universe is the slow cooker. It is set at just the right temperature and time for the perfect outcome. My job is to choose my ingredients and prepare them properly by setting my intentions, asking, giving thanks, and taking appropriate action. Then I put them all into the pot and allow the soup to cook. As I begin to smell it my anticipation builds! *I'm hungry!* It's *good* to be hungry for our best life, our dreams, and our heart's desires!

When we pursue our dreams, our whole "house" is filled with a wonderful aroma. Our lives are rich, colorful, vibrant, and flavorful. So, don't be afraid to experiment, be creative, and have fun with it. Kick it up a notch, throw in some spice, and live well!

As the Leaves Turn

Have the leaves started turning where you live? Here in Texas we are getting our first taste of fall as the temperature finally cools down. The leaves change color later in the South, but they don't miss the opportunity to display their radiance before letting go. In the same way, we move through the seasons of our lives at our own pace, in our own way, as the unique creations that we are. We are affected by our inner and outer environment, which includes our beliefs, attitudes, and circumstances. As the leaves turn around us, we have leaves turning within us.

I am aware of my inner leaves turning as the end of the year approaches and I take stock of my life and work. I glance back on last year at this time, then ahead to where I'd like to be next fall. I stand here now, in the fullness of the present moment, grateful to be alive and well. I hold my dreams lightly, knowing how suddenly life can change. I have learned that even as the leaves change colors, drop to the ground and die, there is an ongoing flow of life within the trees that holds the promise of spring. For the new growth to come, the leaves must fall. I consider this analogy for my own life, and the months that are now behind me. Amid the glory of vibrant color and seasonal beauty is the awareness that this, too, shall pass. So, I pause to absorb the beauty around me, savor the gifts of this season, and allow my awareness and appreciation to expand.

As the leaves turn, the days gets shorter and our to do lists get longer. Now is the time to stop in our tracks and claim our power to navigate the next few months with poise and purpose. There are projects to complete and holidays to plan. Be willing to let go of expectations that may feel heavy or stressful, whether they be your own or others'. Realize that as much as you may cherish certain traditions, you have the freedom to change things up, try something new, and think outside the box. Decide here and now that your life is meant to be savored, not endured. How might you create or discover a new sense of freedom, joy, and fun this holiday season?

Over the past few years, we have been changing up how and where we gather and celebrate. It keeps us open and flexible, which makes the holidays less stressful and more creative. We have realized that the most important thing is being together as family and having fun with friends. We stayed true to our family's holiday traditions for the most part while the girls were growing up, until we decided to break tradition and take a trip to New York City for Christmas! It turned out to be one of our most memorable experiences, and it opened us to trying more new things around the holidays. Now the girls are grown, and our holidays look a little different every year.

Your authentic self seeks creative expression and fulfillment, so don't go through the motions of your life on autopilot. Look for ways to turn over a new leaf, add more color and texture to your daily round, and step outside your comfort zone! This is the season of radiance and release. Move through it mindfully and joyfully, one sacred day at a time.

The Fullness of Silence

"Everything that's created comes out of silence. Your thoughts emerge from the nothingness of silence. Your words come out of this void. Your very essence emerged from emptiness. All creativity requires some stillness."
— Wayne Dyer

You've heard the expression and had the experience of "empty chatter." It is shallow and meaningless. It's just noise. It doesn't add value to anyone or anything. In contrast, have you had the experience of silence? Silence, stillness, awareness. What I have noticed about silence is the inherent fullness. Silence that opens our awareness is full of possibility. It is full of wonder, beauty, comfort, and strength. Therefore, it adds value to the one experiencing it as well as the surrounding environment. By expanding our awareness of both inner and outer beauty, it is fulfilling, satisfying, calming, and empowering.

Silence reveals a greater reality that is ever present but often ignored or unnoticed. It is drowned out by the noise of empty chatter, television, and loud music. We give most of our attention to things that do *not* satisfy, comfort, fulfill, or add value, and we end up feeling empty, cheated, discouraged, and even depressed. We forget that the filling station is at our center, and the way to reach it is through silence.

It begins with outer stillness. Sit still and quiet. Relax. Shift your attention inward and focus on your breath, an image, and/or a word or mantra. Then settle into the silence and just rest. Your eyes may be

289

closed, but your awareness is opened. You begin to sense a fullness of being, calm strength, and peace. Tired nerves and weary mind are soothed in the silence. Your awareness touches the abiding Presence of Divine Love. This is Home. This is the filling station.

> "All you need is deep within you waiting to reveal itself.
> All you have to do is be still and take time to seek for what
> is within, and you will surely find it."
> — Eileen Caddy

This Love created us and continues to sustain us. This is what we are. The more we connect with this source of power and love; the more we will experience it in our everyday lives and relationships.

The practice of silence is a spiritual discipline that transforms us from the inside out. It does take practice and patience to learn to control our thoughts and quiet our busy minds. Once we have learned to find and connect to our center through silence, we can begin to practice carrying the awareness of silence into our conversations and interactions. This will help us be more fully present and attuned to people and situations, listen better, and respond with calm strength. Essentially, we begin to live a more centered and conscious life, and the fullness of silence permeates our lives with beauty, grace, peace, and power.

Scavenger Hunt

Have you ever been on a scavenger hunt? When I was growing up, our church youth group had a scavenger hunt every year around this time. We were divided into teams and given a list of items to search for in the church neighborhood. In addition to ordinary odds and ends, there were unusual or unique items to make it interesting and a bit challenging. For example, the list might include things like a nail, a red leaf, a gum wrapper, a flat rock, a store receipt, a paper clip, a quarter, etc. The church sat in the middle of the downtown area, surrounded by streets, businesses, parking lots, and neighborhoods – good hunting ground for miscellaneous trinkets and treasures. I think kids of all ages (and adults like me) enjoy exploring in search of something interesting or valuable.

Life is like a scavenger hunt. We go into each day with a mental list that we are pursuing; things to do, things to find, and things to create. We are in search of fulfillment every day; physical, mental, emotional, and spiritual. On some level, we know there is more to life than what we can see and hear. When we have a clear idea of what we want we are more likely to find it, but life is full of surprises! I've found that my list pales in comparison to what the Universe has in store for me. This realization keeps me in a state of anticipation, trust, and gratitude as I move through each day. Expect the unexpected! Expect to be surprised by grace. Expect your every need to be met and your heart's desires to be fulfilled. At the same time, surrender your attachment to the outcome. What a way to live!

As I have learned from many spiritual teachers, our lives are a reflection of our thoughts, beliefs, and attitudes. What we think about most will show up and increase in our lives. To attract abundance, we first need to become generous givers and live larger! Yep, we need to expand how we *live* from the inside out. When we learn to think, feel, and act as if we already have what we desire, it will show up as soon as we are truly ready for it. We may not realize we are spending our time and energy scavenging for things that don't really matter, like old wrappers, paper clips, scraps, and nails, when we could have so much more. We need to expand our vision for our lives and deepen our connection to the Source! I believe we get what we expect from life, and we see what we believe. So why not choose to believe that God is good, life is a gift, and the Universe has our backs? Why not look for the good in people and situations?

In that case, life is more like a treasure hunt. This week has been full of sweet surprises, reminding me that unconditional love and divine order are ever present and at work in my life. I have had numerous unexpected gifts, like a visit from my childhood best friend and her mom, some great finds at the bookstore, and an email from my brother in Canada saying that he and his family are planning to come for a visit next month! My heart is full! And when my heart is full of gratitude, joy, and love, my life overflows with good gifts and surprises.

> *"For where your treasure is, there will your heart be also."*
> — Matthew 6:21

The real treasures are within us, and when we discover those our lives will reflect their beauty and bounty.

Today is all we have, and it is full. Treasures abound. Seek, and you shall find. Give, and it shall be given to you. Open yourself to receive a little more. Relax, rejoice, and give thanks. I assure you that the Universe is just waiting for you to say, "*Yes!* I am ready!" Now let the treasure hunt begin!

Halloween Fun

Halloween brings up many happy and fun memories from my childhood, including costume making. My mother was an artist, a seamstress, and an economist, so outfitting three kids in Halloween costumes was a creative challenge. We would come up with ideas and help with the design, utilizing the many dress up and craft supplies we had on hand, plus Mom's sewing skills. The construction of our costumes was at least half the fun of Halloween! When you grow up with that kind of ingenuity, it's hard to settle for a store bought costume. It seems a bit lame. But I've done that, too!

After college I worked for a property management company called Pace Realty. They had a company wide Halloween costume contest one year, and I came up with the idea of doing Pace Picante Sauce. Each person on our staff at the apartments dressed as an ingredient, and I was the jar of salsa. Together we made each costume, and our team *won!* It was great fun. We had a tomato, an onion, a jalapeno pepper, and the jar with the "Pace Picante Sauce" label. It was hard to beat that idea since it used the company name!

When I became a mom, I carried on the costume making tradition as much as possible. Having two girls meant we had plenty of dress up materials! Even though I did buy a few costumes over the years, it was always more fun to make them, especially with the girls' help! I should clarify that I have never been a seamstress, so when I say "costume making," it did *not* involve sewing! It was more like a trip to the craft store, the closets, and Goodwill, with a lot of imagination! Each year the dress up box grew as we added more garb, bobbles, and wigs, so we got a lot of mileage out of Halloween!

In addition to costume making was pumpkin carving, another fun, creative, and very messy undertaking. Designing, digging out, and carving was followed by rinsing and roasting the seeds! My girls enjoyed this activity as much as I did growing up.

Halloween gives us the opportunity to get into a creative and playful frame of mind just before moving into the holiday season! The next two months can get a little crazy, so we need a strategy to keep calm and stay well! The year will be over before you know it, so try to savor each day, and the simple pleasures of the season. Be sure to take time to care for your soul as well as your body.

Have a safe, fun, and playful Halloween, even if you stay in and watch a movie! I plan to make a batch of popcorn and watch my recording of *It's the Great Pumpkin, Charlie Brown!* Some things never get old, and hopefully that includes you!

Anticipation

Anticipation... the magical moxie that makes us tingle from the inside out like bubbly champagne! This is a time of anticipation as the holidays approach and families and friends gather to celebrate the present and remember the past. It's the week before Thanksgiving and Lauren, who has been away at college since the first of August, is flying home tomorrow! That is our joyful anticipation this weekend!

Anticipation is something we can stir up any time we choose to engage our thoughts and feelings in positive expectancy for something in our lives. This activates the Law of Attraction, which is always operating in the universe, but we can direct it with our intention and creativity. According to the Law of Attraction, the energy of our feelings has power, so our thoughts need to be accompanied by feelings as we engage our whole being in the positive expectation of our desires. When we think, feel, and act as if what we desire is already here, we can pull it toward us.

When things don't happen the way that we hoped or anticipated, we can still maintain a positive expectancy by believing and affirming that divine order is at work and something even better is unfolding for us. If we learn to accept disappointment with an attitude of gratitude and openness, we will discover a gift within it. Perhaps the Universe is leading us toward our highest and best good, and we just can't see it yet. All we have is the present, and that *is* the present. We don't need to see the future to trust that it is good and beautiful. Therefore, we can anticipate each new day with joy and gratitude.

As you prepare for the coming holidays, cherish every task, enjoy the simple abundance that surrounds you, and show appreciation and generosity to others wherever you are. Let the joy of living bubble up within you and spill over to everyone around you. If you are going through a difficult or painful season, you can anticipate that this, too, shall pass. A new season is before you. Love surrounds you and sustains you — even when you don't feel it. Ask, believe, and you shall receive.

November Comes with a Full Plate

Standing on the threshold of November, the end of the year is in view. We can't see what life will bring us in the next two months, but we can see our calendar, our hopes and dreams, and our goals. We can feel the joy and anticipation of the holidays, family gatherings, seasonal cooking, celebrations, remembrances, and cherished moments.

November has also brought loss and grief over the past several years. It was at Thanksgiving that we lost my father-in-law many years ago. It was at Thanksgiving that we lost my mother just four years ago, and in September of that year my 49 year old sister-in-law died suddenly of aggressive cancer. In November of last year, I lost a friend without a chance to say goodbye. This time of harvest, thanksgiving, gathering, and celebration is like a canvas, painted with rich, colorful layers of love and longing, laughter and tears, joy and sorrow. It is a time of reflection and release.

November brings with it a full plate. As you prepare for the holidays by making plans, decorating your home, cooking and baking, sending cards, listening to special music, and gathering with friends and family, I'm sure that, like me, your heart and mind are flooded with many feelings, memories, hopes, and ideas. The holidays are loaded with these and can, at times, bring on anxiety and stress. Therefore, your preparations need to include a plan to nurture yourself physically, mentally, emotionally, and spiritually. When you are rested, healthy, and happy, you will have more to give. Fill your tank first, and you will experience a more peaceful, relaxed, and joyful holiday season.

Irish psychotherapist and writer Thomas Moore calls this profound attention to the authentic needs that stir within "caring for our souls." He says that we were created for this very purpose,

> "To love, nurture, nourish, sustain, protect, uplift, inspire, delight, charm, and comfort the beloved presence within each of us. . . It is through 'the small details of everyday life' that we make our souls feels welcome. . . Tending the things around us and becoming sensitive to the importance of home, daily schedule, and maybe even the clothes we wear are ways of caring for the soul."
> — Thomas Moore, *Care of the Soul: A Guide for Cultivating Depth and Sacredness in Everyday Life*

The real key is to be present, notice the beauty and wonder within and around you, and enjoy it. As you embrace favorite traditions, be willing to try something new and different as well. Let Love surprise you. Let Love feed your soul and uplift your spirit. Trust that the presence of Love is embracing and celebrating *you*. As a beloved pastor and friend once told me, "That which you seek is seeking you."

This is a time for connection, reflection, and gratitude. Relax and rejoice; keep it simple and stress free. Find ways to share what you have with others. Realize that you have the creative capacity to bring your ideas and dreams to fruition. This is a season of mystery and miracles.

Awakening Through Gratitude

"Developing a true sense of gratitude involves taking absolutely nothing for granted. Rather, we always look for the friendly intention behind every deed and learn to appreciate it." — Albert Schweitzer

You've probably heard the phrase "attitude of gratitude" for years, and accept its value on a surface level, at least. However, until you have practiced it consistently and made it a habit, you may not realize that it is the key to awakening your heart, mind, and spirit.

A common tool for developing a habit of giving thanks is a gratitude journal. You may have tried this and found it valuable. It is a concrete exercise in which you write down at least five things for which you are grateful each day. Doing this at the end of the day helps you put the day in perspective and identify what made you smile, give thanks, feel good, etc. When you make this a habit, it becomes easier and easier to notice the gifts and graces that each day brings. As you open your eyes and mind to *notice* more good, you open yourself to *receive* more good. You attract more to be thankful for, and the cycle continues. Thus, you awaken to the beauty and bounty of life and your sense of appreciation deepens.

> "Gratitude unlocks the fullness of life. It turns what we have into enough, and more. It turns denial into acceptance, chaos to order, confusion to clarity. It can turn a meal into a feast, a house into a home, a stranger into a friend. Gratitude makes sense of our past, brings peace for today, and creates a vision for tomorrow."
> — Melody Beattie

My experience with gratitude has been expansive. I know it started in my childhood as I grew up in a household in which we were appreciated, valued and praised. When we are appreciated as children, we learn to be appreciators. This is an invaluable gift parents can give their children, as it sets them up to see value in themselves and others and to experience and express gratitude. As I have continued to learn and practice gratitude through all the seasons of my life, I have noticed a deepening of faith and wonder. "Thank you" has become as natural as breathing for me; I say it in my mind and under my breath as a prayer for protection, wisdom, and grace. I say "thank you" in advance whenever I ask God for anything. I say it when I behold the beauty in creation, kindness and compassion in humanity, and the awareness of Divine Love within and around me.

I have had to practice it through many difficult times in my life when my hopes and dreams were dimmed or damaged. I have learned to surrender, let go, and trust that there is something better unfolding in my life, something new being created. Disappointments are detours which can lead us into greater understanding and experience — especially when we let go of our attachment to the outcome and trust that a greater good is on its way to us. If we get stuck in our disappointment instead of moving through it, then we miss the opportunity for growth and awakening that awaits us.

In the midst of darkness, discouragement, and despair we are challenged to see and be the light of the world. Our gratitude is heightened as we realize daily that life is fleeting and fragile. Each day becomes ever more precious, and in seeking God we find that God is drawing us closer. *"In the shadow of Thy wings I sing for joy."* I can give thanks for the awareness of Divine Love that holds me, shelters me, and lifts me up. Continuing to give thanks as a prayer through the darkness opens our eyes and our hearts to the light that leads us and abides with us. It is an act of faith and courage. Gratitude awakens us to the experience of grace.

Wherever you are and wherever you've been, gratitude can still be learned, developed, and woven into the fiber of your being. It's never too late because grace has been holding you all along. Just turn within and open your eyes, your heart, and your spirit. Be still and know that nothing can separate you from the Divine Love that created you. That alone is reason to give thanks. Start there. Say thank you for that Love. Begin to increase your awareness of it in your daily life by practicing gratitude. It will awaken and transform you from within, and your life will appreciate in value and beauty.

When you don't know what else to say or do, how to pray, or how to take the next step, just say thank you. Trust that the Love at the foundation of your being is holding you, guiding, and providing for you. Expect and anticipate abundance and joy, for they follow gratitude like morning follows night.

Get Your Infusion!

Our friend Kim is going through chemo, getting an infusion every other Monday. I've been listening to Dr. Bernie Siegel's audiobook, *Love, Medicine & Miracles*, in which he shares stories of exceptional patients whose positive mindset, faith, and will to live proved to be more powerful than any treatment they received. He testifies to the power of belief in the healing process, as well as the disease process. I have understood this for many years, and yet I continue to discover new ways to apply it in my life. Dr. Siegel says that cancer patients can imagine the chemo infusion pumping healing energy into their bodies instead of toxic drugs, and that can have a positive effect on their treatment! That really got me thinking.

We all have something ailing us, whether it be physical, mental, emotional, or spiritual. What if we could give ourselves an infusion every day to cure our ailment? Well, we can! My meditation today started with this centering thought from Deepak Chopra: *"I am clear that anything is in my power to change."*

I imagined getting an infusion of healing energy, strength, joy, and peace of mind. I smiled at the thought, realizing once again the creative power of my mind and spirit. When we choose to connect consciously with the Source of Life and Love, with God, we get a divine infusion. Just as a cancer patient has to sit and wait while the infusion takes place, we need to take time to sit quietly and allow

ELISA JUAREZ

Divine Life to flow through our veins, filling our cells with energy. We need to trust that if we take that time to connect to the power source, the rest of our day will be more positive, productive, and powerful!

We are entering a very busy time of year when it is easy to get distracted and stressed. There is so much to do, after all! I suggest that you try giving yourself a daily infusion of whatever you need and desire from the Divine Source. Recognize the thoughts and feelings that may be creating tension, stress, and disease, and choose an infusion of healing energy, peace, joy, and love. Is something lacking in your life? Imagine it flowing into you and filling your life. Just as a cancer treatment requires regular infusions for a time, so does self love. Love yourself enough to make it a regular practice. Whatever you think about and focus on will expand, so choose wisely! Take responsibility for your thoughts, your feelings, and your life. Own your power and it will rise within you!

Our true self is creative and powerful, and our essential nature is wholeness. Let us affirm and express this truth as we move through the holy days ahead. Bring your authentic gifts, your presence, and your whole heart to this season. Open yourself to give and receive abundantly. This is the time of gathering, feasting, celebrating, and giving thanks. When you receive regular infusions of light and love, you will become a powerful presence in the world. That is the most valuable gift you can give!

Don't Rub It In!

Yesterday I helped my dad celebrate his 88th birthday with a special outing. After lunch I took him back to his assisted living facility where a group of residents were sitting in the living room. My favorite resident there is Wally, and he and my dad have become great friends. There sat Wally in his favorite armchair, ready to engage in conversation.

Dad began to tell the story about having scarlet fever in the third grade. Dad talked about how he almost died, but he came to believe God had kept him alive for a purpose. He felt that God's Hand had been with him throughout his life, but acknowledged, "There were times I got mud on my face!"

Wally said, "Yes, but He didn't rub it in!"

I looked up from the jigsaw puzzle that I was working on with Raydene, another resident. "Wally!" I exclaimed. "That is so good; I love that!"

Wally smiled and replied, "Yeah, isn't that good? He didn't rub it in!"

I told him I would remember that one. I got to thinking about how we all get mud on our face at times, saying or doing things we regret, and how we are always forgiven. God brushes it off, wipes our face clean, and encourages us to keep going and growing. However, we still tend to rub it in. When we rub it in by obsessing about our mistakes, holding onto them, and carrying them around, they get absorbed into our brains and our bodies, blocking the flow of God's good. We get "stuck in the mud" of our own thinking.

We also do this to others when they say or do things that we find offensive, upsetting, or "wrong." This is especially true with the people closest to us because we have the opportunity to rub things in or brush them off. It's our choice. We may need to speak up, express our feelings, and set some boundaries. However, that is not the same as rubbing the "mud" into someone's face, making them "wrong," and expecting them to carry that burden.

Seniors are like children at times; they speak the truth in simple, refreshing terms that we can all understand and appreciate. I enjoy spending time with these seniors who have various challenges, including confusion and memory issues. This season of their lives is fragile and uncertain, but they carry within them a lifetime of experience. Although their limitations can be frustrating for them, their humility and inner beauty reflect the grace and wisdom of God.

In this month of thanksgiving, look for the gifts of grace within and around you. Look past the failures and shortcomings of others and yourself and *wash your face!* Clear away your judgment, criticism, and disappointments. Allow the light of Love to shine through you. Practice shaking off the dirt that gets thrown in your face at times and keep going. Give love and give thanks.

Patience & Faith

*"Study the cycles of Mother Nature, the garden whispers,
for they correspond with the cycles of your soul's growth.
Quiet your mind. Rope in the restlessness. Be here. Learn
to labor. Learn to wait. Learn to wait expectantly."*
— Sarah Ban Breathnach, *Simple Abundance*

This has been a week of waiting, which means a test of patience and faith. I have two very special and significant projects that have reached the point of letting go and waiting for the next step to unfold. In both cases I have done all I can do; now they are out of my hands. I have to trust things will work out. This has been an area of growth for me because I get very eager for the results! It can be hard to wait, not knowing what the outcome will look like, if it will turn out the way I have hoped and planned, or if it will be yet another disappointment. This is life!

I have had so many opportunities to work on my patience and faith that you would think I'd be an ace by now. I can honestly say I am better at it; my patience and faith are stronger. I have even been able to accept the possibility that things will not work out right now, that I may have to adjust my timeline. Perhaps there is something better unfolding. My life experiences have taught me that when I apply myself through intention, action, visualization, and prayer, then let go of my attachment to the outcome, I experience more freedom, joy, and peace. I have seen how things work out without my control or concern, sometimes even better than I could have imagined.

305

ELISA JUAREZ

So, on this Friday evening, as the day and the week come to a close, I pour myself a glass of wine and give thanks for the gifts of grace and beauty that this week has brought me. I realize the richness of the present moment and choose to absorb it fully, letting go of both the future and the past. I encourage you to do the same.

Release any sense of disappointment, doubt, or anxiety. Trust that the Universe knows exactly what you need, when you need it, and how to deliver it to you. You can only see a small portion of the picture. Embrace the fullness and beauty of the present moment. Practice this affirmation: *"I am safe, I am loved, I am free. All is well, and all shall be well."*

In this season of harvest and thanksgiving, keep your heart and hands open to receive and give freely. Practice this as you wait for your harvest. Cultivate an attitude of gratitude and allow the Universe to surprise you.

Golden Leaves

My mother taught me to recognize and appreciate the seasons of life and cherish them. Life continually moves through seasons. Nothing lasts forever except the Love that holds us. I know she was on my mind and heart when I wrote this, one year after her passing:

Golden leaves are falling like snowflakes in my backyard. The poinsettias I put in the ground last Christmas are robust and turning red. The lingering warm weather in Texas does not change Mother Nature's plans. The season is changing and it's time to let go. Let go of summer, let go of long days and lush gardens. Let go of disappointments and self doubt. Let go of fear. You just can't hold onto that and really live. It will blind you and block your good. Seasons change whether we like it or not. In the dead of winter there is growth within, under, and through. Life doesn't stop; it just has to go through darkness to find depth. Find your own truth in this metaphor. Do not be deceived into believing that that which appears dark and cold and devoid of life will last for one minute when spring rains return and refresh the earth.

> *"Plant your hope with good seed;*
> *don't cover yourself with thistle and weeds.*
> *Rain down, rain down on me..."*
> — Mumford & Sons

Thanksgiving Preparation

As you prepare for Thanksgiving, are you feeling anxious, overwhelmed, or excited? How do you approach the task? Do you like to try something new each year or stick to tradition? For me it's a blend of both. As new people come into the equation, they bring their ideas and favorite things. We learn to be flexible, adapting to change even on these holidays that hold so many traditions and memories for us.

It helps to consider what part of Thanksgiving means the most to you. This is an important question for each of us to answer, partly so that we don't miss the opportunity to cherish it, and partly to help us keep the whole thing in perspective. When family and friends gather, it can be a mixture of joy and stress, comfort and discomfort, laughter and tears. There are so many expectations around the holidays which make it easy to get stressed, hurt, and exhausted. Start by assessing your own expectations for the day; your expectations of yourself, your hopes, your priorities, and your boundaries. Then look at your expectations of others. Sometimes awareness and simple adjustments of our expectations can transform the experience for us and our loved ones.

Life is so full of change and challenge, and yet the seasons continue to come and go, ebb and flow, bringing their reliable gifts – holidays, traditions, memories, celebrations, and opportunities. Within each one is a sense of awakening and anticipation along with familiarity and comfort. They remind us of the rhythm of life, a gentle rocking in the Arms of Love that hold us and carry through this unsteady, vacillating world. Every day we see how shaky life can be, and we long to hold on to all that is good and certain and precious to us.

In this season of thanksgiving, let go of anything that keeps you from giving and receiving fully and freely. Let go of expectations, judgments, and perfectionism by simply embracing the beauty of each moment. Be present with your loved ones and cherish them. Feed not only your body but also your soul. Relax and rejoice. Savor it all! Keep your preparations creative, joyful, and fun! Remember that simplicity is the secret sauce for a stress-free holiday!

Lead Bread Lesson

As we all prepare for Thanksgiving, I thought I would share a funny memory from my childhood that just might contain a little lesson for all of us.

I used to enjoy baking with my mom when I was growing up, and one Thanksgiving she let me make the cranberry nut bread all by myself. I had never made it, but I had seen my mom make all kinds of breads, including yeast breads. I followed the recipe, mixing everything together, and was confused when I saw the consistency of the dough. I thought it should be thicker like yeast bread, not something I could pour into a bread pan. "*Hmm, I must have missed something. There's not enough flour in here!*" I thought to myself. *Well, I can remedy that!* I added more flour until the batter was thick and slightly sticky. I scraped it into the loaf pan and put it in the oven. When the bread came out it was like a brick! We named it "Lead Bread" and had a good laugh. Mom gently explained to me the difference between quick breads and yeast breads; boy, did I feel silly!

There is a lesson in this about trust. Can you think of an experience when you felt things weren't going the way you hoped or expected, or didn't look the way you thought they should, and you decided to take matters into your own hands to ensure a particular outcome? Maybe instead of allowing things to unfold naturally, you thought you had a better way of doing it. Perhaps your words and actions interfered with a process or situation that did not need to be changed.

That recipe did not need to be changed; I just didn't recognize the nature of quick breads and decided to change it. I changed it, all right! And that loaf of "lead bread" ended up being thrown into the backyard!

Life gives us plenty of opportunities to learn to let go and trust. The older I get, the more I experience this deepening trust that carries me through all kinds of situations. Trust gives us a lightness of being by lifting our burdens, worries, and fears. When we refuse to let go of them we become like the lead bread and our life becomes harder than it was designed to be.

Thanksgiving is a wonderful time to share memories of food and family, to work together in the kitchen, and to celebrate the abundance of this season. It is also a time for reflection and gratitude, inviting us to look within ourselves and practice trust. Know that you can trust the Love and Wisdom that created you. Know that you were designed to live fully and freely, to learn and grow continually, and to enjoy and your life.

The Wish List

When I was growing up, the Sears Holiday Catalog would arrive at our house sometime in the fall, usually in late October. Although I don't remember exactly when, I am sure it was not as early as holiday marketing begins nowadays! It was a thick, red, shiny catalog boasting colorful pictures of toys and games, clothing and accessories, and an abundance of gift ideas that inspired our annual wish lists! In our family we would each make a wish list to share with each other, thereby taking the guesswork out of holiday shopping. As children we made long lists to give our parents plenty of ideas and options, and who knows how many items we might receive? It was worth a try to aim high! Oh, and during the Santa years, that list was sent or shared with him in some mysterious way. It was all so magical and exciting!

I tried to carry this forward with Art and our family, but it took years for him to embrace it. If I mentioned something I wanted or needed in the month or two before Christmas, he would often say, "Let's go look at it!" or "Let's go get it!" By the same token, if he thought of something he wanted, he would look it up online or go to a store and get it. I had to work on him for years, telling him that anything that comes to mind in the way of wishes or gifts leading up to Christmas needs to be *noted,* and *saved* for Christmas. He caught on, and I had many a surprise on Christmas morning over the years. He didn't like the idea of telling people what you want, saying that it takes the fun and surprise out of gifting. I can appreciate that, but we still share ideas with each other and our daughters who ask us every year for gift ideas. The combination of getting something we wanted and something unexpected is the best of both worlds!

We all have a wish list of sorts, for the holidays and for our lives. There are things we *want* and things we *need.* I recently saw a wise recommendation about giving gifts to children. It suggested four types of gifts: (1) something they want; (2) something they need; (3) something to play with; and (4) something to read. I think that is a fine idea for adults, as well! When making your wish list, add at least one item from each of those categories. Be willing to share your list with your family members. It is fun to come up with creative and meaningful gifts for each other. Having a few ideas to work with can make the process easier.

There was another type of gift giving which my parents initiated once we were old enough to understand and participate. My mother asked us to write down a non-material gift we would like to give each person in the family. The written note was placed in the person's stocking. Here is where our good intentions to listen better, tease less, help more, complain less, be more kind and cheerful, etc., were expressed. It was a thoughtful exercise for each of us as it taught us the value of giving more of ourselves, our time and energy, and our love to each other. It taught us to look within ourselves for the gifts that are ours to give, and to find ways to be a gift to each other. These gifts were blessed and multiplied as they were shared. The older we get, the more we desire and appreciate these gifts of genuine love and attention. We also realize that they can be the most valuable because of what they require of us. It is learning that *presence* makes the best *present*.

There is joy and delight in finding or creating meaningful gifts that add value to people's lives and inspire them to love, laugh, play, learn, and grow. Consider what your loved one needs, desires, and enjoys. Be open to creative, fun, and unconventional ideas. Make it personal and purposeful. Give from the heart, including a message of love and affirmation with the gift. Do your best to keep the whole process simple, fun, creative, and authentic. This time of year is meant to be savored and celebrated, so don't let stress and anxiety seize the day. Be present with your loved ones; accept and appreciate them for who they are, and you will have given them one of the best gifts you can give. Lift your wish list and your heart's desires to the Universe.

Give thanks in advance. Life is full of surprises and miracles. Keep your eyes and your heart open so that you don't miss them!

Gifting Outside the Box

I am listening to Christmas music as I write this, thinking about how to approach the holidays and gifting with creativity and authenticity. As you read this, please quiet the voice in your head that says, "I'm not creative!" I think we all doubt our creativity at times, but we can share ideas and have fun doing it! There are all kinds of ideas online, in magazines, and in craft stores. This is also a time when holiday bazaars and craft shows are prevalent, providing opportunities to gather ideas and gifts while supporting local artists and entrepreneurs! The older we get the less we need, and the more we enjoy giving gifts that matter. Those are usually gifts that cannot be wrapped in a box or bag, such as acts of service, donations of time and money, and being present with those who need comfort. There are countless ways to give from the heart, and that is the spirit of Christmas.

When I was a young adult, before I was married, my family celebrated Christmas at my parents' house in Indiana. One year when I was stretched financially, I had to really think about how and what to give as gifts. I came up with an idea that ended up being a hit, and my family said they were some of the best gifts I had ever given. I found some photographs I had taken of my mother's childhood home in New Hampshire, and other special photos, and used them to make notecards. I don't remember if I printed them at home or at a print shop, but it was an inexpensive and unique gift. Photos can be used to make all kinds of gifts, especially now that everything is digital. These gifts are personal and affordable. I have made photo calendars and photo books for my parents in the past and they always loved them. So, think about ways to take some family photos and create simple, unique, and personalized gifts for your family and friends.

The most meaningful and lasting gifts are those that express some aspect of yourself, or something that has been valuable to you. Think about what has made a difference in your life and give gifts that will add value to another person's life. I have made quote books and boxes by writing quotes, affirmations, or poetry in colorful journals or on slips of colored paper to fill a decorative box. These are gifts of inspiration that can uplift and encourage people throughout the year. I leave plenty of blank pages in the book so the recipient can add to it. What books have you read or listened to that have impacted your life or made you laugh? Books are timeless gifts that are inexpensive, yet so valuable. If you have someone on your list who is not a reader, then consider finding an audiobook they would enjoy and appreciate, or give them a subscription to Audible, an audiobook app available through Amazon. Think about what you enjoy doing that could be a gift to someone else. If you cook, bake, or enjoy putting food baskets together, go that route! I make salsa every year and give it as gifts. I think everyone enjoys homemade foods!

Okay, you get the idea. It's nothing new or revolutionary, but you know that it is easier to get a gift card than to take a little more time and come up with something personal and original. I just know that the holidays can be more fun and fulfilling if we put ourselves into our giving. Consider giving the gift of time and attention to your family. That means more than anything in a box, I promise. You can take an afternoon that you might spend shopping and battling traffic and lines and use that time to make or do something "outside the box" instead. Give an experience, like a special outing, a massage, or a movie. You don't have to be "creative" like an artist; you just need to be open and receptive. You can copy someone else's idea and make it your own! Ideas are everywhere, but there is only one *you,* and *you* have unique gifts to weave into your holiday giving.

Another option is to give a gift that has a broader impact, such as a donation to a favorite nonprofit in honor of someone. Our family has given Heifer Project gifts for years; this can be done online (www.heifer.org), and they send a card acknowledging the gift. This organization works to end poverty by providing livestock and training in sustainable agriculture to communities throughout the world. You can purchase a gift of livestock in honor of someone and know that your gift will directly impact a community in need. The website explains each of the options in their gift catalog, and how these animals support the livelihood of the people in the community.

Here is one example: A flock of chicks is $20. This helps provide a family in need with a starter flock of 10-50 chicks, along with the training that will empower them to turn your donation into a lifetime of opportunity. Each flock of chicks:

- Provides eggs and protein for nourishment
- Boosts income through the sales of extra eggs and offspring
- Ensures security for generations through Passing on the Gift

I encourage you to check out the website for more information. There are larger gifts that can be made with a group, so if your family

ELISA JUAREZ

or another group you belong to would like to go in together to purchase something more costly, then that is a great option, too!

There are many other non-profits that invite gifting, so consider your favorite causes and organizations and look into ways to support them through a gift in someone's honor. I am partial to those that provide food and shelter since many people are lacking those basic necessities. Local food banks, shelters, and other organizations support families who struggle to make ends meet. Habitat for Humanity is one of my favorites, and they work with families and volunteers to build houses in communities across the country. You can see what they are doing in your area and elsewhere at www.habitat.org. Organizations that support health and wellness through research and education are other great options. I like to support the Alzheimer's Association since my dad is struggling with that disease, and I know that organization is doing significant work to support those affected and to find a cure. Find out more at www.alz.org.

Those are a few ideas for your consideration as you navigate this season of shopping, wrapping, baking, gathering, and celebrating. We can each make a difference in the lives of those who have little, giving out of our abundance with gratitude and compassion. When we give, we receive so much more, and the cycle continues.

Finally, as we learn to embrace simplicity by paring down the clutter we have accumulated in our homes and lives, we are also giving a gift to ourselves. We find more space, energy, freedom, and peace of mind. Who doesn't want *that* kind of gift?

Hold On, It's Harvest Time!

It's one of my favorite seasons of the year — harvest time and Thanksgiving! Unfortunately, as a society we tend to rush this one, minimizing its gifts and its value as we push toward Christmas. We enjoy the food and wine and soon are tempted to check the Black Friday deals and make our lists. It saddens me that so many stores have started opening on Thanksgiving Day to get a jumpstart on Black Friday. This decision has a ripple effect on our society; even if many of us choose to abstain from shopping on Thanksgiving, many more have to go to work on that day. It affects families across our country, and it is completely unnecessary. Sadly, there are plenty of people eager and willing to go out shopping after the feast, so the retailers are rewarded for opening their doors. I say, "Hold on!"

This month we reap a rich harvest of food for our tables, our minds, and our souls by recognizing and celebrating simple abundance with gratitude. It is a time to intentionally increase our awareness of and appreciation for the manifold blessings that surround us. As the days begin to accelerate on the downhill slope to the holidays, I urge and encourage you to *hold on*. Soak up the beauty in every moment and the joy of time with family and friends. Cherish it all, feast on it, and let it fill you up. Nothing in the stores can satisfy like the gift of relationships. Take your time, enjoy it all, give freely, and celebrate the true abundance of this season.

317

Wrap Up November

Thanksgiving has given way to the season of Christmas and Hanukkah, with all its lights, music, décor, celebrations, and gifting. I am one who likes to let Thanksgiving linger for the last week of November before bringing out the Christmas decorations. I have the George Winston *December* cd on which the first piano piece is *Thanksgiving*. I listen to it every year at this time. There is something about music that connects us to the past and enriches the present. Seasonal and holiday music is rich in meaning and memories and has the power to uplift our spirits. Since the holidays can bring on a mixture of feelings, I find it helpful to play the music that is soothing, joyful, and inspiring to me.

As we wrap up November, it's hard not to think about what we're going to wrap in December. One of the most prevalent activities of this season is gift giving. Although we all enjoy giving, we may not all enjoy shopping and trying to find the "right" gifts for our friends and family. It can be challenging, time consuming, and tiring. Sadly, we end up feeling stressed and stretched — mentally, physically, and financially! If we can learn to "think outside the box" for creative and simple ideas, then we can gift "outside the box," too, which will help us enjoy the process and the season much more! All it takes is a shift in perspective and priorities.

As November winds down, take some time to pause and prepare for the month that lies ahead. Open your heart and mind to receive ideas and inspiration for giving, receiving, and celebrating. Consider

SOUL SALSA

what you have to give that doesn't require a user's manual, batteries, or a hit to your bank account. I assure you that your friends and family value *you* — and your time, energy, and attention — more than any material gift that is out there.

AUTUMN RECIPES

Apple Cinnamon Muffins

Adapted from my mother's *Betty Crocker Cookbook*.

- 1 egg
- ½ cup unsweetened almond milk or regular milk
- ½ teaspoon salt
- ½ cup sugar
- 1/3 cup packed brown sugar
- 2 teaspoons baking powder
- ¼ cup melted butter
- 1 cup grated raw, tart apples, not pared
- 1½ cups sifted whole grain flour
- 1½ teaspoons cinnamon
- 1/3 cup chopped nuts

INSTRUCTIONS

1. Beat egg slightly with fork then stir in milk, melted butter, and raw tart apples into beaten egg.
2. Sift together flour, sugar, 1 teaspoon cinnamon, baking powder, and salt and stir into the wet mix. Stir just until flour is moistened. Batter should be lumpy. Do not overmix.
3. Fill greased or lined muffin cups 2/3 full.

4. Mix sugar, chopped nuts, and ½ teaspoon cinnamon and sprinkle over the top.

5. BAKE at 400 degrees F for 20-25 minutes.

Makes 12 medium muffins.

Cranberry Nut Bread

Adapted from the Fanny Farmer Cookbook and my childhood! I learned to make this as a young girl, and it has always been a favorite — especially around the holidays.

- 1 orange
- 2 tablespoons butter
- 1 egg
- 1 cup sugar
- 1 cup cranberries, chopped
- ½ cup chopped walnuts or pecans
- 2 cups flour
- ½ teaspoon salt
- 1½ teaspoons baking powder
- ½ teaspoon baking soda

INSTRUCTIONS

1. Preheat the oven to 325 degrees.
2. Butter a loaf pan.
3. Zest the orange; squeeze the juice into a measuring cup and add enough boiling water to make ¾ cup.
4. Add the orange rind and butter and stir to melt the butter.
5. Beat the egg in another bowl and gradually add the sugar, beating well.
6. Spoon into the pan and bake for 1 hour.
7. Remove from the pan and cool on a rack.

Family Circle Ginger Snaps

These were my Aunt Laurel's favorite cookies when she was growing up, and I must say they were also one of mine!

- 2 cups sifted flour
- 2 teaspoons baking soda
- 1 teaspoon cinnamon
- ½ teaspoon salt
- 2 teaspoons ground ginger
- ¾ cup butter
- 1 cup sugar
- 1 egg
- ¼ cup molasses

Granulated sugar to taste

INSTRUCTIONS

1. Cream butter.
2. Gradually add sugar, and cream until fluffy.
3. Beat in egg and molasses.
4. Combine flour, ginger, soda, cinnamon, and salt into sifter. Sift over creamed mixture, blending well.
5. Form teaspoonfuls of dough into small balls by rolling lightly between palms of hands.
6. Roll balls in granulated sugar to coat entire surface.
7. Place 2" apart on ungreased cookie sheet.
8. Bake at 350 degrees for 12-15 minutes.

Hot Cranberry Bake

This is a delicious dessert for this time of year, and a great one to take to a gathering!

- 4 cups peeled, chopped cooking apples
- 2 cups fresh cranberries
- 1½ teaspoons lemon juice
- 1 cup sugar
- 1-1/3 cup firmly packed brown sugar
- ½ cup melted butter

INSTRUCTIONS

1. Layer chopped cooked apples and fresh cranberries in a lightly greased 2 quart baking dish.
2. Sprinkle with lemon juice and sugar.
3. Combine brown sugar and melted butter. Stir until moistened and crumbly.
4. Sprinkle over fruit.
5. Bake uncovered at 325 degrees F. for 1 hour.
6. Serve warm with vanilla ice cream.

Makes 8 servings.

Oatmeal Cranberry Walnut Cookies

By Elisa Juarez

- ½ lb. (2 sticks) butter, softened
- 1 cup brown sugar
- 1/3 cup granulated sugar
- 2 eggs
- 1 teaspoon vanilla
- 1 - ½ cups flour
- 1 teaspoon baking soda
- 1 teaspoon cinnamon
- ½ teaspoon sea salt
- 3 cups oats
- 1 cup dried cranberries
- ½-2/3 cup chopped walnuts
- 1 cup chocolate chips (white, semisweet, or dark)

INSTRUCTIONS:

1. Heat oven to 350 degrees F.
2. Beat together butter and sugars until creamy.
3. Add eggs and vanilla; beat well.
4. Add flour, baking soda, cinnamon and salt; mix well.
5. Add oats, cranberries, walnuts, and chocolate chips.
6. Drop by rounded tablespoonfuls onto ungreased cookie sheet.
7. Bake 10-12 minutes or until golden brown.
8. Let cool, then transfer to wire cooling rack.

Makes about 4 dozen.

Puerco y Calabacita (Pork & Mexican Squash)

This is a family favorite from Art's side of the family.

- 4 pork loin chops, cut into chunks
- 1 medium zucchini or calabacita (Mexican squash) cubed
- 1 small (8 oz) can tomato sauce
- ½ onion, chopped
- 1 tomato, chopped
- 1 cup frozen corn
- Salt and pepper, to taste
- 1 teaspoon cumin
- Cilantro, chopped (optional)
- 1 teaspoon garlic powder

INSTRUCTIONS

1. Brown pork in oil in large, deep skillet.
2. Sprinkle flour over pork; add salt, pepper, cumin, and garlic powder.
3. Add zucchini, then tomato sauce and water to cover.
4. Add tomato and onion, cover and cook for about 5 minutes.
5. Add corn and cook on medium low for about 10 more minutes.
6. Serve over rice.

Makes 4 servings.

Pumpkin Bread

This recipe is a family favorite, adapted from the *Fanny Farmer Cookbook*.

- 1½ cups unbleached flour
- ½ teaspoon salt
- 1 cup sugar
- 1 teaspoon baking soda
- 1 cup pumpkin puree
- ½ cup canola or coconut oil
- 2 eggs, beaten
- ¼ teaspoon nutmeg
- ¼ teaspoon cinnamon
- ¼ teaspoon allspice
- ½ cup chopped nuts (optional)

INSTRUCTIONS

1. Preheat oven to 350 degrees.
2. Sift together the flour, salt, sugar, and baking soda.
3. Mix the pumpkin, oil, eggs, ¼ cup water, and spices together, then combine with the dry ingredients, but do not mix too thoroughly.
4. Stir in the nuts.
5. Pour into a well buttered 9 x 5 x 3 inch loaf pan (or multiple small loaf pans).
6. Bake 50-60 minutes for large loaf.

7. Check small loaves after 30 minutes, until toothpick inserted comes out clean.

8. Turn out of the pan and cool on rack.

MUFFINS: This recipe can be used to make muffins; just pour batter into a muffin tin, filling each cup 2/3 full, and bake at same temp for 20 minutes, or until toothpick inserted come out clean.

Sausage and Fall Vegetable Harvest

Adapted from a crockpot recipe in the *Everything Slow Cooker Cookbook* by Margaret Kaeter.

- 1 pound acorn or butternut squash
- 2 medium potatoes
- 4 carrots
- 4 ribs celery
- ¼ cup bell pepper, chopped
- 2 yellow onions
- 1 cup zucchini, sliced
- 1 cup fresh or frozen peas
- 1 cup fresh or frozen green beans
- 2 cups fresh or canned beef broth
- 2 tablespoons red wine
- ¼ teaspoon ground black pepper
- 1 teaspoon dried, crushed rosemary (or a few sprigs fresh)
- ½ pound sausage in large round links or patties
- 2 tablespoons flour
- ½ cup warm water

INSTRUCTIONS

1. Peel the squash and cut into ½ inch cubes. (Squash has a very tough skin so use a large, sharp knife and work on a hard surface.).
2. Peel the potatoes and cut into ½ inch cubes.

3. Peel the carrots and cut into 1 inch lengths.

4. Cut the celery ribs into 1 inch lengths.

5. Core the bell pepper and chop with a medium sized knife into pieces about ¼ inch square.

6. Peel the onions and quarter.

7. Cut the zucchini into slices about ¼ inch thick.

8. Combine the squash, potatoes, carrots, celery, zucchini, green beans, broth, wine, black pepper, and rosemary in slow cooker.

9. Cut the sausage into ½ inch slices. If using patties, break them into marble sized chunks.

10. Combine the sausage, peppers, and onions in a frying pan and cook on medium high heat until the sausage and onions are browned. Drain off the grease and lay the mixture on paper towels for 2 minutes to soak up additional grease.

11. Add the sausage, onions, and peppers to the vegetables in the slow cooker. Cook covered on low heat for 6 to 8 hours.

12. One hour before serving, add the peas, and use a fork to mix 2 tablespoons flour and ½ cup water in a small bowl until the mixture is smooth.

13. Add this to the vegetables and sausage, stirring until it is well mixed.

14. Cook covered for 1 additional hour.

Spinach, Goat Cheese, and Roasted Carrot Salad

Adapted from *Food Network Magazine.*

- 1 bunch small to medium carrots with tops, trimmed and halved lengthwise
- 5 tablespoons extra virgin olive oil
- Kosher salt and freshly ground pepper
- ¼ cup sliced almonds
- 2 tablespoons sherry vinegar
- 1½ teaspoons honey
- 1½ teaspoon Dijon mustard
- 1 small shallot, thinly sliced
- 6 cups baby spinach (about 4 oz)
- 1 head red leaf lettuce, torn into large pieces
- 4 oz goat cheese, crumbled
- ¼ cup roughly chopped fresh chives

INSTRUCTIONS

1. Place a baking sheet in the oven; preheat to 450 degrees F.
2. Toss the carrots with 1 tablespoon olive oil, a big pinch of salt and a few grinds of pepper in a large bowl.
3. Spread the carrots on the hot pan and bake until lightly browned and tender, 20 to 25 minutes.

4. Meanwhile, toast the almonds in a small, dry skillet over low heat, stirring frequently for about 5 minutes. Let cool.

5. Whisk vinegar, honey, mustard, and shallot in a large bowl.

6. Slowly whisk in the remaining ¼ cup olive oil until combined.

7. Add the spinach, lettuce and almonds and toss to coat.

8. Season with salt and pepper.

9. Transfer the salad and carrots to a platter.

10. Top with the goat cheese and chives.

CHAPTER FIVE: WINTER II

Winter II

*"The seasonal rhythms correlate with our bodily rhythms...
Our dream life and inner life grow more insistent with the
winter darkness... The old year is put to bed, one's business
is finished, and the harvest of spiritual maturity is reaped
as wisdom and forgiveness."*
— Joan Borysenko, *Pocketful of Miracles: Prayers,
Meditations, and Affirmations to Nurture Your Spirit
Every Day of the Year*

December is like a tapestry of rich color and texture, woven with family and holiday traditions, rituals, celebrations, and memories. Past and present intertwine with hopes, desires, expectations, and sighs. The significance of this season is deep, stirring our souls to embrace its mystery and magic. The light shines in the darkness as our north star, our hope, and our healing. In the midst of frenetic holiday shopping, planning, and socializing, our souls pull us inward for balance, stillness, and reflection. We struggle with the demands upon our time, energy, and finances, longing for that which is Real and lasting, significant and satisfying. The gifts that matter are ours to give and to receive if we recognize them. Open hands and hearts allow us to experience the sweet and sacred treasures that this season brings.

We glance back on the past year for a sense of perspective and purpose as we anticipate the year ahead.

"We start to get a hint of the power and sweetness and
absurdity of life and to see it not as all fragile or harsh, but
as real, the really real. We get buoyancy and, God knows,
sometimes even effervescence. Perspective doesn't reduce
gravitas; it increases reverence."
— Anne Lamott, *Almost Everything*

December is truly a time for reverence, wonder, and miracles. The
ancient stories illustrate humanity's longing for light, love, and hope.
As we light the candles, sing the songs, tell the stories, and share food
and drink, we experience the mysterious connection between divinity
and humanity. We find a deep nourishment for our souls which is,
indeed, like *salsa*, fresh and full of flavor and spice.

ELISA JUAREZ

Season of Lights

The month of December ushers in a season of lights, festivities, and holy-days. Before Christmas ever began, the Jewish faith was on the line. After the Maccabees successfully rebelled against Antiochus IV Epiphanes, the Temple was purified and rededicated. The miracle in this story was the Jewish people had barely enough sacred oil to keep the temple menorah (a candelabrum with eight branches) lit for one day. The purification ceremony was to last eight days, with the candles burning. Miraculously, the candles did burn for eight days straight on that small portion of oil. This amazing incident gave birth to the Jewish holiday of Hanukkah which means "rededication." It is also known as the Festival of Lights, and in the words of author Sarah Ban Breathnach, it is celebrated *"in remembrance of their struggle for religious freedom and the miracle of restoration, symbolized by the abundance of oil."*

In the Christmas story, Jesus is born into a Jewish community by a young, simple Jewish girl who was betrothed to Joseph, a Jewish carpenter, but not yet married. It is noteworthy that God is willing to challenge all the societal and religious rules and norms to reach us.

Although we don't know all the facts of the story, it is full of symbolism and metaphors for our spiritual lives. Divine Love comes to and through the simple, humble, and willing among us. Light from a star provides guidance and direction for those who seek the Christ child. His life is in danger from the start as earthly kings feel threatened by rumors that a new king has been born. The whole story is full of drama, mystery, and miracles.

The holiday lights in our communities, homes, churches, and temples continue to bring a spirit of joy, celebration, and wonder to those whose hearts are humble, open, and willing. It is light shining in the darkness that gives us hope, guidance, and courage. The star and the candles represent the light of Divine Love within us — regardless of the name you give it or the religion you practice. When we are "enlightened," we are awake to this abiding Presence, allowing it to live, love, and move through us. This is what Jesus referred to as "the Way, the Truth, and the Light." He put the two words "I AM" in front of the phrase, which is the name of God. People throughout the ages have misunderstood this statement, interpreting it to mean that Christianity is the only way to God, the only truth; and as a result have essentially turned away from the radical humility, acceptance, and love that Jesus lived and taught.

The season of lights, miracles, gifts, and abundance is for all of us. It is a reminder of who we truly are, and a celebration of the love that miraculously continues to burn within us. Perhaps the small portion of oil is like the mustard seed in its capacity.

> "Sacred oil in a temple. Loaves and fishes on a mountainside. Miracles are of Spirit, not any one faith. Miracles are for anyone who believes. That is the heart of Hanukkah, and the soul of Christmas. The more we allow ourselves to recognize the wisdom and truth in other spiritual paths; the closer to wholeness we become."
> — Sarah Ban Breathnach

The Gifts That Matter

I have another holiday memory to share which has been an important lesson for me throughout my life. My dad was a minister, and when I was growing up we used to call on shut ins as a family during the Christmas season. There were several elderly people in our church who could not get out, so we took homemade cookies, sang Christmas carols, and visited them. When I was a teenager, I had short hair, and with my winter cap on I was mistaken for my brother a few times. How do you think *that* felt? Ugh!

At that age my siblings and I groaned about making these rounds, and my mother would say, "It is a very small and simple thing for us to do, and it means a great deal to them."

It must have been around that same time in my life when my best friend Julie and I decided to stop by the nursing home that was on our way home from school and visit the residents. We walked right by there anyway and found it enjoyable to visit. They loved seeing young people, and they could tell that I was a girl. That felt better!

My parents continued to demonstrate a spirit of service, humility, and compassion throughout their lives. Even when my mother was on oxygen and had difficulty doing the things she used to do, she would still make food for others, call and write notes to people who were sick or hurting, and put others' needs before her own. She believed service is what life is about, and she wanted to be sure she never quit serving until the day she died. She did what she had the power to do and she impacted countless lives, including my own.

As you go through this holiday season, consider the small and simple things you can do for others that would make a difference for them. Whatever resources you have — whether it be time, health, energy, money, or skills — find a way to share them with those who have less. You will find that your joy will increase, and your good will multiply! This can be achieved with a phone call, a handwritten note, some homemade soup, a personal visit, or an offer to take someone where they need to go. Whatever you are inspired to do, do it! These are the gifts that matter. Be open each day to the ideas that come to you and act on them. Do what you have the power to do.

Time and attention are the most valuable commodities we can give these days, and sometimes the hardest to sacrifice. Start and end each day by giving yourself the gift of time and attention so that you can be renewed, inspired, and empowered to give to others. Even a small investment of time for yourself goes a long way. Know that you are worth it, and that you have more to give than you will ever know, especially when you start by loving yourself.

Journey of the Soul

*"Perhaps the Christmas spirit is our souls' knowledge that
things, no matter how beautiful, are only things, . . that we
were created not always to do but sometimes simply to be.
Perhaps the Christmas spirit is a loving reminder that we
must make time for the long, slow journey across the desert;
we must take time to discover the star; we must honor the
time necessary to brood over the coming of the authentic*

ELISA JUAREZ

> women we were created by Love to become."
> — Sarah Ban Breathnach, *Simple Abundance*

As autumn's brilliance fades into the gray, stark landscape of winter, we come to the end of another year. It is a time for letting go of the past year with all its challenges, joys, and disappointments, and clearing ourselves and our lives for a new beginning, for transformation and new growth. It is a time to dream and hope and wonder. That is the inherent gift of the Christmas season. We can relate to the hopes and dreams of the people in Jesus' time, the awe and wonder of the message that was brought to them, and the journey they took to find the Christ child. They believed, they trusted, they followed, they found. New birth, new beginning, renewed hope. The whole story is cradled in the undergirding and all encompassing Love of God. That is the true and ultimate gift, then and now. Will we accept it this time? What will we give? What will we *be* in response to the gift?

These choices are ours to make, and we must make them consciously. Fear and doubt linger in the shadows, ready to snatch us into their grasp. We see evidence of them all around us but often fail to see them *within* us. We are easily deceived into thinking we need them for our own protection, that people and circumstances outside of us are a threat, or that we are not worthy of Love. In truth, that which we allow to separate us from others will divide us from our true selves and our awareness of God.

The journey of faith and wonder leads us to our true selves, our higher purpose, our joy and fulfillment. It is the journey we are called to, the way of the heart, the spirit, and the soul. Like the shepherds and the wise men, we must step out of our comfort zones and let go of our fears. In so doing, we will discover that there is yet more to life, more to give, more to receive, and more to learn. It is an adventure and an awakening.

During this Christmas season, pause long enough to absorb the wonder of God's gift. Embrace the humility and simplicity inherent in the birth of the Christ child. Realize that Christ seeks expression through each of us. So let us say, as Mary did, "Here I am, Lord." Then just give thanks, because you, too, are called to bring light and love into the world. You are equipped, empowered, and anointed. Glory to God!

Meditation

"Being has infinite power, and you are pure Being at your core. Connect to it through meditation, through joyful acceptance of the present moment, and always through Love. Let the light of pure awareness be the transformative power in your life." — Deepak Chopra

Growing up, I was a busy child. I would bring activities to the den while watching TV because I wanted something to do with my hands. And my attention. I could have been an avid reader like my sister if I had been able to sit still and focus long enough. She could sit and read for hours on end, which baffled me. I had to be moving. I was what some would call "hyperactive," although I wasn't high strung, just very energetic. I never really outgrew that high energy wiring; I channeled it into productivity and exercise. I still tend to get up from my chair during TV commercials, which baffles Art. "Where are you going?" he'll ask, and, "*Now,* what are you doing?" But I can find something to do in those 5-10 minutes, rather than waste them in front of the television!

Although my energy has served me well, the practice of meditation has helped me discover and maintain balance in my mind, body, and soul. It has expanded my awareness and increased my overall well-being from the inside out. It has connected me to a deep sense of peace, wisdom, and love which infuses my life at every level. The first step in learning to meditate is sitting still. Once you've mastered that, you're faced with the greater challenge of quieting the mind! Neither came easily for me, but now, all these years later, I find it harder to move once I've settled into meditation. I just want to stay and stay.

I remember when I first learned to meditate. I was in my mid 20s and attending a Unity church led by a fireball female minister, Rev. Linda Pendergrass. She did Wednesday night classes that you didn't want to miss. You didn't even want to be *late.* One of those classes was about meditation, which was new to me.

Here's how it started. Our minister issued a "20-20" challenge for us as an assignment. We were to meditate for 20 minutes each morning and 20 minutes each night. Back then, 20 minutes of sitting still felt like being in time out for an hour! However, I was able to calm my body much sooner than my mind. Our minister taught us to observe the thoughts that came into our heads and let them move through. "Don't let them stop and have babies," she would say. Thoughts will come in and want to stay, so observe without judgment and don't get attached to them. Keep them moving along!

It is a lifelong discipline to control our minds, but it is also the most valuable. The human mind is like a circus, and without a trainer it can run wild!

In time this practice became an anchor for me as a time of connection, grounding, and clarity. I have used various forms and methods including guided meditations, silence, writing, and yoga. The key is to find an inner stillness and focus that connects you to the creative life force or Spirit within. Psychologist, scientist, and spiritual teacher Dr. Joan Borysenko described the effects of being so focused and absorbed in an activity that our breathing slows.

"In this state creativity flowers, intuition leads to a deeper wisdom, the natural healing system of the body is engaged, our best physical and mental potential manifests itself, and we feel psychologically satisfied." — Dr. Joan Borysenko

She explains that spiritual mediation is different, in that it helps you "become aware of the presence of the divine in nature, in yourself and in other people;" and the love and joy of Spirit "will begin to permeate your life."

There are many tools, teachers, and resources available to help you learn to meditate. The two who have been most influential for me are Dr. Deepak Chopra and Dr. Wayne Dyer. Their guided meditations continue to support my practice and expand my awareness.

"On a daily basis, take a moment, or many moments, to center yourself and knowingly rest in the place where you're calm, still, and unaffected by your situation. Consciously

ELISA JUAREZ

> breathe slow, full, deep abdominal breaths. The experience
> may be modest at first, but it is from that still, silent place
> that consciousness generates your power, your personal
> reality, and the infinite possibilities that happen in it."
> — Deepak Chopra

The gifts and benefits are endless, and such a practice will support you through all the seasons of your life in ways you cannot imagine. It is both a *salsa* and a *soothing* for the soul, mind, and body. It will ground you and lift you up, nourish and strengthen you, empower and inspire you. If I could learn it, so can you! Start where you are, as you are, with an open mind and heart. Give this gift to yourself and discover a whole new level of living, loving, and being.

> "Learning to meditate is the greatest gift you can give
> yourself in this life." — Sogyal Rinpoche

In the stillness you become aware of the majestic Presence which indwells you. As you dwell in it, letting it permeate your consciousness and your entire being, you begin to reflect it. You become a mirror of the Light and Love within you. This is the Image likeness and, in this consciousness, you begin to draw to yourself all that you need and desire for your growth, your health, your fulfillment, and abundant life. So go forth in peace and power, walking lightly, gently, and joyfully into the experience of life.

Tackling the To-Do List

How are you feeling? Christmas is drawing near, and I'm realizing how precious is every day leading up to it. I am anticipating the arrival of our daughters and the holiday traditions we will share. Last night my mental "To-Do List" cost me a bit of sleep. This morning Art got up, turned on the coffeepot and our new, little electric fireplace, and a wave of gratitude and joy swept over me. It truly is the simple things in life that warm our hearts and fill our cups.

As you continue to check things off your list are you feeling a sense of fullness and gratitude or lack and frustration? Are you feeling stressed about getting to everything and everyone on your list? I was starting to feel some of that yesterday and in the night, so I took time this morning to write in my journal, the "morning pages" as Julia Cameron calls it. Putting your thoughts and mental clutter down on paper clears your head, calms your mind, and gives you perspective. I highly recommend this daily practice! It will help you to be more focused, peaceful, and productive. Then you may want to reevaluate and rewrite your list. Decide what is really important and what can be "waitlisted" or eliminated.

One thing I have "waitlisted" the past few years is the annual Christmas letter, which I love to write, but which takes time to write, address, and mail, so I do it around the first of the year. By then I have received others' cards and letters and can respond to their news with a handwritten note at the bottom of my printed letter. Sending Christmas cards can be an enjoyable yet time consuming task, so consider a Happy New Year card/letter instead! Share some highlights of the past year and what you are looking forward to in the new year. Just be authentic; keep it real and simple.

Remember to make room (i.e., time, space, and attention) for the real gifts of the season: peace, joy, love, and beauty. Our gifts and celebrations should reflect these treasures and honor their presence in our lives. Think of all the places that turned Mary and Joseph away because there was no room. How often do we do this ourselves? There is often "no vacancy" in our daily lives for the rest, attention, and nourishment that our souls need to thrive. Finally, in the story, they end up in a simple stable with the animals and lots of itchy hay. It's not the Comfort Inn, but that is where the miracle happens. It happens in simplicity, humility, and surrender.

Finally, take a few minutes each day to write your gratitude list. This list is more important and valuable than the others! I recommend doing this at the end of the day, but the start of the day is great, too. Just do it. You will find that it opens your eyes, mind and heart to notice, receive, and enjoy the abundance that is already present in your life. It will also attract more, as what you think about and focus on expands! Consider giving those you love a small gratitude journal and invite them to join you in this practice. It will add value to their lives and increase their capacity to give and receive. You can enclose a note that tells what you appreciate about them.

As you approach Christmas and work with your lists, choose to do the things that bring you joy and fill your cup. We can only give what we have, and when we are full our love and joy spill over to everyone around us. Behold the Light in yourself and others and allow it to fill your home, your relationships, and all your holiday activities.

The Perfect Present

Last night I was relaxing in my armchair, feeling weary and a little blue. I figured it was a combination of a lack of sleep and a shortage of funds in my checking account. My awareness was of *lack* instead of *abundance*. I knew I needed to shift my attention to what I *have*, and I thought about the people who have had devastating losses or other hardships this year. Many have lost their homes to natural disasters, battled health issues, struggled financially, or lost loved ones. Most recently, a family I know through business lost nine male family members in a plane crash the weekend after Thanksgiving. Those mothers and wives lost their husbands, sons, and brothers, who were on their way home from a hunting trip. This family is financially wealthy, but their loss will leave a void that nothing in this world can fill.

I realized once again that I have everything. It's Christmastime and I have my family, my health, and a lovely home. That is more than most.

> *"Gloom we have always with us, a rank and sturdy weed,*
> *but joy requires tending."* — Barbara Holland

Sometimes gratitude needs a gentle nudge to wake up. Gloom can creep into our consciousness when we are feeling a shortage, which is a common experience in December. It can be a lack of energy, ideas, money, or time, all of which are in demand as our attention is fixed on shopping, giving, celebrating, and feasting. As much as we may

ELISA JUAREZ

enjoy it all, it can leave us feeling depleted and overwhelmed. Giving brings such joy, it is easy to feel discouraged when we can't give as much as we'd like. Despite our understanding of the gifts that matter – gifts of time, attention, kindness, and unconditional love — we still want to be able to spend money on our loved ones. When we seek simple, meaningful, and creative gifts, we find that we don't need big bucks to give something precious. Among the best gifts are *experiences*, as they create lifelong memories and build relationships. Additionally, consider authentic gifts that weave together elements of the past and present; for example, photo gifts, handmade crafts or artwork, favorite family stories and games, and pieces of cherished holiday traditions. These are presents that carry the presence of family. They will last longer than a hand mixer.

As Christmas parties ramp up this week, we are faced with more choices. Maintaining balance and peace amid the festivities is an opportunity for us. A quiet evening at home, a massage, a coffee or wine date with a friend, or a walk can help restore our souls and our sanity. At the end of the month, we will feel the effects of how we spent our time as well as our money. As the year comes to a close, we need interludes of solitude and silence to reflect on what is behind us, what we've accomplished, how our lives are unfolding, and where we are headed. I highly recommend writing these things in a journal to give you perspective, both now and a year from now when you look back once again. A blank book/journal makes a great gift to yourself, and your loved ones!

With the "countdown to Christmas" well underway, I am challenged daily to stay centered and grounded in the now. The *present* is the real gift, *the perfect present*. It is where all the good stuff resides.

It is the portal to presence, peace, joy, and beauty. We cheat ourselves when we let our minds hold us in the past or pull us into an uncertain future. We are here now, and God is here now. Jesus taught us in Luke 17:21 that the kingdom of God is present, here and now, *"in the midst of you."* No shortage, no lack. Let the holidays be a reminder of the holiness that holds us in wholeness. As we shift our awareness from shortage to supply, we connect to the fullness of God's Presence in the midst of us. Here we find the perfect present.

Christmas Has Come

Now that the salsa has been made, a pot of beans is simmering on the stove, and a batch of apple cinnamon muffins is cooling on the counter, I am sitting down with a glass of wine to pen this message. When I started my kitchen projects this morning, Lauren put on some old home movies and I began to wonder if I would get anything done. We were captivated, humored, and filled with nostalgia as we watched first Christmases, first steps, birthdays, recitals, and visits with grandparents. So many rich memories! I told Lauren that all those years are stored in my heart like a treasure chest and I feel so full. As Christmas comes again, we find joy in the memories, traditions, and relationships that have enriched our lives.

Each year I read a quote from *Simple Abundance* that Sarah Ban Breathnach found and shared from an anonymous source. It is a treasure itself, as it points us to the mystery of life and the essence of our authentic selves.

"If, as Herod, we fill our lives with things, and again with

> *things; if we consider ourselves so unimportant that we*
> *must fill every moment of our lives with action, when will*
> *have time to make the long, slow journey across the desert*
> *as did the Magi? Or sit and watch the stars as did the*
> *shepherds? Or brood over the coming of the child as did*
> *Mary? For each one of us, there is a desert to travel. A star*
> *to discover. And a being within ourselves to bring to life."*
> — Anonymous

Perhaps sometime during your Christmas holiday you will find time to sit in stillness and reflect on your own journey. I bet you've come a distance this year, overcoming obstacles and taking courageous steps into the darkness. As you look ahead to the new year, know that you are stronger now than you were at this time last year. Know, too, that the Universe is already preparing the way for you, lining up some sweet surprises and new discoveries for you. What an adventure, this life! We must learn to cherish it *more* each day, to really embrace the wonder of it all, and to feel the energy of Divine Love that is ever present within us!

The Christmas story holds so much mystery and metaphor for us. It is a universal story of humanity, as it calls us to discover and embrace the divine within us. It calls us to follow our own star, to trust that we belong to God, and to give birth to our authentic selves. Christmas Eve is upon us. Let us stop the busyness that has filled this season and kneel before the Presence that is born anew within us. Let us rest in the knowing that all is well, that we are held in the Everlasting Arms, and that we are enough. This is enough. The Light of Wisdom and Grace is shining upon you this night. Behold the gift and rejoice!

Merry Christmas.

WINTER II RECIPES

Gingerbread Raisin Pancakes

This is a recipe from my childhood. My mother used to make the most wonderful, nutritious pancakes, and these were some of my favorites!

- 2½ cups unbleached flour
- 5 teaspoons baking powder
- 1½ teaspoons baking soda
- 1 teaspoon cinnamon
- ½ teaspoon ginger
- ¼ cup molasses
- 2 cups milk
- 2 eggs, slightly beaten
- 6 tablespoons butter, softened
- 1 cup raisins

INSTRUCTIONS

1. Mix and sift flour, baking powder, baking soda, salt and spices.
2. Combine molasses and milk; add eggs; stir in melted butter.
3. Add molasses mix to flour mix; stir only until moistened.
4. Stir in raisins.
5. Cook on a hot griddle, using ¼ cup batter for each pancake.
Makes 20 pancakes.

Gingerbread People

This recipe was adapted from the *Fanny Farmer Cookbook*, like so many of my favorites, and it was a holiday tradition while I was growing up! We loved making these, decorating them, wrapping them in clear plastic wrap with a ribbon, and giving them as gifts. We also loved eating them, and the house smelled wonderful when they were baking! They are called "Gingerbread Men" in the cookbook, but we renamed them "Gingerbread People" because we made girls, as well, by adding skirts and bows. We did this by putting the icing into waxed paper piping bags that we made ourselves.

- ½ cup molasses
- ¼ cup sugar
- 3 tablespoons butter
- 1 tablespoon milk
- 2 cups flour
- ½ teaspoon baking soda
- ½ teaspoon salt
- ½ teaspoon nutmeg
- ½ teaspoon cinnamon
- ½ teaspoon ground cloves
- ½ teaspoon ground ginger

CONFECTIONERS FROSTING:
- 3 tablespoons melted butter
- 1 teaspoon vanilla

- 2 ½ cups sifted confectioners' sugar

INSTRUCTIONS:

1. Preheat oven to 350 degrees F.

2. Butter some cookie sheets or line with parchment paper (or use nonstick pans).

3. Heat the molasses to the boiling point, then add sugar, butter, and milk.

4. Mix the flour, baking soda, salt, nutmeg, cinnamon, cloves, and ginger.

5. Add to the molasses mixture and blend well.

6. Add a few tablespoons of water (enough so that the dough holds together and handles easily).

7. Roll or pat out the dough until it's about ¼ inch thick.

8. Cut into large or small gingerbread people, using special cookie cutters, or a very sharp knife.

9. Bake for 5-7 minutes.

10. Make frosting: Put melted butter and vanilla in small bowl, then add confectioners' sugar. Beat with mixer for several minutes until very creamy. *Note: To make it thinner, just add water 1 teaspoon at a time and mix well. Makes 1 cup.*

11. When cookies are cool, frost and decorate with candies, raisins, white chocolate chips, etc.

Sugar Cookies

The recipe for the dough is from Carmen Estep, a woman I met in an early childhood parenting group years ago. It has become our favorite sugar cookie, and a holiday tradition for our girls. The icing recipe is my own.

- ¾ cup butter, softened
- 3 oz pkg. cream cheese, softened
- 1¾ cups confectioners' sugar, sifted
- 1 egg
- ½ teaspoon vanilla extract
- ½ teaspoon almond extract
- 2 cups unbleached flour
- ¾ teaspoon baking powder

ICING:

- 1 stick butter, softened
- 2 cups confectioners' sugar, sifted
- ½ tsp almond extract
- 2 tbsp (more or less) almond milk (or regular milk) for moisture
- Beat until smooth.

INSTRUCTIONS:

1. Mix together all ingredients until well combined.

2. Chill 2 - 4 hours.
3. Roll out, cut, and place on cookie sheets.
4. Bake at 350 degrees for 7 - 9 minutes.
5. Allow to cool before adding icing.

ELISA JUAREZ

Mrs. Dahlman's Swedish Nut Balls

This recipe is a family favorite from my childhood, and now, it is a favorite for my girls. This is one of the simplest recipes I've ever seen, and we make them every year during Christmastime.

- 3 tablespoons sugar
- 1 teaspoon vanilla
- ½ cup butter
- 1 cup flour
- ½ cup pecans, chopped

INSTRUCTIONS:

1. Combine all ingredients and blend well.
2. Roll in small balls.
3. Bake at 350 degree for about 25-30 minutes.
4. Roll in confectioners' sugar while still hot.
5. Let cool.
6. Finish by rolling in confectioners' sugar again once cool.

Grammie Rand's Scotchies

- 1 cup unbleached flour
- ½ teaspoon baking soda
- ½ teaspoon salt
- ½ cup butter
- 1 cup brown sugar
- 1 egg
- 1 cup rolled oats
- ½ cup pecans, chopped
- 1 cup coconut

INSTRUCTIONS:

1. Sift together flour, soda, and salt.
2. Cream butter and beat with sugar. Add egg and vanilla and beat until light and fluffy.
3. Stir in flour mixture, oats, pecans, and coconut.
4. Use teaspoon to drop onto greased cookie sheet.
5. Flatten to 1/8" with bottom of glass dipped in flour.
6. Bake at 325 degrees for 12-15 minutes.
7. Remove from pan immediately.

ABOUT THE AUTHOR

Elisa holds a B.A. in Psychology and a master's degree in Social Work. In addition, she has continued to study nutrition, wellness, and personal/spiritual development. Her work experience includes counseling, community education, volunteer coordinating, recruiting, network marketing, and retail management. Her joy comes from writing, reading, cooking, yoga, meeting new people, wine tasting, and doing crossword and jigsaw puzzles. She and her husband, Art, are happily married and have two grown daughters.

Writing has helped her to take what life dishes out and create something to share and savor. These "somethings" live on her blog, *Spoonful of Salsa*, at www.spoonfulofsalsa.com. It is a creative expression of her passion for writing, cooking, and healthy living, as well as a prelude to *Soul Salsa*. She invites her audience to that "table" where they will find nuggets of nourishment for body, mind and soul.

Elisa J. Juarez
Email: elisaj@spoonfulofsalsa.com
Facebook: @spoonfulofsalsa
Instagram: @spoonfulofsalsa31

Made in the USA
Monee, IL
31 August 2020